Oak Alley Plantation
Vacherie, Louisiana

Houmas House
Burnside, Louisiana

Bon Appétit!

Curt M. Böhringer

Fine Dining

Louisiana Style

by John M. Bailey

Louisiana Strawberry Dessert
Juban's Restaurant, Baton Rouge

**Recipes from over one hundred
of the most outstanding chefs
at some of the finest restaurants
and bed and breakfast inns in Louisiana**

John M. Bailey

About the author:

Author of "FINE DINING MISSISSIPPI STYLE" and
"FINE DINING TENNESSEE STYLE."
Graduate of the University of Mississippi.
Associate Member of the American Culinary Federation.
Member of the Southern Foodways Alliance.
John and his wife Ann reside in Germantown, Tennessee.

Back cover photos beginning with Welcome to Louisiana and going clockwise:
Welcome to Louisiana Sign
Lafayette Welcome Center
Commander's Palace
Fleur' de Lis'
Water Lily
Alligator
Peacock
Hodges Gardens
Joan of Arc
Vieux Carré Police Precinct
Cooking Crawfish (center photo)

Copyright 2002 John M. Bailey

ISBN 0-942249-24-0
Library of Congress: 2002111648
First Printing September 2002

Cover photograph of Greenwood Plantation,
in West Feliciana Parish near St. Francisville, by John M. Bailey
Cover design by Jacob Fasano

Published by
Toof Cookbook Division
STARR★TOOF
670 South Cooper Street
Memphis, Tennessee 38104
800-722-4772

Ann Bailey admiring the Louisiana State Flower - the Magnolia.

This book is dedicated to:
My wonderful wife Ann for her continued love and support for my projects

Beautiful Oleander Shrub - Monroe – PHOTO BY JOHN BAILEY

Introduction

This is the third in a series of cookbooks that showcase the fine chefs, restaurants and bed & breakfast inns that are found across the Southern states. Louisiana is known for its music, great food and the friendliness and warmth of its diverse culture. After spending many months in Louisiana researching this book, I can attest to that!

In this book, we have divided the state into 5 distinctly different regions. Northern Louisiana is referred to as Sportsman's Paradise, Crossroads for the center of the state, Cajun Country for south Louisiana, Plantation Country for the river road area and Greater New Orleans for the southeastern part of the state. The New Orleans area is further subdivided into the Metro and North Shore areas.

I hope that you enjoy your visits to this great state as much as I enjoyed working this project. The year 2003 will be a great year to visit Louisiana because it will be the 200th anniversary of the signing of the Louisiana Purchase! I also hope that you use this book as a guide to the great chefs, wonderful restaurants and bed & breakfast inns across this state. These recipes have been tested over the years in restaurants and bed & breakfast inns throughout Louisiana. Now enjoy them in your home. They are on the house, compliments of the Chef!

Bon Appetit!

John M. Bailey

Acknowledgments:

I would like to thank the following people:

- **The Chefs of Louisiana for all of their great recipes.**
- **The local chapters of the Louisiana Chamber of Commerce for their help.**
- **Bill Williams Jr. AIA for the use of his wonderful pen & ink drawings.**
- **Martha Miller Designs for the use of her beautiful pen & ink drawings.**
- **The Louisiana Department of Tourism for the use of their historical information and descriptions.**
- **Chef James Graham for taking me out in his canoe to take pictures in the Louisiana bayous.**
- **My longtime friend Larry McIntire for showing me around New Orleans.**
- **Tim and Ashley Francis for their hospitality and help.**
- **I would also like to thank the following for their help on this project: W. Jett Wilson, attorney & Ed Neal, CPA**
- **Susan Hawkins for restaurant information about South Louisiana.**

JMB

TABLE OF CONTENTS

Please note all recipes were written and contributed by the finest chefs, restaurants and bed and breakfast establishments in Louisiana. These recipes are not written for the inexperienced cook. If there are any questions about cooking terms, please refer to the extensive glossary beginning on page 189. Some minor editing was done for added clarity on each recipe.

John M. Bailey

Louisiana State Museum – the Cabildo – PHOTO BY JOHN BAILEY

Lacy iron balconies in the Vieux Carré – PHOTO BY JOHN BAILEY

Jackson Square – PHOTO BY JOHN BAILEY

Stop off at Emeril Lagasse's NOLA restaurant

Lush tropical courtyard courtesy of Broussard's restaurant– PHOTO BY JOHN BAILEY

North shore of Lake Pontchartrain – Photo by John M. Bailey

Egret in Louisiana Swamp – photo by John Bailey

Oak Alley, Vacherie, Louisiana – PHOTO BY JOHN BAILEY

250+ year old live Oak – PHOTO BY JOHN BAILEY

One of the local residents – PHOTO BY JOHN BAILEY

Beautiful Louisiana bayou – PHOTO BY JOHN BAILEY

Sabine Parish – Hodges Scenic Gardens waterfall and lake – PHOTOS BY JOHN BAILEY

Natchitoches Historic District — PHOTO BY JOHN BAILEY

Cane River, Natchitoches — PHOTO BY JOHN BAILEY

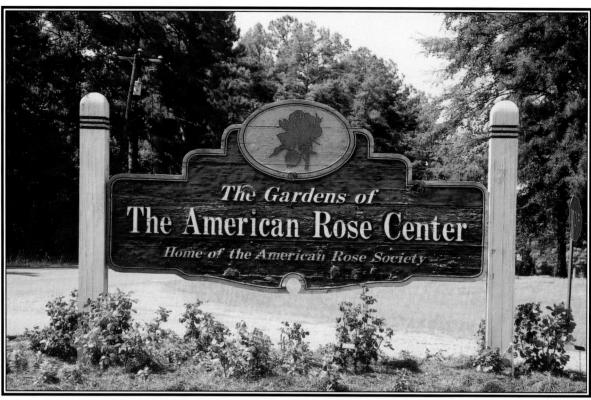

The American Rose Center, Shreveport – PHOTO BY JOHN BAILEY

Over 40 acres of Blooming Beauty! American Rose Center – PHOTO BY JOHN BAILEY

Crawfish Étouffée, courtesy of Lafayetté's Restaurant – PHOTO BY JOHN BAILEY

Follette Pottery celebrates the Ruston Peach Festival– PHOTO BY JOHN BAILEY

Monroe's Biedenharn Museum– PHOTO BY JOHN BAILEY

Biedenharn Gardens – PHOTOS BY JOHN BAILEY

NEW ORLEANS is the second oldest settlement in the Louisiana Purchase Territories. The Cabildo in the Vieux Carré is the site of the Louisiana Purchase transfer in 1803 and home to a variety of exhibits and artifacts including a bronze cast of Napoleon's death mask. New Orleans' French Quarter, also called the Vieux Carré was a thriving cultural center way before the 1803 Louisiana Purchase made it an American city. Step into the past on these old brick streets and slate alleyways, and you'll find every kind of antique and collectible you can imagine, from Confederate dollars to plantation silver. But also look beyond the lacy iron balconies and enticing shop windows into the secluded, mysterious world of Creole courtyards—you can take a courtyard tour and let the secrets of 18th and 19th century New Orleans unfold before you.

The mystique of New Orleans only begins in the French Quarter—so let the rhythms carry you through the city as far as your imagination and sense of adventure will take you. The Warehouse District, the Garden District, Uptown, the West Bank, Chalmette—the list goes on and on, each area sporting its own architecture, history, culture, and style.

On the edge of the Quarter you'll really get below sea level at one of the country's top five aquariums, the Audubon Aquarium of the Americas. Visit the new *Frogs!* exhibit, featuring more than 25 species of the most colorful frogs you've ever seen—they go way beyond green! And next door, the Entergy IMAX Theatre takes you on larger-than-life adventures to exotic locations in 2D and 3D. Also nearby is the state's only land-based casino.

Along the streetcar line, the Warehouse District offers New Orleans' answer to Soho, with art galleries, museums and boutiques. Be sure to splash in the footsteps of American soldiers at the inspirational D-Day Museum, where you'll stand in awe before a Higgins landing craft (They were built in New Orleans!) and hear heroic stories of those who served. You'll also see World War II planes, a Sherman tank, a German staff car and more. Then explore the rare Southern-made swords, personal items of Robert E. Lee and Jefferson Davis, and other memorabilia across the street at Memorial Hall Confederate Museum. It was established in 1891, just 26 years after the end of the Civil War, and many of the artifacts were donated to the museum by the soldiers themselves! Next door is the Ogden Museum of Southern Art, a superb showcase of visual arts of the American South and the largest collection of its kind.

Hop aboard a streetcar and head to the Garden District and Uptown. Many of these magnificent mansions along St. Charles Avenue were built by wealthy Americans who moved to town after the Louisiana Purchase. Across St. Charles from the hallowed halls of Tulane and Loyola Universities you'll find Audubon Park, an expanse of moss-draped oaks that extends all the way to the river. From here you can catch a riverboat back to the Quarter or other destinations, or you can stay on the grounds and visit the world-class Audubon Zoo, home of the real-live Louisiana Swamp Exhibit. Also Uptown is famous Magazine Street, offering miles of gorgeous architecture as well as art galleries, antiques, cafés and watering holes. In New Orleans, where life is lived to the fullest, the dead remain a beloved part of the cultural landscape, from lively local jazz funeral traditions to the ornate architecture of the historic above-ground cemeteries. Take a tour of these hauntingly beautiful "cities of the dead," and see tombs of pirates, politicians, riverboat gamblers, and voodoo queens. Hear stories of flamboyant lives and sometimes, mysterious deaths.

There's no counting the deaths of aristocratic young men under the Dueling Oaks in City Park, formerly a plantation and now one of the largest inner-city parks in the country. Here in the old days, a rude remark or a slap on the face with a glove often culminated in swords or pistols at dawn. Steps away from the site is the stately New Orleans Museum of Art, one of the South's premier art collections. Take a jaunt out farther—you choose the direction—to discover gems like Chalmette Battlefield, site of the 1815 Battle of New Orleans and home to an annual reenactment in January. Drive to the San Bernardo Scenic Byway to the Los Islenos Village, where you can delve into the culture of these Spanish colonists who came from the Canary Islands in the 1700s. At the bayou town of Jean Lafitte (named for the gentleman pirate) take an eco-tour by boat, Cajun style, through mysterious swamplands and winding bayous, past tiny isles shrouded in foliage, and you'll understand why no one could find Jean Lafitte unless he wished it. In April you can catch the colorfully decorated boats and family festivities of the Blessing of the Shrimp Fleet.

Across the Mississippi River, the West Bank has more to explore. See how floats are made at Mardi Gras World. Cool off at the wavepool or take a canoe ride at Bayou Segnette State Park. Or visit the old town of Gretna (now a suburb of New Orleans) to learn about the exciting days of railroad expansion at the Louisiana Railroad Museum, housed in the circa-1905 Texas Pacific Depot.

KENNER – Rivertown, U.S.A. is a must for those traveling with children. There are eight museums, including a Mardi Gras museum, a life-size NASA space station prototype and planetarium, and the largest collection of toy trains in the country. You can also relive great football moments at the New Orleans Saints Hall of Fame or catch a Broadway musical at the Rivertown Repertory Theatre.

METAIRIE – If you're looking for great shopping, check out the many malls of Metairie, New Orleans' oldest suburb. Restaurants are never far from shopping spots, and every kind of cuisine from Cajun to Vietnamese can be found in the Metairie area. Plus, the Jefferson Performing Arts Society offers Broadway-quality productions with a full pit orchestra, touring classical dance and orchestral companies, and a locally revered annual production of *The Nutcracker.*

Ralph Brennan's

BACCO

310 Chartres Street
New Orleans, LA 70130
(504) 522-2426

BACCO'S Italian cooking offers guests a dining alternative to the Creole and Cajun food that New Orleans is famous for. BACCO has a delicious assortment of homemade pastas, wood-fired pizzas and fresh regional seafood selections for its guests. BACCO is housed in a historic building in the heart of the French Quarter on Chartres Street. New Orleans magazine ranked BACCO "Best Italian" 1995. Gambit Weekly's reader's poll rated BACCO with "Best Ambiance" The Zagat survey ranked BACCO "One of New Orleans Best Italian Restaurants and "One of New Orleans Most Romantic Restaurants" 1999. The Times Picayune gave BACCO its "4 Beans" rating and Food Critic Tom Fitzmorris gave BACCO 4 stars. Where New Orleans' Visitors Choice Poll voted BACCO'S "Best Italian Restaurant" 1998, 1999 & 2000!

Haley Gabel, Executive Chef

In 1993 Haley Gabel broke new ground as the first woman to head up a Brennan Family (of Commander's Palace fame) kitchen. Chef Gabel is a graduate of the Culinary Arts Academy of Cincinnati, an affiliate of the Culinary Institute of America. The cuisine vibrates with the essence of authentic Italian cooking in scrupulously fresh, well chosen regional ingredients that pulse with flavor!

FETTUCINE CON TARTUFI NERO (BLACK TRUFFLE FETTUCCINE)

4	ounces fresh fettucine	½	ounce white truffle oil
1	ounce black truffle puree	½	ounce unsalted butter
1	ounce Reggiano Parmesan cheese, shaved		Pinch of salt Pinch parsley, minced
½	ounce extra virgin olive oil		

Drop fettucine in a large pot of boiling salted water. While pasta is cooking, mix all ingredients except parsley in a mixing bowl. Drain pasta and toss with mixed ingredients. Empty contents from mixing bowl using a pasta fork to spin fettucine into the center of a large hot pasta bowl. Top pasta with shaved cheese and sprinkle minced parsley. Serves 1. This recipe is for one appetizer. For an entrée size, double all ingredients.

Serves 1.

VERMOUTH STEAMED MUSSELS

¼	cup red onions, julienned	2	teaspoons green onions
¼	cup olive oil	1	teaspoon crushed red pepper
¼	cup pancetta, diced		
¼	cup butter, unsalted	½	cup sweet vermouth
½	cup tomatoes, diced	24	cleaned mussels
¾	cup chicken stock Salt & pepper to taste	2	Tbsp. minced garlic

Method: In a sauté pan, heat the olive oil with the garlic, pancetta and the red onions. Add the mussels. De-glaze with the sweet vermouth and add the chicken stock, season with the salt and pepper. Cover with another sauté pan and steam the mussels open. Remove the mussels and add the diced tomatoes, butter and green onions. Adjust seasoning. Pour the sauce over the mussels and serve with a piece of grilled bread.

Serves 2.

Continued Page 21

ROSEMARY AND GARLIC MARINATED PORK TENDERLOIN

MARINATED PORK TENDERLOIN:

8	ounces pork tenderloin, cleaned	4	ounces garlic mashed potatoes
1	ounces sweet-and-sour prune sauce	½	ounce unsalted butter
¾	ounce rosemary/garlic paste	3	ounces wilted escarole
5	prunes		

Method: Rub pork tenderloin with rosemary/garlic paste. Roll tenderloin on grill and put into oven at 350 degrees. Cook until medium-rare or medium. Set aside and rest for 5 minutes and slice. Add 1 ounce of sweet-and-sour prune sauce with 5 prunes and reduce by half. Add butter and mix well. Sauté escarole. Place sliced pork on escarole and coat with sauce and prunes. Serve with garlic mashed potatoes.

ROSEMARY/GARLIC PASTE:

2	cups olive oil	8	ounces rosemary, finely chopped
6	ounces chopped garlic	1	ounces cracked black pepper

Method: Puree all ingredients in a food processor.

SWEET AND SOUR PRUNE SAUCE:

2⅔	cups water	1	pound pitted prunes
1	pound sugar		
½	bottle sherry vinegar		

Method: Place all ingredients in a saucepan. Bring to boil and remove from stove.

WILTED ESCAROLE:

3	ounces escarole, cleaned and cut	½	ounce unsalted butter
¼	ounce minced garlic	½	ounce olive oil
		1	pinch crushed red pepper

Method: Over medium-high heat, add oil, garlic and crushed red pepper. Add escarole and butter. Toss until escarole is wilted.

GARLIC MASHED POTATOES:

8	peeled russet potatoes	6	ounces unsalted butter
½	cup roasted garlic puree	6	ounces scalded milk Salt and butter to taste

Method: Boil potatoes until tender, drain, let dry for 5 to 8 minutes and place in mixer. Pulse at high speed for 30 seconds. Add butter, roasted garlic puree, salt and pepper. Slowly add milk until smooth. Do not over-whip potatoes, or they will become very sticky and gummy.

BON TON CAFÉ

401 Magazine
New Orleans, LA 70130
(504) 524-3386

Chefs Wayne and Debbie Pierce

Owner/Operator

Wayne and Debbie operate the oldest Cajun restaurant in New Orleans. Wayne, having grown up in south Louisiana, was well aware of this wonderful lifestyle, culture and cuisine of the Cajun people. Wayne's aunt and uncle first operated Bon Ton and he has continued the tradition established by them. Contributing to his continued success is his ability to resist being influenced by new trends that alter the style of traditional Cajun cooking. Bon Ton Restaurant received the 5 Star International Award of Excellence for their culinary accomplishments. On Sunday, July 19, 1998 Bon Ton Restaurant hosted a private dinner party for former President William Jefferson Clinton.

BON TON SHRIMP REMOULADE SALAD

32	large Gulf shrimp, unpeeled	2	cups olive oil
4	4-ounce jars Creole mustard	2	tablespoons sugar
4	4-ounce jars Grey Poupon mustard	1	tablespoon paprika
4	green onions, chopped with stems	1	pkg. crab boil
		2	quarts water
			Salt to taste
			Romaine lettuce (for 8 salads)
		4	ripe tomatoes

Pour water and crab boil into pot and add salt and pepper to taste. Bring mixture to a boil and add shrimp. Bring back to a boil and cook 8-10 minutes or until shrimp are cooked. Strain and allow shrimp to cool. Peel and de-vein shrimp.

Make remoulade sauce by combining both mustards with chopped onions, olive oil, sugar and paprika. Mix together until blended to smoothness. (A small amount of water may have to be added to achieve this). Place shrimp over bed of chopped lettuce and cover with remoulade sauce. Garnish with fresh tomato wedges.

Eight servings.

BON TON HOMEMADE TURTLE SOUP

1	gallon water	½	dozen eggs hard boiled and diced
2	cups tomato sauce		
2	cups whole peeled tomatoes (cut up)	1	lemon cut into 5-7 slices
2½	cups dried onions	1	cup chopped parsley
5	bay leaves		Salt & pepper to taste
2½	pounds turtle meat cut, almost diced, into small pieces (may substitute beef such as brisket)	1	cup cooking sherry wine
		3	cups of roux (2 cups flour, 2 cups vegetable oil)
¼	cup cloves (wrapped in tightly sealed cloth)		

Bring one gallon of water to boil in appropriate sized pot. Add tomato sauce, whole tomatoes, dried onions, bay leaves and bring to simmer. Make a roux by combining flour and oil in a separate skillet and heat over low to medium flame, stirring often. Allow mixture to come to a golden brown color. Stir often to prevent burning of roux on bottom of skillet. You may have to add oil to keep the consistency of roux slightly loose. Once roux becomes golden brown, remove from heat. Add roux to simmering mixture and stir until the two are thoroughly combined. Add turtle meat and simmer for one hour. Add eggs, lemon slices, sealed cloth containing cloves, salt and pepper. Continue to simmer ½ hour stirring frequently to keep roux well dissolved and mixture evenly distributed. Turn off heat, add parsley and sherry wine and sample for seasoning. Mixture may have to be reduced more to concentrate flavors or may be thinned by adding additional water, if desired.

Yield: 8 – 10 cups (Double quantities if you want to freeze for future use.)

Continued Page 23

CRABMEAT IMPERIAL

2	pounds fresh picked jumbo lump crabmeat	1	cup olive oil
1	cup green onions chopped with bulbs and stems	½	cup sliced mushrooms
¼	cup pimentos chopped	½	cup sherry wine
		¼	cup chopped parsley
			Salt to taste

12 Toasted bread points – from French bread cut in lengths to a point (toast points should be approximately 4" in length)

Sauté green onions and mushrooms in 1 cup of olive oil until clear or limp. Add crabmeat, pimento and sherry and allow to marinate until warm throughout. Season with salt to taste. Place 3 toast points per serving on plate with wide ends of toast meeting in the middle and points facing out as a star. Mound crabmeat on top of toast. Sprinkle lightly with parsley.

Yield: 4 servings

STEAK CUBED WITH MUSHROOMS IN CABERNET WINE SAUCE*

4	cups cooked rice	½	cup chopped parsley
1	teaspoon flour	1	cup beef broth
4	10-ounce sirloin strip steaks, trimmed	2	cups red wine (Cabernet)
2	sticks margarine		Salt & pepper to taste
2	cups sliced mushrooms		

Cut each sirloin into 5 equal cubes, giving 20 pieces. Season with salt and pepper. In a large skillet, melt 1 stick of margarine over a high flame. Place steak cubes in hot margarine and brown on both sides. Add sliced mushrooms. (Use additional margarine if you feel it is needed.) Add beef broth and wine. Remove steak cubes when cooked to desired wellness. Add 1 teaspoon of flour to sauce and stir until reduced to desired thickness. Place steak cubes (5) around rice pilaf. Spoon sauce with mushrooms onto steak and around rice. Sprinkle with chopped parsley and serve.

Yield: 4 servings.

*Original recipe: The Bon Ton Café, New Orleans, LA Wayne Pierce, Proprietor.

OYSTERS ALVIN

1	dozen oysters (freshly shucked)	½	cup beef broth (bouillon)
2	cups flour	¾	quart frying oil
½	stick margarine		Juice of ½ lemon
1	teaspoon paprika		Salt to taste (¼ teaspoon)
1	teaspoon chopped parsley		Pepper to taste (½ teaspoon)

Dust oysters in flour. Deep-fry in pre-heated oil (350 degrees) until golden brown. Remove and drain. Melt margarine in skillet. Add beef broth and simmer until mixture thickens slightly. Place fried oysters in mixture. (The bottom of the oysters become soaked while the tops remain crisp). Season with salt, pepper and lemon and sprinkle lightly with paprika. Place in broiler until oysters brown slightly. Sprinkle with parsley and serve around bouillon rice, adding sauce from oysters.

Yield: 1 serving

BOUILLON RICE

1	cup cooked rice – (place on side)	¼	cup chopped mushrooms
1	teaspoon margarine	¼	cup chopped onion
¼	cup beef broth (bouillon)	¼	teaspoon salt
		¼	teaspoon pepper

Sauté margarine, onions, broth, mushrooms, salt and pepper until onions are clear. Add to cooked rice and stir over low heat until rice absorbs the liquid. Mound rice onto plate, surround with Oysters Alvin, and serve.

Continued Page 24

BON TON BREAD PUDDING WITH WHISKEY SAUCE

BREAD PUDDING:

1	loaf French bread	2	tablespoons vanilla
1	quart milk	3	tablespoons
3	eggs		margarine
2	cups sugar	1	cup raisins

Soak bread in milk; crush with hands until well mixed. Add eggs, sugar, vanilla, raisins and stir well. Met margarine in thick baking pan, then add bread mixture to pan. Bake at 350 degrees until slightly firm throughout and lightly browned on top. Allow to cool, cut into individual sized servings. When ready to serve, heat, then pour whiskey sauce on top and place under broiler for a couple minutes to heat sauce. (Use as much sauce as individual likes).

WHISKEY SAUCE:

2	sticks margarine	Bourbon whiskey
2	cups sugar	to taste (1 to 2
2	eggs	ounces)

Cream sugar and eggs until well mixed. Melt margarine and add to creamed mixture. Add whiskey to taste which should make sauce creamy smooth.

- Est. 1953 -

Bon Ton Café

New Orleans Oldest Cajun Restaurant

SPINACH SALAD DRESSING

1	quart mayonnaise		Salt and black	
2	tablespoons		pepper to taste	
	currant jelly	½	tablespoon	
1½	tablespoons		tarragon, dried.	
	balsamic vinegar			

Combine all ingredients into a mixer. Cover and place in a refrigerator. Shelf life: 1 week.

SOFT SHELL CRAB DORÉ

Sprinkle salt, pepper and lemon juice on (6) cleaned crabs. Sauté in butter until done or until crabs turn red. Set aside on a dish and keep warm.

SAUCE DORÉ

1	pound cleaned shrimp	½	cup heavy cream
1	cup sliced mushrooms	¼	cup lemon juice
¼	cup chopped shallots	¼	cup green onions
½	cup white wine	½	teaspoon chopped garlic
		¼	cup butter, salt and pepper

Sauté shrimp in wine for 2-3 minutes add shallots, green onions, mushrooms, lemon juice and garlic. Slowly cook for 3 more minutes. Add heavy cream and butter. Cook until it becomes a sauce. Add salt and pepper to taste and place sauce in the center of 6 warm plates. Top with warm crabs and garnish with chopped parsley, a lemon slice and fresh dill sprig.

Yield: 6 servings.

POMPANO NAPOLEON

1	tablespoon butter	1	teaspoon granulated garlic
1	tablespoon shallots, minced	1	teaspoon dried oregano
3	ounces capers, drained, liquid reserved	1	teaspoon dried thyme
8	ounces cream	1	teaspoon dried basil
3	ounces Creole mustard Salt & pepper to taste	3	pompano fillets, 6 ounces each
½	cup sweet paprika	12	large dry-pack scallops
1	tablespoon black pepper	12	large shrimp, peeled, de-veined
1	teaspoon cayenne pepper	6	puff pastry rounds, 3 inches each, baked

In heavy saucepan, melt butter; sauté shallots and capers. De-glaze pan with caper liquid; add cream. Bring to simmer; whisk in mustard. Season with salt and pepper. Keep warm. Combine paprika, black pepper, cayenne pepper, garlic, oregano, thyme and basil to make Creole seasoning. Slice fillets in half lengthwise; pound gently. Dust fillets, scallops and shrimp with Creole seasoning; grill to desired doneness. Split pastry round in half; arrange bottom part on plate. Place fish on top followed by shrimp and scallops; spoon on sauce. Top with pastry round.

Yield: 6 servings.

CRABMEAT BROUSSARD'S

8	jumbo shrimp, peeled and butterfly	¼	cup white wine
1	tablespoon butter	2	cups chicken stock
1	ounce olive oil	1	cup heavy cream
1	small onion, diced	3	ounces Brie cheese
2	artichoke hearts, chopped	¾	pound jumbo lump crabmeat
1	clove garlic, minced	½	cup breadcrumbs
¼	cup flour	1	tablespoon whole thyme leaves
		3	tablespoons olive oil

Preheat oven to 400 degrees. In large skillet, melt butter and sauté shrimp. Set aside to cool. In heavy saucepan, heat 1 ounce of olive oil. Sauté onion, artichoke and garlic over medium heat until onion becomes limp. Sprinkle flour and mix well. De-glaze with white wine then add stock. Reduce heat and simmer 3 minutes. Add heavy cream and simmer another 5 minutes. Remove from heat and let stand 2-3 minutes. Take Brie and scrape off white "skin" and cut into small pieces. Add Brie to cream sauce and stir until all cheese is melted and mixed well. Let cool. Mix breadcrumbs, thyme and olive oil and set aside.

After cheese mixture has cooled, gently fold in crabmeat. Place one shrimp in the center of 2½-ounce oven-proof dish, so that it stands. If you have a problem, make butterfly cut deeper. Spoon crabmeat mixture around shrimp and sprinkle with breadcrumb mixture. Repeat with remaining shrimp. Place dish on pan and place in preheated oven for 15-20 minutes or until hot and bubbly.

Serve 8.

Continued Page 26

CREPES BROUSSARD

1	10-ounce package frozen strawberries	12	medium fresh strawberries, hulled and halved
¼	cup white sugar		
¼	cup water	12	dessert crepes
½	cup strawberry liqueur		

Puree the frozen strawberries in a blender. In a saucepan, dissolve the sugar in water and the strawberry puree. Cool for 5 minutes. Add the liqueur and cook until it becomes a thickened sauce. Use fresh strawberries cut in half to enhance the sauce. Using 12 precooked crepes, layer them flat on a work surface. Make a filling in the blender using the following ingredients.

Filling:

¾	cup cream cheese	1	teaspoon lemon juice
¼	cup whipping cream		
2	tablespoons sugar	½	cup chopped walnuts, folded in by hand

Pipe the filling into the crepes, roll and heat in the strawberry sauce. Place 2 crepes per person in a deep dish and serve.

Yield: 6 servings.

SHRIMP AND CRABMEAT CHEESECAKE

3	(¼-ounce) packets unflavored gelatin	2	teaspoons tarragon leaves (soak 1 hour in white wine and drain)
¼	cup water		
¼	cup cider vinegar		
2	cups mayonnaise	2	teaspoons minced, roasted garlic
2	cups sour cream		
¼	cup fresh lemon juice	1	cup sliced green onions
½	cup Dijon mustard	2	teaspoons paprika
5	tablespoons chopped fresh dill or	¾	pound cooked shrimp, peeled and chopped
1	tablespoon dried dill, or to taste	¼	pound jumbo lump crabmeat

FOR THE PIMENTO SAUCE:

1	can or jar (12 to 14 ounces) whole red pimentos	8	ounces cream cheese
½	cup heavy cream	1	teaspoon salt
		2	tablespoons fresh dill

FOR THE PECAN MIXTURE:

2	tablespoons butter	1	teaspoon Worcestershire sauce
1	cup pecan pieces		
½	teaspoon salt Pinch of cayenne pepper		

In a small, heavy saucepan, combine gelatin, water and vinegar and set aside. In a large bowl, combine mayonnaise, sour cream, lemon juice, mustard, dill, tarragon, garlic, green onion and paprika. Mix well. Fold in chopped shrimp. Place gelatin mixture over very low heat, stirring constantly until dissolved. Pour gelatin slowly into shrimp mixture and mix well. Quickly but gently fold in crabmeat. Pour into 8- or 9-inch springform pan. Cover and refrigerate overnight..

To make pimento sauce: Drain pimentos and place in blender with heavy cream, cream cheese and salt. Puree and pour into glass bowl., mixing in the dill. Cover and refrigerate overnight..

To make pecan mixture: Melt butter in skillet; add pecans, salt, cayenne pepper and Worcestershire sauce. Sauté 2 to 3 minutes, being careful not to burn. Cool and chop coarsely. Set aside, but do not refrigerate.

To assemble: Remove side of springform pan and spread pimento sauce over top of cheesecake. Press chopped pecans into sides of cheesecake. Chill until ready to serve.

Makes 15 servings.

Broussard's

Continued Page 27

BOUILLABAISSE

For broth:
½	cup olive oil
½	pound carrots, sliced diagonally
½	pound celery ribs, sliced diagonally
½	pound onions, chopped
¼	cup garlic, chopped
¼	cup shallots, chopped
½	pound fennel, peeled, sliced diagonally
½	pound green peppers, peeled, sliced diagonally
½	cup tomato paste

1	gallon fish or shrimp stock
2	cups tomatoes, peeled, chopped
⅛	ounce saffron
	Salt & white pepper to taste
3	bay leaves
1	pound medium shrimp, peeled, de-veined
1	cup raw oysters
½	cup lump crabmeat
½	pound crawfish tail meat
½	pound fresh trout or pompano, cubed
½	pound scallops
18	fresh mussels

Heat oil; sauté carrots, celery, onions and fennel until half cooked. Add green peppers, garlic and shallots; cook 1 minute. Add tomato paste; cook 10 minutes. Add stock; tomatoes, saffron (steeped in a little hot water), salt, pepper and bay leaves. Bring to boil; remove from heat. At service, heat broth, add seafood; cook 5 minutes. Servings: 6 to 8.

EGGS NEW ORLEANS

1	stick butter
2	tablespoons flour
2	cups of Pet evaporated milk
1	cup water
½	teaspoon salt
⅓	teaspoon cayenne pepper

1	teaspoon Worcestershire sauce
1	pound white crabmeat (thoroughly picked)
6	hard-boiled eggs
1	tablespoon chopped parsley
	Paprika and parsley

In a medium saucepan melt butter. Add flour; stir well and cook about 5 minutes. Add the milk, slowly stirring constantly. Add the water, cooking slowly until the mixture thickens. Add the salt, cayenne pepper, Worcestershire sauce and crabmeat. Cook for 5 minutes. Pour into a glass baking dish. Cut the eggs in half and place eggs cut side up onto the crabmeat mixture. Sprinkle a little paprika and parsley over the top. Bake in 375-degree oven for 10 minutes.

Yield: 12 servings.

CHICKEN CLEMENCEAU

3	6-ounce boneless and skinless chicken breasts (cut in cubes)
	Salt & pepper
3	tablespoons butter
½	cup white wine
1	tablespoon chopped garlic
2	cups diced white potatoes

1	cup sliced mushrooms
½	cup cooked green peas
1	teaspoon chopped parsley
½	teaspoon paprika
	White pepper

Season chicken with salt and pepper. In large frying pan, melt butter; add chicken and stir. Let cook for 5 minutes. Add wine, garlic and potatoes. Cover; let cook for another 5 minutes. Potatoes should be soft and wine just about cooked out. Uncover and add mushrooms, stirring well. Sauté until mushrooms begin to get soft. Add peas, parsley and paprika. Cook until well blended, being careful not to mash vegetables. Add salt and white pepper to taste.

Yield: 4 servings

CLANCY'S

6100 Annunciation Street
New Orleans, LA 70118
(504) 895-1111

John Vodanovich
General Manager/ Co-owner

Brad Hollingsworth
Founder/ Co-owner

Executive Chef Brian Larson

*Brad opened Clancy's in 1987 and since then, Clancy's has been dedicated to preserving the Creole tradition in a fine dining atmosphere. Clancy's has cultivated a strong local clientele that has made it one of the most popular restaurants in New Orleans as well as a "must go" for tourists and conventioneers. A few of the awards and ratings recently received are: "Four Stars" by locally renowned restaurant critic Tom Fitzmorris, "Four Beans" by **Times Picayune Publishing**, Restaurant Guide, "Top Ten" in popularity by New York's Zagat Survey", "Award of Excellence" by "**Wine Spectator**" magazine and "Fodor's Choice" by Fodor's – New Orleans – 2001.*

PAN FRIED LOUISIANA SOFT SHELL CRAB / SAUTÉED CRAWFISH TAILS & MEUNIERE SAUCE

To prepare soft shell crab:
With a pair of kitchen shears cut across the "face" of crab, removing eyes & mouth. Raise "wings" of crab & cut out lungs. Turn crab on backside and remove paddle shaped "key". Season cleaned crab with salt, pepper, paprika and cayenne mix.

Batter for crab:
Dust crab thoroughly in white flour (under wings also). Immerse in beaten egg wash. Dust crab again in white flour.

In a hot skillet over medium heat with olive oil or clarified butter, lay crab on back side and sauté until golden brown (2-3 minutes). Turn crab and drop pan in 350-degree oven for 4 to 5 minutes. While crab is in oven, prepare your cleaned crawfish tails. Season tails with salt & white pepper & cayenne paprika mix. Sauté tails in whole butter. Splash with white wine & add a pinch of sliced scallions, set aside. When tails are ready, prepare your meuniere sauce. In a small skillet put 3-4 tablespoons whole butter. Allow butter to begin to brown, pull off heat and immediately add a pinch of fresh chopped parsley and 1 teaspoon fresh lemon juice, then add 5-6 dashes Lea & Perrins Worcestershire sauce. Bring crab out of oven, having already assembled your plate with sautéed fresh asparagus & roasted new potatoes (or your favorite starch & vegetable).

Place crab on plate. Top crab with sautéed crawfish tails and dress with sizzling meuniere sauce. Serve immediately!

Serves one.

LEMON ICE BOX PIE

Crust:

4	ounces Graham cracker crumbs	1½	ounces fresh unsalted butter, gently melted
1	ounce white sugar		
2	tablespoon brown sugar		

Mix above ingredients until well blended. Form mixture into a non-greased 9-inch pie pan. Bake at 400 degrees for 5 minutes until crust is firm. Cool.

Filling:

4	egg yolks	2½	cans sweetened condensed milk
2	cups fresh squeezed lemon juice		

Blend and mix all filling ingredients. Pour mixture evenly into crusts. Freeze immediately. When frozen, cut & serve.

Yield: 1 pie

EMERIL'S DELMONICO RESTAURANT AND BAR

1300 St. Charles Ave.
New Orleans, LA 70130
(504) 525-4937

Delmonico Restaurant had been in business since 1895 and closed its' doors in February 1997. The restaurant re-opened in May, 1998 under the ownership of Chef Emeril Lagasse. The building went through an extensive renovation under the direction of Trapolin Architects in New Orleans. The two-story structure, located in the Garden District includes three main dining rooms, a bar and private party rooms. The cuisine at Emeril's Delmonico is classic Creole. Chef de Cuisine Neal Swidler oversees the kitchen operation.

Emeril's Delmonico

VEAL MARCELLE

6 tablespoons butter	1 tablespoon Creole mustard
4 cups sliced Exotic mushrooms	Cayenne pepper
Salt & freshly ground black pepper	½ pound butter, melted and warm
1 tablespoon minced garlic	16 spears of fresh pencil asparagus, blanched
½ pound lump crabmeat, picked over for cartilage	8 veal loin cutlets (about 2½ ounces each)
¼ cup chopped green onions	1 cup flour
4 egg yolks	4 thin slices of fresh lemon
1 lemon, juiced	1 tablespoon finely chopped fresh parsley leaves
1 tablespoon water	

In a large sauté pan, over medium heat, melt 3 tablespoons of the butter. Add the mushrooms. Season with salt and pepper. Sauté for 2 minutes. Remove from the heat and stir in the green onions. Set aside and keep warm. In a stainless steel bowl set over a pot of simmering water over medium heat, whisk the egg yolks with the lemon juice, water and mustard. Season with salt and cayenne. Whisk the mixture until pale yellow and slightly thick. Be careful not to let the bowl touch the water. Remove the bowl from the pot and whisking vigorously, add the butter, 1 teaspoon at a time, until all is incorporated. Keep warm. In a large sauté pan, melt 1 tablespoon of the butter. Add the asparagus. Season with salt and pepper. Sauté for 2 minutes. Remove from the heat and keep warm. Place each piece of veal between a sheet of plastic wrap. Using a meat mallet, pound out very thin. Season both sides of the veal with salt and pepper. Season the flour with salt and pepper. Dredge each piece of veal in the flour, coating each side completely. In another large sauté pan, over medium heat, melt the remaining 2 tablespoons of butter. Add the veal and pan-fry for 1 minute on each side. Remove from the heat. To serve, lay two pieces of the veal in the center of each plate. Spoon the Hollandaise over the veal. Lay four spears of asparagus over each plate of veal. Place a spoonful of the relish in the center of the asparagus. Garnish with the pieces of lemon and parsley.

Serves 4.

COMMANDER'S PALACE

1403 Washington Avenue
New Orleans, LA 70130
(504) 899-8221

Nestled in the middle of the Garden District, stands this turquoise and white Victorian fantasy of a building – complete with turrets, columns, and gingerbread. Since 1880, Commander's Palace has been a New Orleans landmark known for the award winning quality of its food, service and commodious dining rooms. When Ella, Dottie, Dick and John Brennan took over personal supervision of the restaurant in 1974, they began to give the splendid old landmark a new look. It was decided to design rooms and settings indoors which complemented and enhanced the lovely outdoor setting; so the décor was planned for a bright, casual airiness. Walls were torn out and replaced with walls of glass, trellises were handcrafted for the garden room to complement and accent this particular color and design

Particular attention was paid to the heart and soul of the restaurant – the kitchen and the dishes created there. Commander's cuisine reflects the best of the city and both Creole and American heritages, as well as dishes of Commander's own creating. Seafood, meats, vegetables, and everything is as fresh as it possibly can be.

Among the many accolades and awards that Commander's Palace has received: James Beard Foundation – Lifetime Outstanding Restaurant Award DiRoNa – Fine Dining Award 2002 – 1988 Zagat Survey/New Orleans Most popular Restaurant (15th Straight Year) 2001, 1997 & 1995 Food & Wine Magazine Reader's Choice Award, #1 Restaurant in America, 1999 – Robb Report – Chosen #2 Chef in the World, 1997 Southern Living Magazine – Reader's Choice Awards, #1 City Restaurant

Tory McPhail, Executive Chef

Chef Tory graduated from the ACF accredited cooking school at Seattle Community College. Upon graduation, school counselors recommended he go to New York City or New Orleans. Since New Orleans has Mardi Gras, the Big Easy won hands down. Once he arrived in New Orleans, Tory was hired by Executive Chef Jamie Shannon of Commander's Palace. A quick study, Tory moved through all the stations in the kitchen. In 1995, Tory became Sous Chef at Palace Café, which was then a part of the Commander's Palace Restaurant Group.

Two years later, Tory decided to broaden his culinary knowledge and moved to Palm Beach, Fl to work at the Breakers, where he quickly became Restaurant Chef. Still wanting to acquire European cooking experience, Tory moved to London to work in the Two-Star (Michelin) restaurant Picasso Room and it's One-Star sister L'Escargot.

Tory left Britain to help open Commander's Palace in Las Vegas. With Tory as Chef De Cuisine, CPLV garnered widespread acclaim. Due to the tragic illness of Tory's friend and mentor Jamie Shannon, Tory was asked to come home and help run the kitchen with the New Orleans team. "We're glad to have him here to continue the evolution of Creole cuisine….he's no stranger to Commander's kitchen," says co-owner Lally Brennan.

OYSTER VELOUTÉ

2½ onions, diced	¼ gallon of milk
2½ leeks, half mooned	2 pounds Gruyere cheese
1½ pounds of butter	
3½ cups of flour	2 cups of chopped fresh herbs
2½ cups of dry vermouth	Salt & pepper
2 gallons of oyster liquor	

Sweat veggies in butter. Add flour making a roux and cool on low for 5-10 minutes. Add vermouth and oyster liquor. Cook for 20 minutes. Add milk and cheese. Cook until all of the cheese has melted. Finish with fresh herbs and salt and pepper.

Continued Page 31

1½ ounce diced tasso
1½ ounce chopped artichoke hearts

1 tablespoon breadcrumbs
3 ounces of the veloute

Place all of the ingredients in a hot cast iron crock pot and top with breadcrumbs. Heat in a 350-degree oven for 5 minutes.

Serves 12.

CHEF TORY'S SEARED REDFISH AND CHILI GLAZED SHRIMP SALAD

¼ cup mangos, diced
2 lemons (juiced)
¼ cup Karo syrup
¼ cup vegetable oil
⅛ teaspoon salt
1½ tbsp. Commander's Creole Seasoning
2 ounce New Orleans Rum
1 Serrano chili, minced
¼ teaspoon red chili flakes

1½ cups baby greens
½ ounce red onions, shaved
¼ cup hearts of palm, sliced thin
2 jumbo shrimp (head on)
3 ounce medallion redfish, smoked
½ ounce black pepper Brioche Croutons
Salt & pepper to taste

Method:

Vinaigrette — Combine ⅛ cup of mangos, lemon juice and half of Karo syrup in blender. Puree until smooth. When blending, slowly pour in vegetable oil in a steady stream to emulsify. Season with salt.

Heat a heavy bottom skillet over medium heat and add oil. While pan is heating, season shrimp and redfish on both sides with Commander's Creole seasoning. Sear shrimp and redfish in pan for 1½ minutes on both sides. Remove redfish and shrimp and set aside. Deglaze pan with rum (make sure to remove pan from the flame while deglazing). Place pan back on the stove and add Serrano chilis, red pepper flakes and remainder of Karo syrup. Reduce pepper mixture to a sauce consistency. Add shrimp back to the pan and set aside.

Combine baby greens, hearts of palm, red onion, croutons and mango vinaigrette in a mixing bowl. Season with salt and pepper to taste. Place salad mixture on a plate. Place the redfish on the greens. Place the glazed shrimp atop the redfish. Finish the plate with mango vinaigrette.

Serves 1.

DICKIE BRENNAN'S STEAKHOUSE
716 Iberville Street New Orleans, LA 70130 (504) 522-2467

In just three short years, Dickie Brennan's Steakhouse has received nation accolades. In addition to receiving the Wine Spectator Award of Excellence this year, Dickie Brennan's Steakhouse has recently been named one of the Top 12 Steakhouses in America by national foodwriter John Mariani.

Dickie Brennan's Steakhouse features USDA Prime beef exclusively – a fact that sets it apart from other steakhouses. Executive Chef Gus Martin and Chef de Cuisine Chris Barbato lead the culinary team at the French Quarter restaurant. Straightforward USDA Prime Steaks with a New Orleans Touch, fresh seafood and innovative Creole dishes define the cuisine.

HOUSE FILET

8 ounces creamed spinach (recipe follows)
4 ounces Pontalba potatoes (recipe follows)

1 8-ounce beef filet, cooked to desired temperature
1½ ounces Béarnaise Sauce
5 fresh oysters, fried golden brown

Spread creamed spinach across the entire bottom of a plate, in a circle. Place Pontalba potatoes in small circle in center of plate. Place filet on top of the potatoes. Ladle the Béarnaise sauce over the filet. Place fried oysters around the filet.

Serves 1.

BÉARNAISE SAUCE:

4 tablespoons fresh tarragon, chopped
½ gallon hollandaise sauce

To make Béarnaise sauce: Fold tarragon into hollandaise sauce; set aside.

Continued Page 32

CREAMED SPINACH

1	tablespoon unsalted butter	½	cup Béchamel sauce (see recipe following)
3	ounces yellow onion, sliced	¼	cup heavy cream
12	ounces fresh spinach, picked clean		Creole seasoning to taste

In sauté pan, melt butter. Add onions and fresh spinach and sauté until wilted. Add Béchamel sauce and heavy cream and stir. Season to taste with Creole seasoning.

Serve immediately in a dip dish. Serves 2.

BÉCHAMEL SAUCE:

2	ounces unsalted butter	1	bay leaf
2	ounces all-purpose flour	2	whole cloves
1	cup whole milk		Kosher salt to taste
4	ounces yellow onion, chopped		White pepper to taste

In medium size pan, melt butter. Add flour and make a white roux by whisking thoroughly. In medium sauce pot, combine milk, onion, bay leaf, cloves, salt and pepper; bring to a simmer over low heat. Slowly add white roux by whisking it in, and allowing sauce to thicken. Strain sauce, set aside to cool and then add to spinach mixture. Serves 2.

PONTALBA POTATOES

1	medium potato	2	ounces will mushroom mix (shiitake, crimini, oyster, etc.)
3	cups vegetable oil		
1½	tablespoons unsalted butter		
2	ounces yellow onion, julienne	½	ounce green onions, finely chopped
1	ounce tasso, diced small		
½	tablespoon, fresh garlic, chopped	1	tablespoon brandy Creole seasoning to taste

Wash potato and bake in an oven at 350 degrees for 40 minutes. Cool potato, peel and cut into medium size cubes (½" x ½"). In large pot, add oil and bring to 350 degrees. Add potatoes and fry until golden brown (about 4 minutes). Strain and set aside over paper towels to absorb extra oil. In sauté pan, melt butter over medium heat, add onion and cook until slightly brown. Add tasso and garlic and cook until garlic is lightly toasted. Add mushrooms and cook until tender. Add fried potatoes, green onions, brandy and seasoning, toss to mix and serve. Serves 1.

CREOLE ONION SOUP

6	ounces unsalted butter	½	quart heavy cream
1½	pounds yellow onions, julienne	2	bay leaves
2	ounces, all-purpose flour	2	tablespoons Kosher salt
1	quart chicken stock or broth	1	teaspoon white pepper, fresh ground
8	ounces white wine	18	ounces Cheddar cheese, shredded
½	quart milk		

In large pot, melt butter over medium heat. Add the julienne onions and cook until translucent (do not brown). Add flour to pot and cook for 8 minutes, stirring constantly. Do NOT brown the flour! Add chicken stock or broth, white wine, milk, cream and bay leaves and bring to a boil. Reduce to low heat and allow soup to simmer for 20 minutes. Remove bay leaves, add salt and pepper. With a hand mixer or blender, puree soup, add Cheddar cheese slowly until dissolved. Serve immediately. Yield: 1 gallon.

PRIME BEEF TENDERLOIN

18	ounces seasoned beef tenderloin, cooked to temperature and sliced	1	red bell pepper, roasted, cooled, peeled, julienne
2	ounces oil	1	tablespoon brandy
1	teaspoon fresh garlic, chopped	9	ounces brandy cream sauce (recipe follows)
4	ounces wild mushroom mix (shiitake, oyster, crimini –all sliced.)	1	teaspoon Creole seasoning
		2	quarts water
		12	ounces Capellini pasta

In large sauté pan, over medium – high heat, blacken beef tenderloin to desired temperature, then remove and cool in refrigerator. In a sauté pan at medium heat, add oil, then garlic. Lightly toast the garlic, and add wild mushroom mix. Then add the julienne roasted peppers and sauté until tender. Add sliced beef, then remove pan from fire and add brandy, carefully return to fire and flame it. Add the brandy cream sauce and bring to a boil. Add Creole seasoning to season mixture. In large pot, bring 2 quarts of water to a boil, and cook pasta al dente. Remove and drain. Plate the pasta splitting it into size portions of 2 ounces each. Spoon about 3 ounces of the beef mixture over the pasta. Serve immediately. Serves 6 appetizer portions.

Continued Page 33

BRANDY CREAM SAUCE:

2	tablespoons unsalted butter	1	tablespoon carrots, diced small
2	tablespoons fresh shallots, chopped	½	cup red wine
1	teaspoon fresh garlic, chopped	1	cup veal demi-glace
		½	cup brandy
1	tablespoon celery, diced small	½	cup heavy cream
		½	teaspoon salt
		½	teaspoon white pepper

In sauce pan at medium heat, melt butter, then add shallots, garlic, celery and carrots. Sauté all items until tender, then add red wine and bring mixture to a boil, and reduce it by three-quarters its volume. Add veal demi-glace and brandy, bring to a boil and reduce by half its volume. Add heavy cream, bring to a boil and reduce by half its volume. At this point the sauce has gone through a natural reduction and is ready to be seasoned with salt and white pepper to taste. Strain the sauce. Add sauce to sauté pan to be used in Prime Beef Tenderloin appetizer recipe. Yields: 8 to 10 ounces of sauce.

CRAB AND AVOCADO CHARLOTTE WITH SWEET CORN COULIS AND ASPARAGUS

4	ripe avocados	1	tablespoons chopped cilantro
1	bunch asparagus, blanched	1	tablespoons sesame oil
2	teaspoons pureed ginger		Salt & pepper to taste
1-2	teaspoons pureed garlic	1	tablespoons red topiko (smelt roe)
1-2	tablespoons lemon juice	1	cup picked crabmeat (lump or claw meat)
1-2	tablespoons lime juice		
½	cup diced red onion		

Smash avocados once peeled. Add everything except asparagus, crabmeat & topiko. Mix well. Check for seasoning. Fold in crabmeat. Place in ring mold on center of plate. Line asparagus tips around the circle. Corn coulis in between each spear. Garnish top of Charlotte with more crabmeat and the topiko, and a sprig of cilantro.

CORN COULIS:

6	spears of corn		Pinch of salt and pepper
1	tablespoon olive oil	1	bay leaf
1	tablespoon canola oil		Water or clear broth

Shave corn kernels off of cob, sauté in oil lightly. Add water or broth, approximately 3 cups. Cover, cook until tender. Remove cobs. Strain corn—keep the liquid. Put strained corn in blender, adding some of cooking liquid, just enough to form sauce-like consistency. Check for seasoning. Strain liquid through a fine wire mesh strainer.

EMERIL'S RESTAURANT

800 Tchoupitoulas Street New Orleans, LA 70130 (504) 528-9393

Chef Emeril Lagasse opened Emeril's Restaurant in March 1990 in the Warehouse District. This highly successful restaurant uses only the freshest ingredients available. They are purchased from local farmers, ranchers and fisherman. Lagasse refers to his food as "new New Orleans" cuisine. Chef de Cuisine Chris Wilson oversees the daily operation of the kitchen. Emeril's was renovated by renowned New York design company, the Rockwell Group in 2000.

BANANA CREAM PIE WITH CARAMEL DRIZZLES AND CHOCOLATE SAUCE

There're a few secrets necessary to successfully making this pie (which, incidentally, has been on the menu at Emeril's since Day One, and continues to be one of the most requested desserts). First, the bananas, while ripe, need to be firm, so that they hold their shape when pushed into place. Second, the pastry cream needs to be very stiff, so that when sliced, the pie will not crumble or slide. It's also important to cover the bananas completely with the last layer of pastry cream to prevent them from discoloring. And while at Emeril's they pipe the whipped cream over each individual slice before serving, feel free to spread your whipped cream over the whole pie, if you'd prefer.

Makes one 9-inch pie, 10 servings

4	cups heavy cream	½	cup cornstarch
1½	cups whole milk	1	recipe Graham Cracker Crust, recipe below
1½	cups plus 2 teaspoons granulated sugar		
1	vanilla bean, split in half lengthwise and seeds scraped	3	pounds (about 9) firm but ripe bananas, peeled and cut crosswise into ½-inch-thick slices
3	large egg yolks		
2	large eggs		

½	teaspoon pure vanilla extract Caramel sauce, recipe below Chocolate sauce, recipe below		Shaved chocolate, for garnish Confectioner's sugar, for garnish

Combine 2 cups of the cream, the milk, ½ cup of the sugar, the vanilla bean and the vanilla seeds in a large heavy-bottomed saucepan over medium heat. Bring to a gentle boil, whisking to dissolve the sugar. Remove from the heat. Combine the egg yolks, eggs, cornstarch and 1 cup of the sugar in a medium bowl and whisk pale yellow in color. Set aside.

Whisk 1 cup of the hot cream mixture into the egg yolks. Gradually add the egg mixture to the hot cream, whisking constantly. Bring to a simmer, stirring constantly with a large wooden spoon to cook out the cornstarch and the mixture thickens, about 5 minutes. (The mixture may separate slightly. If so, remove from the heat and beat with an electric mixer until thick and smooth.) Strain through a fine mesh strainer into a clean bowl. Cover with plastic wrap, pressing down against the surface to prevent a skin from forming. Chill in the refrigerator for about 4 hours.

To assemble, spread ½ cup of the custard over the bottom of the prepared crust, smoothing with the back of a large spoon or rubber spatula. Arrange enough banana slices (not quite one-third) in a tight, tiled pattern over the custard, pressing down with your hands to pack them firmly. Repeat to build a second layer, using ¾ cup of the custard and enough bananas to cover, smoothing down the layer evenly. For the third layer, spread ¾ cup of custard over the bananas and top with the remaining bananas, starting 1-inch from the outer edge and working toward the center. Spread 1 cup of custard evenly over the bananas to prevent discoloration. Cover with plastic wrap and chill for at least 4 hours or overnight. In a medium bowl, whip the cream until soft peaks form. Add the remaining 2 teaspoons of sugar and the vanilla extract and whip until stiff peaks form.

Remove the pie from the refrigerator. With a sharp knife dipped in hot water, cut the pie into 10 equal slices. Transfer the slices to dessert plates. Fill a pastry bag with the whipped cream and pipe onto each slice. (Alternately, spread the whipped cream evenly over the pie before cutting.) Drizzle each slice with the caramel sauce and chocolate sauce, sprinkle with the chocolate shavings and confectioners' sugar, and serve.

Continued Page 35

GRAHAM CRACKER CRUST

Makes one 9-inch crust

1¼ cups graham cracker crumbs
¼ cup sugar

4 tablespoons unsalted butter, melted

Preheat the oven to 350 degrees F. Combine the graham cracker crumbs and sugar in a medium bowl and mix well. Add the butter and mix well. Press the mixture into a 9-inch pie pan. Top with aluminum pie tin and with a circular motion, press the crust tightly into the pan. Bake until browned, about 25 minutes. Cool for 10 to 15 minutes.

CARAMEL SAUCE

Makes a generous ¾ cup

¾ cup sugar
2 tablespoons water
½ teaspoon fresh lemon juice

½ cup heavy cream
2 tablespoons to ¼ cup whole milk

Combine the sugar, water and lemon juice in a medium, heavy saucepan over medium-high heat. Cook, stirring, until the sugar dissolves. Let boil without stirring until the mixture becomes a deep amber color, 2 to 3 minutes, watching closely so it doesn't burn. Add the cream, whisk to combine, and remove from the heat. Add the milk, 2 tablespoons at a time, until the desired consistency is reached. Remove from the heat and cool to room temperature before serving with the pie. (The sauce will thicken as it cools.)

CHOCOLATE SAUCE

Makes 1½ cups

¾ cup half-and-half
1 tablespoon unsalted butter

½ pound semisweet chocolate chips
¼ teaspoon pure vanilla extract

Scaled the half-and-half and butter in a small, heavy saucepan over medium heat. Remove from the heat. Place the chocolate and vanilla in a medium, heat-proof bowl. Add the hot half-and-half and let sit for 2 minutes, then whisk until smooth. Serve slightly warm. (The sauce can be kept refrigerated in an airtight container for several days, but it must be returned to room temperature before serving.

Emeril's

RESTAURANT
NEW ORLEANS

GALATOIRE'S RESTAURANT

209 Bourbon Street
New Orleans, LA 70130
(504) 525-2021

*October 2001 – Hot Off the Press: The October 2001 issue of **Gourmet** Magazine names Galatoire's as one of the nation's Top Fifty Restaurants! "We are truly honored to be recognized by so honorable and respected a publication as **Gourmet**," said Melvin Rodrigue, general manager of Galatoire's. "Throughout the 96-year history of the restaurant the Galatoire family has consistently strived to provide the very finest, most memorable dining experience possible."*

*The Gourmet article places Galatoire's at Number 24 in the nation for fine dining experiences. Galatoire's is also the proud recipient of numerous awards including the coveted Year 2000 DiRoNa Award, issued for general restaurant excellence. The Nation's Restaurant News elected Galatoire's to its Hall of Fame in 1981 – this honor has been bestowed upon fewer that 200 restaurants in the United States. In May 1988, Inside America: The Sophisticated Guide to American Travel listed Galatoire's as the best restaurant in New Orleans. In 1990, 1991 and 1992, the **Conde Nast Traveler** elected Galatoire's to one of fifty Distinguished Restaurants, an honor that begins with the nomination by Mimi Sheraton of Taste: **The New Yorker's** Candid Guide to Restaurants.*

*Executive Chef Milton Prudence and Chef d'Cuisine Ross Edwards lead the fine culinary team in the kitchen. Chef Prudence is a veteran of more than thirty years with Galatoire's. On average, Galatoire's employees spend ten years with the restaurant.
Employee loyalty contributes greatly to the success of Galatoire's.*

SHRIMP REMOULADE

1	bunch celery	1	cup red wine
1	bunch green onion		vinegar
1	bunch parsley	2	teaspoons
½	large yellow onion		Worcestershire
1	cup ketchup		sauce
1	cup tomato puree	½	cup salad oil
1	cup Creole mustard	1½	ounces paprika
2	tablespoons		Jumbo boiled
	horseradish		shrimp
	(prepared)		

Mince celery, green onion, parsley and onions in a food processor. Add ketchup, tomato puree, Creole mustard, red wine vinegar, horseradish and oil to the vegetables, and mix all ingredients in the food processor, adding paprika last. Allow the sauce to stand refrigerated 6-8 hours before serving and taste again. Adjust horseradish if necessary. Evenly coat the shrimp with the sauce in a mixing bowl, and serve on a bed of lettuce.

Serves 12.

CRAB SARDOU

Hollandaise sauce	12	artichokes
(see below)	2	pounds jumbo
Creamed spinach		lump crabmeat
(see below)	½	cup clarified butter

In a large pot, submerge the artichokes in water and boil for approximately 30 minutes, until the stems are tender. Allow the artichokes to cool, and peel the leaves from the hearts. Using a spoon or your thumb, remove and discard the hearts, leaving the bottom of the artichokes. While waiting for the artichokes to cook and cool, prepare the Hollandaise sauce and creamed spinach, placing both of these items on the side. Sauté the crabmeat in the clarified butter until hot, being careful not to break the lumps. Remove from heat. Arrange serving plates and spoon equal portions of the creamed spinach onto the plates. Place 2 peeled artichoke bottoms into the bed of spinach. Drain excess butter from the crabmeat, and spoon equal portions into the cavities of the bottoms. Finally, top with a generous portion of the Hollandaise sauce.

Serves 6.

Continued Page 37

HOLLANDAISE SAUCE:

6	egg yolks	1	teaspoon lemon juice
7	tablespoons solid butter (cut into small pieces)	1	teaspoon red wine vinegar
	Salt (pinch)	2	tablespoons cold water
	Cayenne pepper (pinch)	2	cups clarified butter

In a double boiler, combine egg yolks with the solid butter, salt, cayenne pepper, lemon juice and red wine vinegar. Over medium heat, whisk the ingredients continuously until the mixture increases in volume and achieves a consistency that adheres to the whisk. Using a ladle, slowly whisk the clarified butter into the mixture. If the sauce appears to be too thick, add a touch of the cold water to bring it back to a proper consistency. Yields 3 cups.

CREAMED SPINACH:

3	cups cooked spinach	1	cup Béchamel sauce (see below)
			Salt & pepper

In a sauté pan, fold the spinach and béchamel sauce together and simmer over low heat. Salt and pepper to taste. Serves 6.

BÉCHAMEL SAUCE:

⅛	pound of butter	¼	cup of flour
1	cup of milk		

Heat milk until it simmers. Melt the butter and add the flour to make a roux. Continue whisking on a low heat to cook the flour but do not allow it to remain on the heat long enough to change from a blonde roux to a brown roux. Add ½ of the heated milk to the roux while constantly whisking. This mixture will become thick like a paste. Add the remaining milk and whisk until smooth.

CHICKEN CLEMENCEAU

1	fryer chicken	1	15-ounce can petit pois, drained
3	tablespoons minced garlic	¼	cup clarified butter
2	Idaho potatoes		Salt and white pepper to taste
1	pint jumbo button mushrooms, sliced		

Preheat your oven to 400 degrees. Rinse your chicken and cut into four quarters. Salt and pepper chicken and bake for approximately 30 minutes until golden brown. During the cook time of your chicken, begin preparing your Brabant potatoes. Peel the potatoes and cut them into ¾ inch cubes. Deep fry the potatoes in vegetable oil until golden brown and remove to a paper towel to drain.

In a large sauté pan, begin to sauté sliced mushrooms in clarified butter until tender. Add minced garlic, Brabant potatoes, petit pois and salt & pepper to taste. After you have checked the seasoning of the garnish, begin putting the chicken quarters into the sauté pan with the garnish and sauté an additional 3 to 5 minutes for the chicken to absorb the flavors of the garnish. Place the quartered chicken pieces onto serving plate. Using a slotted spoon, drain excess butter from garnish and top the chicken with equal portions.

GW FINS

808 Bienville Street
New Orleans, LA 70112
(504) 581-FINS (3467)

Gary Wollerman
Tenney Flynn
Proprietors

Tenney Flynn
Executive Chef

GW Fins is a global seafood restaurant, which serves the highest quality seafood that is available throughout the world, every day. As such, the following is a list of some of the seafood that you may find on GW Fins menu on any given day, along with its place or origin. The menu changes daily, based on the freshest and best seafood that is available at that moment: The following are examples of seafood that may be available: Sea Bass from Chile, Cold water lobster tails from New Zealand, Dover Sole from Holland, Mackeral from Japan, Sockeye, King and Coho Salmon from Alaska, Halibut from Alaska, Snapper from Florida, Speckled Trout and pompano from the Gulf of Mexico, Haddock and Skate from New England, farm raised catfish from Mississippi and the list goes on and on!

CREOLE TOMATO, CUCUMBER AND VIDALIA ONION SALAD

3 ounces Creole tomato filets, peeled and seeded
2 ounces cucumbers, peeled, seeded *cut on the bias and macerated in seasoned rice vinegar
2 ounces Vidalia onions, cut in ⅜" julienne
1 ounce Maytag blue cheese, macerated in rice vinegar
1 sprig fresh basil
2 ounces sherry vinaigrette (recipe follows)

Toss together the tomato filets, marinated cucumbers and onions and 2 tablespoons of the dressing and place in a 4" salad ring. Top with the blue cheese and the basil sprig and remove the ring. Spoon the remaining tablespoon of dressing around the salad.

Makes 1 serving.

*Tomatoes should be held at room temperature unless very ripe.

SHERRY VINAIGRETTE

⅓ cup sherry vinegar
1⅞ teaspoons Dijon mustard
1⅞ teaspoons sugar
⅝ teaspoon salt
⅝ teaspoon freshly ground black pepper
⅞ teaspoon herbs - parsley, chervil, chives, thyme, etc.
½ cup olive oil
⅓ cup Pomace oil

Place all ingredients except oils in a 2 gal. container. Blend with a mixer and slowly add oils to emulsify.

Makes 5 servings.

HORSERADISH CRUSTED DRUM

4 each prepped drum* fillets (prep instructions follow)
1 cup fried parsnips (recipe follows)
12 each fried spinach leaves (recipe follows)
8 ounces truffled potato sauce (recipe follows)
Oil and butter for sautéing
Truffle oil

Preheat a large nonstick sauté pan. Add about 2 tablespoons olive oil and 1 tablespoon butter and place the prepared fillets crumb side down. Cook until golden brown, turn and lower heat. Cook on low heat until done – about 2-3 minutes. Ladle 2 ounces of potato sauce on the side of the plate and place the drum fillet in the center. Mound ¼ cup fired parsnips on top of the fish, drizzle a few drops of truffle oil on top of the sauce and top with 3 fried spinach leaves.

Yield: 4 servings.

*If drum is not available, substitute snapper, grouper mahi mahi, redfish or your favorite fish.

Continued Page 39

Prep for Horseradish Crusted Drum

4	each 7-8 ounce drum fillets (grouper, snapper, mahi mahi, redfish)	2	cups panko (Japanese breadcrumbs)
½	cup Dijon mustard	1	tablespoon dried parsley
½	cup prepared horseradish		Salt & pepper

Mix the above ingredients and coat the fillets.

Crispy Fried Parsnips

| 4 | each large parsnips, peeled and cut in strips, using the peeler | | Ice water Vegetable oil for frying Thermometer |

Peel the parsnips, place in ice water, dry and fry in vegetable oil at 300 degrees until crispy.

Yield: 4 servings.

Fried Baby Spinach

| 12 | each perfectly shaped spinach leaves | | Vegetable oil for frying Thermometer |

Pick small washed spinach leaves (a few extra wouldn't hurt) wash and dry. Cut the stems about an inch long. Heat about two cups of oil to 300 degrees and place the leaves one at a time in the hot oil. Stir gently to separate the leaves and carefully remove them when they become translucent and place them on a paper towel to drain. Reserve uncovered at room temperature.

Yield: 4 servings.

Mashed Potatoes for Truffle Sauce

2	each large Idaho potatoes, peeled, cut 2" cubes		Salt & pepper
2	ounces butter	4	ounces half and half, warmed
4	ounces half and half, warmed	2	teaspoons truffle oil

Place potatoes in a sauce pan and cover with cold water. Place on high heat and bring to a boil. Cook until fork tender. Drain and leave in the hot pot to steam dry. Mash with a potato masher or fork removing all lumps (before adding any liquid). Stir in butter and 4 ounces of warmed cream. Season to taste with salt and pepper. Thin with the other 4 ounces of warm cream, add truffle oil and strain through a sieve. Reserve warm.

Yield: 4 servings.

Mashed Sweet Potatoes
With Bananas, Bourbon and Vanilla

2	pounds sweet potatoes, peeled, cut 2" cubes	2	each ripe bananas
		½	tablespoon salt
1	cup heavy cream	2	tablespoons soft butter
1	each vanilla beans, split	½	cup freshly squeezed orange juice
½	cup honey		
½	cup brown sugar		

Place sweet potatoes in a thick bottomed saucepan, add cream, salt and the split and scraped vanilla bean. Cover and cook on low heat until potatoes are soft, about 45 minutes. You may need to add a tablespoon or two more of cream, but the main thing is to cook at a bare simmer. Add hone, brown sugar, orange juice and bananas. Increase the heat and cook mashing all ingredients until somewhat smooth. Remove vanilla bean and remove from heat. May be made in advance and reheated.

Yield: 6 servings.

HERBSAINT

701 St. Charles Ave.
New Orleans, LA 70130
(504) 524-4114

Susan Spicer, Chef & Co-owner
Donald Link, Chef & Co-owner

Chef Susan Spicer of Bayona restaurant teams up with Chef Donald Link to offer French-American bistro fare at this sleek eatery. Entrées range from sautéed port tenderloin with smothered greens to duck confit galette. Vegetarian dishes are available, as well as fine wines by the glass.

SHRIMP BISQUE

1	tablespoon butter	1	pint shrimp stock
1	cup chopped onion	1	pint water
1	cup chopped celery	¼	cup rice
½	cup chopped carrot	1	sprig tarragon
½	cup scallions		Dash of brandy and Herbsaint
1	teaspoon paprika		
1	teaspoon salt	2	teaspoons salt
2	cups chopped tomatoes	½	cup heavy cream
		1	tablespoon butter
5	each whole shrimp cut up with shells on		

In a heavy bottom saucepot sauté the onion, carrot, celery and scallion with the spices until soft. Add tomatoes and shrimp and cook until tomatoes break down, about 15-20 minutes. Add shrimp stock and water and simmer an additional 10 minutes then add the rice and cook another 15 minutes. Add the tarragon about 5 minutes before removing soup to strain. Put soup in small batches in a blender and blend until smooth, then strain. Return to heat and finish with a dash of brandy and Herbsaint, salt, cream and butter. A little hot sauce never hurts.

SHRIMP WITH GREEN CHILE GRITS AND TASSO CREAM SAUCE

SAUCE:

2	tablespoons + 2 tablespoons whole butter	4	tablespoons all-purpose flour
½	cup diced onion	1	cup shrimp stock
½	cup diced celery	1	cup heavy cream
½	diced tasso		Dash of lemon juice and hot sauce to finish
1	tablespoon fresh chopped thyme		
1½	teaspoon salt & black pepper each	2	pounds of large shrimp (more or less depending whether this is an appetizer or entrée)
¾	teaspoon cayenne pepper		
¾	teaspoon chopped garlic		

Melt 2 tablespoons of butter in a sauce pan over medium heat, add onion, celery, tasso, chopped thyme, cayenne, paprika and garlic and cook until vegetables are soft. Add other 2 tablespoons of butter and melt into pan, then add your flour to blend in with vegetables in the pan. Then add shrimp stock and reduce by half, add cream and reduce again until a nice thick cream sauce has formed. Finish with the lemon juice and hot sauce. When sauce is done set aside and cook your shrimp in whatever oil or fat you desire for a couple of minutes on each side until they are almost all the way cooked and ladle sauce over shrimp and simmer for 5 minutes. To serve spoon over warm grits with roasted peppers and cheese mixed in.

(Serves 4-6)

Tip: Whenever making sauce that has some sort of roux in the base always add your liquids in stages so that you don't make your sauce too thin, the sauce is always easier to thin out than thicken.

LE PARVENU

509 Williams Blvd.
Kenner, LA 70062
(504) 471-0534

Chef Dennis Hutley, Proprietor

Chef Dennis is the Founding President of the ACF Junior Chapter (1976) and Sargent at Arms – New Orleans ACF Chapter 1978. He cooked for the Papal Entourage during Pope John Paul II's visit to New Orleans in 1987. Chef Dennis has been featured in Great Chefs Series "Louisiana New Garde" 1990 (3 Episodes) and recognized in **"Gastronomy World Star" – Mumm Champagne 1991**

Le Parvenu Restaurant was established in April 1996. It is located at 509 Williams Blvd. very near the Mississippi River in the Historic District of Rivertown. It is a 55 year old house with four dining rooms and a small bar area. It's fronted by a white picket fence, large covered porch, and surrounded by a spacious yard & garden. The fare is award winning and labeled "Innovative American Creole Cuisine". It is fine dining in a business casual atmosphere.

In just 6 years of operation, Le Parvenu Restaurant has gotten the awards… "Best New Restaurant" – New Orleans, 1996, "Zagat Survey" Top Ten in New Orleans, 1997 to present. "Four Stars" by local food writer Tom Fitzmorris, "DiRoNA Award", 2002, "Fodor's Choice" – Fodor's Travel Guide, 1997 to present and "AAA Recommended Dining" – Triple A Tour Book, 2001.

MIRLITON, SHRIMP AND CRAB BISQUE

4	ounces butter	3	cups crab, shrimp & mirliton stock
2	ounces flour	2	cups cream, heated
⅓	cup diced carrots	¾	cup Sauternes wine (sweet wine)
¼	cup diced celery		
¼	cup diced onion	1½	teaspoons salt
1	tablespoon garlic	½	teaspoon white pepper
2	medium bay leaves		
3	medium mirlitons, peeled & diced		

Use gumbo crabs, shrimp shells and mirliton parings for "stock". Melt butter, add flour and cook gently for 2 or 3 minutes. Add carrots, celery, onions, garlic and bay leaves and cook 3 minutes without browning. Add mirlitons, mix well and heat through. Whisk in strained stock, bring to a simmer and cook about 5 minutes. Whisk in cream, simmer 5 minutes, then add wine and cook another 5 minutes., season with salt and pepper, stir well. To serve, place boiled shrimp and lump crabmeat in soup cups or bowls and ladle in soup, garnish with a dollop of freshly whipped cream and serve.

Yield: 2 quarts.

TOASTED GARLIC DRESSING

6	egg yolks	1	cup garlic vinegar
1	teaspoon mustard powder	½	teaspoon salt
		3	cups olive oil
1	teaspoon Worcestershire sauce	1	cup fine julienne elephant garlic, toasted under a broiler, cooled
½	teaspoon ground black pepper		

Whisk together the yolks, mustard powder, Worcestershire, pepper, vinegar and salt. Put this mixture in a blender and at high speed add the olive oil slowly (as for making mayonnaise) to emulsify. Stir in elephant garlic, store in a clean container and chill. Stir well before using. (To make garlic vinegar, put whole cloves of peeled regular garlic on a sheet pan or cookie sheet, "toast" gently under the broiler, tossing and mixing as they brown. Chill well, put in a jar and cover amply with white vinegar, allow to "steep" about 2 weeks before using.

Yield: about 1 quart.

Continued Page 42

CREOLE DIPPING SAUCE / SHRIMP PARFAIT

2	cups raw 50/60 ct. peeled shrimp, pureed	2	teaspoon brandy
½	cup tomato puree	1	cup concentrated shrimp stock
2	tablespoons lemon juice	½	tablespoon chopped garlic
1	tablespoon dry sherry	½	tablespoon chopped shallots

Combine above ingredients and cook over medium heat until nearly dry, but still moist puree in a blender, place in a bowl and chill. Then add 2 cups heavy (regular) mayonnaise, ½ teaspoon paprika and ¼ cup green cayenne relish and refrigerate.

To serve as "dipping" sauce, skewer large raw shrimp and season. Grill, un-skewer, then serve warm with cold "dipping sauce" on the side maybe with a little mixed lettuce and garnish of some sort to present.

To make "parfait": Marinate cold, peeled boiled shrimp with sliced green onions, chopped garlic & shallots, lemon juice, a little liquid crab boil and a little olive oil, chill for a while and then put in each glass a little shredded lettuce, a layer of boiled shrimp, a little sauce, some more boiled shrimp and some more sauce until glass is full with layers, garnish as desired and serve.

Yield: 1 quart.

le Parvenu

Innovative American Creole Cuisine

LOUISIANA CRAB CAKES

2	cups heavy cream	1	pound jumbo lump crabmeat
½	cup slice green onions		About 2½ to 3 cups finely shredded French bread
1	tablespoon chopped garlic		Salt & white pepper to taste
¼	cup brandy		
1	teaspoon liquid crab boil		

In a skillet combine cream, green onions, garlic, brandy and liquid crab boil, then bring to a boil and cook about 3 or 4 minutes, add lump crabmeat with salt and pepper and mix in very gently. When thoroughly heated, remove from heat and very carefully fold in breadcrumbs. Spread mixture on a pan and allow to cool slightly. Spoon or scoop into 16 equal portions and then shape into "cakes" without "pressing" to facilitate a light texture. Place on a lightly buttered or greased pan and broil under medium high heat until browned. Serve with your favorite sauce and choice of vegetables. Note: Add the bread carefully and in two steps if possible, it might take more or less to get the mixture just to where it will "form."

Yield: About 8 servings.

CLASSIC CRÈME BRÛLÉE

7	egg yolks	1	fresh vanilla bean, split & scraped into cream
4	ounces sugar		
3	cups heavy cream		

Preheat oven to 300 degrees. Combine egg yolks & sugar and whip to a ribbon stage. Meanwhile heat cream (with vanilla bean) just to a boil. Gradually whisk hot cream into egg yolks and sugar, skim any foam that appears. Ladle mixture into 4-ounce ramekins, place ramekins into a shallow pan containing about a ½ inch of warm water. Place the pan in the oven and bake approximately 1½ hours, or until just "set." Remove ramekins from water bath and chill in the refrigerator. To serve, spread a thin layer of light brown sugar on top of the chilled cream and glaze under the broiler until caramelized and slightly burnt. Note: The "secret" is slow cooking.

Yield: 6 servings

LEE CIRCLE RESTAURANT

#3 Lee Circle
New Orleans, LA 70130
(504) 962-0915

Chef/Owner of Le Parvenu Restaurant, Dennis Hutley, with Clancy's Restaurant of Uptown New Orleans, owners Brad Hollingsworth and John Vodanovich, with Chef de Cuisine Scott Snodgrass have teamed up to open fine dining on the historic site of Lee Circle in uptown New Orleans at 936 St. Charles Ave. The contemporary design features Elegant Creole Cuisine with abundant local favorite selections of veal and seafood done in a "cutting edge" elegance. Scott Snodgrass has been named Executive Chef for Lee Circle Restaurant.

SHRIMP LEE CIRCLE

2	pounds 16/20 ct. Biloxi Bay Shrimp (peeled, tail on & de-veined)	2	tablespoons minced fresh garlic
1	cup artichoke hearts, chopped	1	tablespoon ground white pepper
½	small yellow onion, chopped	1	tablespoon ground cayenne pepper
1	bunch green onions, chopped	1	tablespoon fresh thyme leaves
1	cup fresh basil leaves	2	tablespoons Kosher salt
½	bunch fresh curly parsley	1	cup Herbsaint (licorice liqueur)
		½	pound softened, unsalted fresh butter

Combine artichokes, onions, herbs & spices in a food processor and blend on high speed until mixed thoroughly (about 30 seconds). Add Herbsaint and blend about 15 seconds more. Add butter & blend until creamy (about 15-30 seconds more). Reserve this stuffing and chill in refrigerator. Arrange 5 shrimp in a small casserole so the tails meet in the center of the dish. Using your hands, lift one shrimp tail and place about ½ ounce of the stuffing on top of the head and let the tail fall back over the top of the stuffing. Repeat this process for each of the five shrimp in each dish so that each shrimp is "stuffed" individually and arranged in a circle with the tails up. When every shrimp is stuffed, place dishes in a 400-degree oven and bake for 12-15 minutes, or until shrimp are cooked through. Remove from oven and top with your favorite butter or Hollandaise sauce. Garnish with finely diced red bell peppers and serve.

Yield: 6 servings

BARBEQUED OYSTERS

30	large Louisiana oysters, well drained	½	cup Abita Amber beer
2	tablespoons minced garlic	½	cup Lea & Perrins Worcestershire sauce
1	tablespoon fresh thyme leaves, finely chopped	½	lb. softened butter
1	tablespoon fresh rosemary, finely chopped	2	tablespoons fresh lemon juice
½	cup very dry sherry	1	tablespoon Kosher salt
½	cup oyster liquor (juice from container)	2	ounces pure olive oil

Note: Make sure to have all ingredients ready before starting since this dish will cook very quickly.

Place a 16" skillet over high heat for about three minutes, or until very hot, then add olive oil. Oil should begin to smoke immediately, but if not, allow to heat to a smoking temperature before going to the next step. Add oysters to pan reserving all the liquor for later use. (You may want to let your oysters sit in a colander for a few minutes before this step, as a drier oyster will give a better finished product). The oil should flame up when you add the oysters, this is a very important step in achieving the BBQ flavor. Allow oysters to sauté alone for one minute, then add the garlic, thyme & rosemary and sauté for another minute. Add sherry, oyster liquor, beer and Worcestershire. Let liquid come to a boil and allow oyster to cook for 1-2 minutes, or until firm. Remove from heat, remove oysters and reserve. Return liquid to heat, allow to boil and reduce by ⅔ in volume. Add lemon juice and salt and cook down by half. Add butter and reserved oysters, bring to a boil and serve over white rice.

Yield: 6 servings

LILETTE RESTAURANT

3637 Magazine Street
New Orleans, LA 70115
(504) 895-1636

John Harris, Chef/Owner

Growing up with an Italian mother, Chef John Harris' fondest childhood memories are of the kitchen. Later while working his way through college in restaurants, Harris couldn't resist the lure of cooking school, which would lead him to stints at Café Allegro in Pittsburgh, and Spiaggia in Chicago. After moving to New Orleans John began working as Sous Chef under Susan Spicer at Bayona Restaurant, who sent him to France to apprentice at Amphyclese and Le Pre Catalin, both Michelin rated 2 star restaurants. During his apprenticeship John lived with the Mauri family, whose matriarch Lilette instilled in him a love of traditional cooking, and is also the namesake of the restaurant.

Upon returning from France John took over as Executive Chef at Gautreau's Restaurant. During his tenure there he received mentions in Food & Wine and Southern Living, and a 4 bean rating from S.M. Hahn in the Times Picayune. After his departure from Gautreau's Chef Harris worked with Gerard Maras of Gerard's Downtown, while making plans for opening his own restaurant.

John fell in love with the intimate space at 3637 Magazine Street that would become his own distinctive offering, Lilette. After being open for only a few months, Lilette garnered 4 beans from local Times Picayune food critic Brett Anderson. In September 2001 John was named Chef of the Year by New Orleans magazine and has also received mentions in Southern Living and Bon Appetit.

GRILLED BEETS WITH GOAT'S CHEESE AND WALNUTS

6	large whole beets	¼	cup chives (cut into matchsticks)
½	pound goat cheese (soft)	½	stick of butter
1¼	cups walnuts		

MARINADE:

¼	teaspoon salt	⅛	teaspoon dry oregano
¼	teaspoon black pepper	⅛	teaspoon onion powder
¼	teaspoon dry thyme leaves	⅛	teaspoon garlic powder
¼	teaspoon paprika	¾	cup vegetable oil
¼	teaspoon dry basil leaves		Pinch cayenne pepper

VINAIGRETTE:

1½	ounces red wine vinegar	1	ounce walnut oil
2	ounces pomace olive oil		Salt and pepper to taste

GRILLED BEETS PREPARATION INSTRUCTIONS:

Cover beets by 3 inches with cold water in a large saucepot. Bring water to a boil and simmer until paring knife slides out of beet when pricked. Strain and let cool. While running under water, rub beets with towel to remove skin. Slice beets into ½ inch rounds. Prepare marinade by combining all dry ingredients in large bowl. Mix well and add vegetable oil. Toss sliced beets and hold. To prepare the walnuts, melt butter in a 10 inch skillet and add walnuts. Cook, stirring occasionally, for 5 minutes and season well with salt and pepper. Reserve left over butter. For the vinaigrette add all ingredients and the walnut butter. Whisk well. To finish, grill beets on both sides for 2 minutes and toss in vinaigrette. Place 4-6 slices of beets on each plate and drizzle with vinaigrette. Add 5 dollops of goats' cheese (1 to 2 ounces) per serving, sprinkled with walnuts and chives.

Makes 4 to 6 servings.

Continued Page 45

MARINATED ANCHOVIES WITH BASIL BRUSCHETTA AND STEWED VIDALIA ONIONS

½	pound marinated Spanish anchovies	1	baguette
4	cups julienned Vidalia onions	4	ounces fresh basil
2¾	cups extra virgin olive oil	6	garlic cloves (smashed)

To prepare the stewed onions, put 2 cups extra virgin olive oil and 4 cups of julienned onions in small saucepot. Bring to a boil, reduce heat and simmer for 20 minutes. Add 5 smashed garlic cloves and simmer an additional 20 minutes. Season with Kosher salt and fresh cracked black pepper. Let cool. Note: Olive oil should be about halfway up the onions in the pot. After simmering, the liquid will cover the onions. To make the basil puree, pick basil leaves (rinse & pat dry). Place in blender with ¾ cup extra virgin olive oil and 1 garlic clove. Pulse until blended but still bright green. (Color will dull if blended too long). To serve: Slice baguette on bias into long croutons. Spread liberally with basil puree and grill for 2 minutes on each side. Place two slices on a plate, scoop 2 tablespoons of room temperature stewed onions onto each slice of baguette. Arrange 6 anchovies, (3 on each slice) and garnish with fresh cracked pepper.

Makes 4 servings.

CEDAR PLANK FISH WITH CITRUS HORSERADISH CRUST

¼	cup white wine		Zest and juice of two lemons
	Juice from one lemon		Zest and juice of two oranges
1	bay leaf	4	tablespoons chopped cilantro
8	peppercorns		
½	teaspoon chopped fresh thyme		Kosher salt
¼	cup heavy cream		Sugar to taste
8	ounces cold butter, cubed	2	(8 ounce) trout fillets, skin off
	Salt and pepper		Drizzle of olive oil
2	pounds horseradish, grated	2	(10 inch) untreated cedar planks

Preheat the oven to 400 degrees. In a saucepan, combine the wine, lemon juice, peppercorns, bay leaf and thyme. Bring the liquid to a boil and reduce by half, about 2 to 3 minutes. Whisk in the butter, a cube at a time, until all the butter is incorporated. Season the sauce with salt and pepper. Strain the sauce through a fine mesh strainer and keep warm. Bring a small pot of salted water to a boil. Blanch the lemon and orange zest for one minute. Remove the zest from the water and shock in an ice bath. Remove the zest from the ice bath and pat dry. In a mixing bowl, combine the horseradish, blanched zest, lemon juice, orange juice and cilantro. Season the crust with the Kosher salt and sugar. Season the fillets with Essence. Rub the top of each plank with olive oil. Place each fillet on each plank. Divide the crust in half and cover the top of each fillet with the crust. Place the planks on a sheet pan and place in the oven. Bake the fillets for 12 to 15 minutes or until the crust is golden and the fish is flaky. Serve the planks with butter sauce.

Yield: 2 servings

MR. B'S BISTRO

201 Royal Street
New Orleans, LA 70130
(504) 523-2078

Cindy Brennan, Owner
Michelle McRaney, Executive Chef

Nestled in the heart of the French Quarter, Mr. B's Bistro is located at the intersection of Royal Street and Iberville, one of New Orleans' most celebrated food corners. In 1979, Mr. B's Bistro opened at this historical location and beckoned the culinary world inside. Since 1979, Mr. B's has been an integral part of an on-going process of redefining New Orleans cooking. New Orleans' location and growth as a port city has allowed many cultures to harmoniously blend together, utilizing the foods of South Louisiana, to create a style of cooking referred to as "Creole Cuisine." Mr. B's kitchen has attempted to revive the distinct qualities of Louisiana's varied cultural influences…adapting and incorporating local and regional ingredients into innovative culinary creations. Quality and farm freshness predominate. Mr. B's has been named "Best Business Lunch" in **Gourmet** *and* **Food & Wine**.

NEW ORLEANS BARBEQUED SHRIMP

8	each jumbo shrimp, with shell and head	1	teaspoon Creole seasoning
6 to 8	ounces cold unsalted butter, cut into cubes	½	teaspoon chopped garlic
1	teaspoon ground black pepper	4	tablespoons Worcestershire sauce
1	teaspoon cracked black pepper	3	tablespoons water
			Juice of ½ lemon

In a sauté pan over medium-high heat place all ingredients except butter. Cook until shrimp turn pink (3/4 cooked). Turn heat down to medium and add butter, an ounce at a time, stirring constantly. When all butter is melted, remove from heat. Place shrimp in a bowl and pour sauce over shrimp. Serve with slices of French bread for dipping.

Yield: 1 Serving.

CREOLE SEASONING:

½	cup salt	⅓	cup dried thyme
⅓	cup granulated garlic	⅓	cup dried oregano
¾	cup ground black pepper	1½	cups paprika
¼	cup cayenne pepper	⅓	cup powdered onion
		⅓	cup dried basil

Blend all ingredients in a mixing bowl. Store in a sealed container.

Yield: 4 cups

GUMBO YA YA

1	pound unsalted butter	1	teaspoon ground black pepper
1	pound all-purpose flour	1	teaspoon crushed red pepper
2	each red bell pepper, medium dice	1	teaspoon chili powder
2	each green bell pepper, medium dice	1	teaspoon thyme
2	medium yellow onions, medium dice	1	tablespoons chopped garlic
		2	bay leaves
2	stalks celery, medium dice	2	tablespoons Kosher salt
1¼	gallon chicken stock	1	pound Andouille sausage
2	tablespoons Creole seasoning	1	whole chicken, roasted and de-boned

First you make a roux! Over medium-low heat in a 12 quart stockpot slowly cook the flour and butter until you have a dark mahogany roux. This may take an hour or more. Add the peppers, onions and celery and cook for 5 minutes. Stir in the chicken stock (make sure it's hot), bringing it to a boil. Fold in the rest of the seasonings and cook for another 45 minutes. Continually skim the fat from the top while the gumbo is cooking. Add the Andouille and chicken and cook for approximately 15 minutes.

Yield: ½ gallon.

Continued Page 47

CREOLE SEASONING
(YIELDS FOUR CUPS):

½ cup Kosher salt	⅓ cup dried thyme
⅓ cup granulated garlic	¾ cup dried oregano
	1⅓ cups paprika
¾ cup ground black pepper	¼ cup granulated onion
¼ cup cayenne pepper	½ cup basil

Blend all ingredients in a mixing bowl. Store in a sealed container.

BREAD PUDDING WITH IRISH WHISKEY SAUCE

6 to 12" Po-boy loaves (or French bread)	1 teaspoon ground nutmeg
24 large eggs	1 cup dark raisins
6 cups heavy cream	4 tablespoons unsalted butter
2½ cups sugar	
1 tablespoon + 1 teaspoon ground cinnamon	

Preheat oven to 250 degrees. Cut the loaves of bread into 1½-inch thick pieces. Discard ends. Place one layer of bread in bottom of pan. Sprinkle the raisins on the bread, then top with one more layer of sliced Po-boy loaves. Beat the eggs, cream, 2 cups of sugar, 1 tablespoon of cinnamon and nutmeg until smooth. Pour over the bread layers Before placing in the oven, top with ½ cup sugar, 1 teaspoon of cinnamon and butter. Bake at 250 degrees for 1½ - 2 hours. Serve warm with Irish whiskey sauce drizzled over the top.

Yield: 1 – 10"x12" pan, 10 – 12 servings.

IRISH WHISKEY SAUCE:

2 cups heavy cream	15 egg yolks
2 cups milk	½ cup Irish whiskey
1 cup sugar	

In a medium saucepan scald the cream and milk together. In a bowl whip the sugar and egg yolks together. Incorporate the milk mixture into the sugar mixture and cook in a double boiler for 10 – 15 minutes, or until thick. Add the Irish whiskey and blend.

PALACE CAFÉ

605 Canal Street
New Orleans, LA 70130
(504) 523-1661

*Palace Café has earned national critical acclaim since it opened in 1991 with Best New Restaurant awards from **Esquire** magazine and **USA Today**. Since then, Palace Café won the prestigious Ivy Award from **Restaurants and Institutions** magazine, naming the restaurant as one of the top dining experiences in the United States. **The New York Times, Food & Wine, Cooking Light, Fine Cooking, Travel and Leisure, Wine Spectator,** TV Food Network's **In Food Today,** and CNN's **On the Menu** have also recognized the restaurant.*

*Palace Café's new cookbook **Palace Café: The Flavor of New Orleans** is available at Palace Café and select bookstores. This new book of more than 170 home-cook friendly recipes offers an intimate look at one of New Orleans' best restaurants from the "first family of Creole." The restaurant's highly anticipated first cookbook is a collaborative effort by Dickie Brennan, who tells the story of Palace Café in the introduction and notes throughout the book, with recipes from Executive Chef Gus Martin.*

CRABMEAT CHEESECAKE WITH PECAN CRUST

PECAN CRUST:

¾	cup pecans	5	tablespoons butter, chilled
1	cup all-purpose flour		
¼	teaspoon salt	3	tablespoons ice water

For the Crust: Preheat the oven to 350 degrees. Grind the pecans fine in a food processor. Add the flour and salt and process to mix. Remove to a large mixing bowl and cut in the butter with 2 knives until the mixture resembles small peas. Add the ice water and mix just until the dough holds together. Roll the dough ⅛ inch thick on a lightly floured surface. Press into a lightly greased 9-inch tart pan, starting with the side and then the bottom. Bake for 20 minutes or until golden brown.

FILLING:

½	cup finely chopped onion	2	eggs
1	tablespoon butter	1	tablespoon Crystal hot sauce
4	ounces crabmeat		Kosher salt and white pepper to taste
8	ounces cream cheese softened		
⅓	cup Creole Cream Cheese or sour cream		

For the Filling: Reduce the oven temperature to 300 degrees. Sauté the onion in the butter in a sauté pan until translucent. Add the crabmeat and cook just until heated through; remove from the heat. Beat the cream cheese in a mixer fitted with a paddle or with a wooden spoon until smooth. Add the Creole Cream Cheese and mix well. Mix in the eggs one at a time. Fold in the crabmeat mixture gently. Stir in the pepper sauce and season with Kosher salt and white pepper. Spoon the filling into the prepared crust and bake for 30 to 40 minutes or until firm to the touch.

MEUNIERE SAUCE WITH MUSHROOMS:

1	lemon, peeled, cut into quarters		Kosher salt and white pepper to taste
½	cup Worcestershire sauce		
½	cup Crystal hot sauce	2	cups sliced mixed wild mushrooms
¼	cup heavy whipping cream	2	tablespoons butter
1	pound (4 sticks) butter, chopped		Sautéed crab claw fingers for garnish

For the Sauce: Combine the lemon, Worcestershire sauce and pepper sauce in a heavy saucepot. Cook over medium heat until thick and syrupy, stirring constantly with a wire whisk. Whisk in the cream. Reduce the heat to low and add 1 pound butter one piece at a time, mixing until completely incorporated before adding more butter. Remove from the heat and stir until very smooth. Season with Kosher salt and white pepper. Strain through a fine strainer and keep warm. Sauté the mushrooms in 2 tablespoons butter in a skillet until the mushrooms are tender and the moisture has completely evaporated; excess

Continued Page 49

moisture from the mushrooms may cause the sauce to break when the mushrooms are added. Stir the mushrooms into the sauce. To serve, slice the cheesecake and place on serving plates. Top each serving with the warm sauce and garnish with 3 sautéed crab claw fingers.

Serves 8.

CREOLE CREAM CHEESE

(Makes about 2 cups)

8	cups (½ gallon) skim milk	12	drops liquid rennin, or ¼ rennin tablet
		¼	cup buttermilk

Heat the skim milk to 80 to 90 degrees in a saucepot, using a thermometer to determine the temperature. Stir the rennin into the buttermilk in a bowl; if using tablet rennin, stir until the tablet dissolves. Add the buttermilk mixture to the skim milk and mix well. Pour into a clean container and let stand, uncovered, in a place that is not in a direct flow of hot or cold air for 24 to 30 hours to curdle. Pour the curds into a large strainer lined with cheesecloth and placed over a bowl. Place in the refrigerator to drain for 2 days or until liquid no loner drains from the curds; discard the liquid. Store the Creole Cream Cheese in the refrigerator for up to 1 week.

ANDOUILLE-CRUSTED FISH WITH CAYENNE BUTTER SAUCE

CHIVE AIOLI:

¼	cup chopped garlic	2	egg yolks
⅔	cup blend of 80% vegetable oil and 20% olive oil	1	teaspoon Dijon mustard
1	bunch chives		Juice of 1 lemon
2	tablespoons chopped parsley		Salt to taste

For the Chive Aioli: Cook the garlic in the oil blend in a saucepan over medium heat for 20 minutes, stirring frequently; do not brown. Strain into a bowl and cool. Reserve 8 chive pieces for garnish. Puree the remaining chives and parsley in a food processor. Add the egg yolks and pulse to mix well. Add the garlic oil gradually, processing constantly. Add the Dijon mustard, lemon juice and salt and mix, adding a small amount of water if necessary for a thin mayonnaise-like consistency. Spoon into a pastry tube or plastic squeeze bottle and chill for up to several days.

CAYENNE BUTTER SAUCE:

¾	cup Crystal hot sauce	1	cup (2 sticks) butter, chopped, chilled

For the Butter Sauce: Cook the hot sauce in a small saucepan over medium heat until reduced by ⅓. Reduce the heat to low and whisk in the butter a few pieces at a time, mixing well after each addition. Keep warm.

ANDOUILLE-CRUSTED FISH

6	ounces Andouille sausage or smoked pork sausage, coarsely chopped	1	cup breadcrumbs
1	onion, coarsely chopped	4	(8-ounce) skinless boneless fish fillets Kosher salt and white pepper to taste
2	tablespoons blend of 80% vegetable oil and 20% olive oil	3	tablespoons blend of 80% vegetable oil and 20% olive oil

For the Fish: Grind the Andouille in a food processor. Sauté the ground Andouille with the onion in 2 tablespoons oil blend in a skillet over medium heat until the sausage is brown and the onion is transparent. Puree the mixture in a food processor. Add the breadcrumbs and pulse until mixed. Preheat the oven to 350 degrees. Season the fish on both sides with Kosher salt and white pepper. Heat 3 tablespoons oil blend in an ovenproof skillet over high heat. Add the fish fillets and sear for 2 minutes. Turn the fillets over and drain the skillet. Press the Andouille mixture into the fish to form a crust. Bake for 5-10 minutes or until the fish flakes easily and the crust is golden brown.

To Serve: Ladle the butter sauce onto each serving plate. Place 1 fish fillet on each plate and drizzle the chive aioli across the fish in a zigzag pattern. Top with the reserved chive pieces.

Serves 4.

Continued Page 50

WHITE CHOCOLATE BREAD PUDDING

PUDDING:

6	cups heavy whipping cream	15	egg yolks
2	cups milk	1	(24-inch) loaf stale French bread or fresh French bread that has been sliced and dried in a 275-degree oven
1	cup sugar		
20	ounces white chocolate, broken into small pieces		
4	eggs		

For the Pudding: Combine the whipping cream, milk and sugar in a large heavy saucepot and mix well. Bring to a boil then remove from the heat. Add the white chocolate pieces and let stand for several minutes or until the chocolate melts; stir until smooth. Whisk the eggs and egg yolks in a large mixing bowl. Whisk in the warm chocolate mixture in a slow steady stream; scrape the saucepot with a rubber spatula to remove all the chocolate. Preheat the oven to 350 degrees. Cut the French bread into thin slices and place in a 9x12 inch metal baking pan. Pour half the chocolate mixture over the bread and let stand for about 5 minutes. Press the bread into the chocolate mixture with a rubber spatula or fingers to saturate well. Pour the remaining chocolate mixture over the bread and stir to mix well. Cover the pan with foil and bake for 1 hour. Remove the foil and bake for 30 minutes longer or until golden brown. Cool to room temperature and chill, covered, in the refrigerator for 6 to 8 hours or until set.

WHITE CHOCOLATE GANACHE:

½	cup heavy whipping cream	8	ounces white chocolate, broken into small pieces

For the Ganache: Bring the whipping cream to a boil in a small saucepan. Remove from the heat and add the white chocolate pieces. Let stand until the chocolate melts and stir until smooth. Loosen the pudding from the sides of the pan with a knife and invert onto a work surface. Cut into squares, then cut the squares diagonally into triangles. Place the triangles on a baking sheet and reheat at 275 degrees for 15 minutes or until warm. To serve, place the pudding triangles on serving plates and top with the ganache. Garnish with dark chocolate shavings.

Serves 12.

The Natchez
New Orleans, Louisiana

K-Paul's Louisiana Kitchen

416 Chartres St.
New Orleans, LA 70130
(504) 524-7394

Chef Paul Prudhomme, Chef/Owner
Chef Paul Miller, Executive Chef

Born and reared on a farm near Opelousas in Louisiana's Acadiana country, Paul Prudhomme was the youngest of 13 children. When the last girl left home, he was, at age seven, old enough to help his mother in the kitchen, and it was at her side that he learned the value of fresh, quality products. "We didn't have electricity, so of course there was no refrigeration. Therefore, we used only what was fresh and in season. I learned to appreciate herbs and vegetables right from the garden, freshly slaughtered chickens and fish and crawfish just caught in nearby streams and bayous. This bounty, plus my mother's natural talent as a cook, our whole family's love of cooking and eating, and the joy we shared at meals, all influenced me as a chef," he said.

From a very early age, Paul Prudhomme knew that he wanted to make preparing food his life's work. After completing school, he traveled for several years, working as a cook in all kinds of restaurants, and learning as much as he could about the ingredients and styles of cooking in different parts of the country. "Sometimes, when I thought the food was too bland, I'd sneak in a few dried herbs and spices," he said. "When customers complimented the dishes from my station, I'd try to remember exactly what I'd used, but that was hard, so I began keeping little notes on good mixes in my pockets. Sometimes I'd get caught, and this didn't make me popular with the head chefs."

His wanderlust temporarily satisfied, Prudhomme came to New Orleans, a mere 90 miles from his home, where he honed his skills and built a following at a noted Garden District restaurant. Then, in 1979, he and his late wife, K Hinrichs Prudhomme, opened K-Paul's Louisiana Kitchen. A small restaurant on Chartres Street in the French Quarter, it was originally envisioned as a casual eatery for local customers. Word soon spread of the magic being created in the little kitchen, though, and it wasn't long before customers, both natives and tourists, began lining up to sample some of the amazing dishes created by Chef Paul Prudhomme. Two of his signature creations—Blackened Redfish and Blackened Steak—are widely imitated.

Now one of this country's best-known chefs, Prudhomme has often appeared on national television. He's been seen with Bryant Gumbel on The Today Show, with Joan Lunden on Good Morning America, on CBS This Morning with Forest Sawyer, on 20/20, Live with Regis and Kathie Lee, Donahue, Late Night with David Letterman, with Tom Brokaw on NBC Nightly News, on Larry King Live, Nightwatch with Charlie Rose and the QVC shopping channel.

*All of the **Magic Seasoning Blends** contained in the following recipes are available by contacting: Magic Seasoning Blends, Inc., 824 Distributors Row, New Orleans, LA 70183-0342 or by calling: 1 (504) 731-3590 or Fax 1 (504) 731-3576 or e-mail info@chefpaul.com*

Continued Page 52

VEGETABLES IN A SWEET POTATO CREAM WITH PASTA

Makes 6 cups, enough for 6 side-dish servings

The taste of the sweet potatoes is critical to the appeal of this dish, so choose carefully. We like to use Burgundy variety, a delicious Louisiana product that is available in many markets across the country.

2	medium-size sweet potatoes, about 1¼ pounds total weight
2	tablespoons unsalted butter
1½	cups onions, peeled and cut into ½ inch pieces.
1	cup red bell peppers, cut into ½ inch pieces
1	cup yellow bell peppers, cut into ½ inch pieces
1	cup green bell peppers, cut into ½ inch pieces
1	cup carrots, peeled and cut into
½	inch pieces
½	teaspoon dill weed
5	teaspoons *Chef Paul Prudhomme's Vegetable Magic*
2	bay leaves
1	medium zucchini, peeled, cut into six equal wedges, then cut into ½-inch pieces, about 2 cups
½	cup heavy cream
1½	cups vegetable stock (or chicken stock or beef stock), in all
3	cups cabbage, cut into 1-inch pieces

Preheat the oven to 350 degrees.

Place the sweet potatoes on a sheet pan and bake until they are soft all the way through, 45 minutes to 1 hour. When they are cool enough to handle, peel and puree them in a food processor. If the puree is stringy, force it through a strainer. Set aside.

Melt the butter in a 14-inch nonstick skillet over high heat. When the butter sizzles, add 1 cup of the onions, all the bell peppers, and the carrots. Stir well, then add the dill weed, Vegetable Magic and the bay leaves. Cook, stirring frequently, until the vegetables have a light golden coating from the seasoning, but are still bright in color, about 8 minutes.

Add the puree, stir well, then add the zucchini and the remaining onions. Cook, stirring frequently, until the mixture makes large slow bubbles, about 4 minutes. Add the cream and 1 cup of the stock and stir well until blended in. Bring mixture to a boil and simmer, stirring frequently, until the liquid is thickened and reduced, about 7 minutes.

Fold in the cabbage and continue to cook, stirring frequently, until the cabbage is cooked but still slightly crisp, about 6 minutes. Add the remaining ½ cup of stock. Stir well, then bring back just to a simmer and remove from heat.

MANGO LIME VINAIGRETTE

½	mango, ripe, peeled and seeded	1	teaspoon lime zest
1	cup vegetable oil	¼	teaspoon white pepper
⅓	cup lime juice, fresh	1	tablespoon salt
6	tablespoons lime simple syrup	½	teaspoon pink peppercorns
2	tablespoons shallots, minced	2	tablespoons mirin (Japanese rice wine)

Puree mango in blender. Combine with remaining ingredients and whisk until ingredients are well mixed.

LIME SIMPLE SYRUP

6	tablespoons sugar		Zest of ½ lime
¼	cup water		

Combine all ingredients in a saucepan and bring to a boil, stirring constantly. Cool and set aside.

CHICKEN AND ANDOUILLE SMOKED SAUSAGE GUMBO

Makes 6 main-dish or 10 appetizer servings

1	(3-4 pound) chicken, cut up		About 7 cups chicken stock or water
1	tablespoon plus 2 teaspoons *Chef Paul Prudhomme's Meat Magic*	½	pound Andouille smoked sausage or any other good pure smoked sausage such as Polish sausage (Kielbasa), cut into ¼-inch cubes.
1	cup finely chopped onions		
1	cup finely chopped green bell peppers		
¾	cup finely chopped celery	1	teaspoon minced garlic
1¼	cups all-purpose flour		Hot cooked rice (preferably converted)
	Vegetable oil for deep frying		

Remove excess fat from the chicken pieces. Rub a generous amount of *Meat Magic* on both sides of each piece, making sure each is evenly covered. Let stand at room temperature for 30 minutes.

Meanwhile, in a medium-size bowl combine the onions, bell peppers and celery, set aside. Thoroughly

Continued Page 53

combine the flour with 1 tablespoon of *Meat Magic* in a paper or plastic bag. Add the chicken and shake until pieces are well coated. Reserve ½ cup of the flour.

In a large skillet (preferably not a nonstick type) heat 1½ inches oil until very hot (375 degrees to 400 degrees). Fry the chicken pieces until crust is brown on both sides, about 5 to 8 minutes per side; drain on paper towels. Carefully pour the hot oil into a glass measuring cup, leaving as many of the browned particles in the pan as possible. Scrape the pan bottom with a metal whisk to loosen any stuck particles, then return ½ cup of hot oil to the pan. Place pan over high heat. Using a long handled metal whisk, gradually stir in the reserved ½ cup flour. Cook, whisking constantly, until roux is dark red-brown to black, about 3½ to 4 minutes, being careful not to let it scorch or splash on your skin. Remove from heat and immediately add the reserved vegetable mixture, stirring constantly until the roux stops getting darker. Return pan to low heat and cook until vegetables are soft, about 5 minutes, stirring constantly and scraping the pan bottom well. Set aside.

Place the stock in a 5½-quart saucepan or large Dutch oven. Bring to a boil. Add the roux mixture by spoonfuls to the boiling stock, stirring until dissolved between additions. Add the chicken pieces and return mixture to a boil, stirring and scraping pan bottom often. Reduce heat to a simmer and stir in the Andouille and garlic. Simmer uncovered until chicken is tender, about 1½ to 2 hours, stirring occasionally and more often toward the end of cooking time. When the gumbo is almost cooked, adjust the seasoning if desired with additional *Meat Magic*. Serve immediately.

TRADITIONAL POTATO SALAD

2	tablespoons plus 1 teaspoon *Chef Paul Prudhomme's Vegetable Magic* or *Meat Magic*	6	hard-boiled eggs, peeled and finely chopped
1	teaspoon salt	¼	cup finely diced onions
1½	cups salad dressing or mayonnaise	¼	cup finely diced celery
4	medium-size white potatoes, cooked, peeled, and diced into ½-inch cubes	¼	cup finely diced green bell peppers

Blend the *Chef Paul Prudhomme's Magic Seasoning Blend* and salt into the salad dressing or mayonnaise in a large bowl, then add all the remaining ingredients. Mix well and refrigerate until ready to serve.

Makes 6 to 8 side-dish servings.

Copyright 1992 by Paul Prudhomme

Note: A suggested way to serve these 2 dishes is to put a scoop of potato salad into the bowl of gumbo and stir to blend.

FROM CHEF PAUL PRUDHOMME'S *PURE MAGIC*

PASTA PRIMAVERA

Makes 6 to 8 servings

Primavera means "spring," and this pasta dish takes its name from the tender young asparagus tips or snow peas that used to be available only in early spring. Not, thanks to modern all-weather farming methods and rapid transportation of produce, you can enjoy this treat any time of year. Leave out the prosciutto for a great vegetarian dish.

9	ounces uncooked pasta (your favorite)	6	tablespoons unsalted butter
2	tablespoons olive oil	1	teaspoon minced fresh garlic
1	cup thin strips prosciutto (about ¼ pound)	3	tablespoons plus 1 teaspoon *Chef Paul Prudhomme's Pork and Veal Magic*
2	cups cauliflower florets	1	cup asparagus tips or ¾ cup snow peas
2	cups sliced fresh mushrooms	1	cup chopped green onions
½	cup diagonally sliced carrots	3	cups heavy cream
2	cups sliced zucchini		

Cook the pasta according to package directions, drain and set aside.

Heat the oil in a 12-inch skillet over high heat. When the oil is very hot, add the prosciutto, cauliflower, mushrooms, carrots and zucchini. Add the butter, and as it melts stir in the garlic and Pork and Veal Magic. Stir in the asparagus tips or snow peas and onions, mix well, and cook just until the vegetables are crisp-tender, about 4 to 5 minutes. Stir in the cream and bring to a boil. Lower the heat to medium and cook until the sauce thickens a bit, about 3 minutes. Add the drained pasta, toss well and serve immediately.

Continued Page 54

BANANA BLISS

Makes about 4 cups of sauce, enough for 8 servings.

We developed this sauce for ice cream, but it's also great over pound cake, gingerbread or pudding.

SEASONING MIX:

1   tablespoon *Chef Paul Prudhomme's Sweetie Magic*

½	cup pecans, roasted and coarsely chopped	½	teaspoon ground ginger
4	medium size bananas, slightly ripe	1	teaspoon vanilla
		2	tablespoons crème de banana liqueur
½	cup water	2	tablespoons Bailey's Irish Cream liqueur
½	pound unsalted butter		
1	cup dark brown sugar, lightly packed	1	tablespoon cognac
		1	teaspoon sesame oil
½	teaspoon salt		Vanilla ice cream

Peel the bananas and cut them into diagonal slices about ½-inch thick. Set aside. In a small nonstick skillet over medium heat, roast the pecans, stirring constantly, until they begin to darken and give off a rich toasted aroma. Remove from heat and set aside.

In a 10-inch skillet, whisk together the water, butter and sugar. When the butter melts, add the seasoning mix and bring to a boil, whisking frequently. Whisk in the remaining ingredients, then add the reserved bananas and pecans. Continue to cook, stirring gently for 4 minutes. Remove from the heat and serve warm.

To serve: Ladle ½ cup of the sauce over 2 large scoops of vanilla ice cream. Be sure the ice cream is very cold and the sauce is still very warm.

CHEF PAUL PRUDHOMME'S ®
MAGIC
Seasoning Blends ®

PERISTYLE

1041 Dumaine
New Orleans, LA 70116

Chef Anne Kearney, Chef/Proprietor
Tom Sand, Co-Proprietor

"Food of Love," it's Chef Anne Kearney's motto and it says it all, keeping the young chef and her staff ever mindful their mission to provide culinary excellence upon every plate passing through the kitchen door at Peristyle. For Kearney the words strike close to her heart. Her passion for culinary creativity and the sense of place she feels in the kitchen will always be the cornerstones for her dedication to her chosen career.

Fresh out of the Greater Cincinnati Culinary Art Academy, Chef Anne Kearney came to New Orleans to work under the late Chef John Neal at the acclaimed **Bistro at the Maison de Ville Hotel.** *When Neal left to open* **Peristyle** *in late 1991, he took Kearney along as his Sous Chef. Kearney credits Neal for her tutelage in classic French cooking techniques as well as perfecting her own palate and prompting her discovery of tastes and the depths of flavor.*

In 1992, Kearney took leave of Peristyle for a three-year tenure with superstar Chef Emeril Lagasse. Kearney spent nearly two years sweating it out on the **Emeril's** *restaurant cook line, working at the frenetic pace only an institution of that caliber could command.*

Kearney purchased Peristyle shortly after the April 1995 death of Chef John Neal. Though she made the menu her own immediately upon taking over the helm she is ever mindful to incorporate Chef Neal's legacies whenever possible. In 1998, Kearney married Thomas Sand Jr. He became not only her life partner but business partner, as well.

Continued Page 55

The accolades for Kearney's work have poured in during her tenure. Kearney is one of five chefs honored in 2000 with a James Beard Foundation "Southeast Regional Best Chef" nomination. **Lagniappe** *"5 Beans" Brett Anderson, Oct. 5, 2001 InsideNewOrleans.com* **"...eating here is such a pleasure. It's new-old. My favorite kind of restaurant."** *Tom Fitzmorris September, 2001 – Zagat "America's Top Restaurant Survey 2000 – James Beard Foundation Awards, 1999, 2000, 2001* **American Express Best Chef: Southeast** *nominee.* **Gourmet** *" Voted Top Food New Orleans" October, 1998 – Robert Mondavi* **Culinary Award of Excellence,** *"Top Bistro/Casual Chef in America" September 1998 –* **Food & Wine** *"America's Top Chef" 10 best New Chefs in America July 1998 –* **Wine Spectator** *"America's Rising Star Chef" March 31, 1998 –* **Lagniappe** *"5 Beans" Craig LaBan February 27, 1998. – Zagat – Rated #2 in New Orleans for Food 1998 America's Top Restaurants Survey. James Beard Foundation – 7th Annual James Beard Foundation Awards 1997*

ARUGULA SALAD WITH APPLES, RICOTTA SALATA AND POPPYSEEDS:

1	pound arugula, picked free of stems, washed and air dried	1	ounce grated ricotta salata (firm Italian table cheese)
1	tablespoon small diced shallots	2	Granny Smith apples*

*Wash the apples and cut into ¼" thick slices. Toss the apples slices in 1 tablespoon light olive oil and roasted for 10 minutes on a sheet tray at 350 degrees. Cool and slice into ¼" thick strips, discard the seeds and core as you slice.

POPPYSEED DRESSING:

1	tablespoon white wine vinegar	1½	teaspoons diced shallots
1½	teaspoons Dijon mustard	1½	tablespoons sugar
	Juice of ½ lemon	½	cup peanut oil
1	teaspoon white wine	1	tablespoon light olive oil
1	tablespoon poppyseeds		Salt and white pepper to taste

In a medium stainless steel mixing bowl, using a whisk, combine all ingredients, except the oils. Mix well to break down the sugar. While whisking slowly add the oils in a thin stream and whisk until uniform. Season with salt and pepper. This will keep for up to 1 week, refrigerated.

Assembly: In a large salad bowl, gently toss the arugula, shallots and apples with ⅓ cup of the dressing. Season to your liking. Place the arugula in the middle of 6-8 chilled salad plates, slightly mounding the arugula in the center of each plate. Sprinkle each salad with the apples that may have fallen to the bottom of the bowl, then top with the cheese.

POACHED OYSTERS IN A SAFFRON-TOMATO COULIS:

60	large freshly shucked Louisiana Oysters, preferably P&J	⅛	teaspoon cayenne pepper
1	tablespoon vegetable oil for cooking	1½	teaspoons chopped saffron threads, measure after you chop
1	cup medium dice yellow onions	4	cups fresh tomato concasse, save juices (if the fresh ones are not up to your standards use a nice can of diced tomatoes.)
½	cup medium dice celery		
½	cup medium dice fennel bulb		
1	tablespoon chopped garlic	2	tablespoons unsalted butter
2	cups white wine		Kosher salt and white pepper
1	bay leaf		

*Try garnishing this dish with sizzled leeks, crumbled bacon, grated cheese, chopped green onions or your favorite herbs. Pick whatever looks best to you at the market that day.

Continued Page 56

In a medium sauce pot, heat the oil and gently sweat the onions, celery, fennel and garlic until very tender. Add the white wine, bay leaf, cayenne and saffron. Stirring occasionally. Reduce the wine until half remains, add the tomatoes. Bring this mixture to a boil, reduce the heat and simmer for 15 minutes. Remove from the heat and cool for 20 minutes. Place this mixture in a blender, pulsing the blender off and on until the mixture is very smooth (do this with extreme caution, it will still be hot). Set aside until needed. Refrigerate if needed.

At service time: Place the sauce in a 6 quart sauce pot and slowly bring it to a boil, add the oysters, stir to distribute. Cook the oysters until they begin to firm up, about 2 minutes. Add the butter, stir to incorporate and adjust the seasonings. You could serve this with boiled rice or even Brabant potatoes. Garnish and go, Yum.

Serves 6.

CHILLED CHAMPAGNE-STRAWBERRY SOUP WITH MINT ICE CREAM:

4 cups Louisiana strawberries, hulled and quartered	1 cup slightly sweetened whipped cream
1 750ml bottle of good quality Champagne or California sparkling wine	1 pint of homemade mint ice cream or your favorite mint ice cream
2 cups unsweetened apple juice	8 mint sprigs for garnish Powdered sugar to dust
1 cup spring water	
1 cup sugar	
½ vanilla bean, split Honey (if necessary)	8 chilled shallow "soup" bowls
	8 plates to use as liners for bowls
2 tablespoons chiffonade fresh mint leaves	

Procedure: In a medium non-reactive sauce pot, combine the first 6 ingredients and bring to a boil. Simmer for 10 minutes. Remove the vanilla bean and allow this mixture to cool for 30 minutes. Puree in batches in a blender for 3 minutes until very smooth. Strain through a small hole china cap and chill for 2

hours. Adjust the sweetness if needed using a little honey. Place a dollop of the whipped cream in the center of each bowl, top with a 2-ounce scoop of ice cream, garnish with mint and ladle the chilled soup around the ice cream like a "moat". Dust with sugar and serve on the liners.

RALPH BRENNAN'S RED FISH GRILL

115 Bourbon Street
New Orleans, LA 70130
(504) 598-1200

Casual New Orleans Seafood

Ralph Brennan's RED FISH GRILL, under the culinary direction of the Executive Chef Robert Gregg Collier, boasts a variety of fresh seafood selections, including an abundant supply of fresh Gulf shell fish, fin fish, a raw oyster bar and many other New Orleans classic seafood dishes.

A state of the art kitchen has been installed and the focal point is the hickory wood burning grill which will impart the signature rich, smoky flavor and taste to all of RED FISH GRILL'S grilled seafood, meat and vegetable menu items.

The RED FISH GRILL has won many awards and accolades:

"Best Seafood Restaurant"
Where New Orleans,
Reader's Survey, 2001, 2000, 1999, 1998 & 1997

"Best Grilled Fish"
New Orleans Magazine,
Readers Poll, 1998

Honor Award –
American Institute of Architects 1997

"Best New Restaurant"
Gambit Weekly's *Best of New Orleans 1997*

BARBEQUED OYSTERS

(One serving)

6	oysters	3	tomato slices
	Seasoned breading	2	ounces BBQ oyster
1	8" Po'Boy loaf		sauce (recipe
1½	ounces blue cheese		below)
	dressing (recipe	1	teaspoon chopped
	below)		parsley
½	ounce julienned	4	red onions, thinly
	lettuce		sliced

Method: Coat oysters in seasoned flour and fry until golden. Toss with BBQ oyster sauce and parsley. Dress po-boy with blue cheese dressing, lettuce, tomato and red onion.

BBQ OYSTER SAUCE:

5	ounces Crystal hot sauce	3¼	tablespoons clarified butter
2½	tablespoons honey		

Method: Combine the margarine and the honey and warm to 100 degrees. Using a mixer, add hot sauce in a steady stream. Sauce will emulsify. For serving, sauce should be warmed slowly but not heated or sauce will break.

BLUE CHEESE DRESSING

5	ounces crumbled blue cheese	2	tablespoons salad oil
1	cup mayonnaise	½	teaspoon black
1	ounce sour cream		pepper
2	tablespoons heavy cream	½	teaspoon white pepper
1	tablespoon white vinegar		

Method: Mix all ingredients & blend well.

Continued Page 58

SWEET POTATO CATFISH WITH ANDOUILLE CREAM DRIZZLE

4	(8- to 9-ounce) catfish fillets, trimmed as needed
1	teaspoon Creole seasoning
16	ounces sweet potato crust
4	ounces clarified butter
12	ounces spinach, cleaned
	Creole seasoning to taste
	Salt & pepper to taste
6	ounces Andouille cream drizzle (recipe below)

Method: Sprinkle the catfish with salt and Creole seasoning. Spread the sweet potato crust on the top of the fish. In a hot skillet, add the clarified butter and add the fish crust side up. Remove fish, to sizzle skillet and finish in salamander. When fish is done, crust should be nicely browned. Sauté spinach in clarified margarine and season with Creole seasoning, salt and pepper. Drain spinach and put in center of plate, lay catfish on top allowing the spinach to be seen on either side of the fish. Drizzle the sauce around the fish and spinach. Garnish the fish with chopped green onions.

Serves 4.

SWEET POTATO CRUST:

1¼	pounds roasted sweet potato flesh
½	cup mayonnaise
¼	teaspoon salt
1	dash black pepper
2	teaspoons breadcrumbs
⅜	teaspoon Creole seasoning

Method: Roast sweet potatoes. Peel and place roasted sweet potato flesh and remaining ingredients in mixer and mix to incorporate. Reserve.

Serves 4.

ANDOUILLE CREAM DRIZZLE:

¼	pound Andouille sausage, diced ¼"
¾	ounce vegetable oil
1	tablespoon Creole seasoning
1	tablespoon honey
½	quart heavy cream
1½	ounces bourbon
1½	tablespoons blond roux

Method: Sauté Andouille in oil until lightly browned. Add Creole seasoning. De-glaze with bourbon. Reduce. Add honey and cream. Add roux and let simmer until flour taste is gone. Salt and pepper to taste.

Serves 4

CHOCOLATE BREAD PUDDING

3	cups milk (do not use low-fat or skim)
3	cups whipping cream
1½	cups sugar
12	ounces semisweet chocolate, chopped
12	eggs, lightly beaten
1½	tablespoons vanilla extract
½	cup chopped pecans
1½	pounds day-old bread cubes (1-inch pieces)

TOPPING:

¼	cup sugar
¼	pound butter, cut into pieces

Method: In a medium saucepan combine milk, cream and sugar and cook over medium high heat, stirring until sugar dissolves and mixture comes to a boil. Remove from heat, add chocolate and stir until smooth and completely melted. Beat eggs and vanilla in large bowl to blend. Gradually whisk in chocolate mixture; add bread cubes and let stand until bread absorbs some of the custard, stirring occasionally, about 30 minutes. Stir in pecan pieces. Pour into baking dish and top with sugar and butter. Bake for 1 hour at 250 degrees.

Serves 8.

RENÉ BISTROT
RENAISSANCE PERE MARQUETTE HOTEL

817 Common Street
New Orleans, LA 70130
(504) 525-1111

An Authentic French Bistrot

French Master Chef René Bajeux

*Chef René has opened his own bistro in the central business district to rave reviews! He is the former Executive Chef at the Grill Room in the Windsor Court Hotel. He was awarded the Master Chef of France in 1996, the Chef of the Year in Los Angeles that same year and the Hotel Chef of the Year by the American Tasting Institute for 2002! Chef Bajeux has been featured in **Food and Wine, Zagat Survey, Food Network, Great Chefs of America, Esquire** Magazine and **Life of Rich and Famous.***

BOUILLABAISSE

Serves 4

FISH STOCK:

2	pounds fish bones	½	leek cleaned and diced
1	quart water		
1	quart dry white wine	1	cup diced celery
1	carrot peeled and diced	2	bay leaves
		8	black peppercorns
1	onion peeled and diced		

Combine ingredients and bring to a boil, then simmer for 20 minutes, strain with a china cap and set aside.

BOUILLABAISSE:

1	onion diced	4	ounces diced fennel
1	leek diced and cleaned (Use both the green and white part)	2	ounces diced snapper
		2	ounces diced tuna
1	cup celery diced	3	ounces diced peeled shrimp
10	ounces diced tomato		
2	teaspoons saffron	4	ounces diced mussels
1	ounce Pernod or any other anise liquor	3	ounces diced monkfish

Place all seafood in a large pot, top with the fish stock, cover and simmer for 8 minutes. Season to taste.

ROUILLE:

3	ounces olive oil		Tabasco to taste
1	ounce garlic puree	1	egg
2	ounces sundried tomato	1	tablespoon Dijon mustard

Blend all ingredients in a blender until smooth, season to taste.

GARLIC CROUTON:

One large loaf ciabatta cut in ¼ inch pieces, brush with garlic butter, sprinkled with Parmesan, bake until brown. To assemble dish, place the bouillabaisse in a large bowl, croutons on top. Rouille on the side. Rouille is usually mixed with the hot Bouillabaisse to add extra flavor.

TUNA PASTEUR

6	pieces Tuna	2	pounds mashed potatoes
1	ounce basil		

FOR THE KIM CHEE CABBAGE:

10	ounces diced Napa cabbage	1	tablespoon pureed garlic
4	tablespoons hot sauce	3	tablespoons chopped chives
		8	ounces fish sauce

Continued Page 60

FOR THE ROUILLE:

1	ounce mayonnaise	Tabasco to taste	
½	ounce sundried tomatoes		

Blend all ingredients in blender

FOR THE SPRING ROLL:

8	pieces Spring roll wrappers	1	ounce crushed peanuts
10	ounces diced smoked chicken	4	ounces julienned carrots
1	package glass noodles	8	ounces julienned snow peas
4	tablespoons soy sauce	2	quarts peanut oil for frying

FOR THE VINAIGRETTE:

2	ounces olive oil	1	ounce Champagne vinegar
1	ounce diced carrots		Salt & pepper to taste
¼	ounce basil		
4	tablespoons pureed ginger		

Sear the tuna on four sides in a cast iron pan until desired temperature. Set aside at room temperature. Make the mashed potatoes and add the pureed basil and set aside. **For the Kim Chee:** place all ingredients in a non-reactive crock and mix well. Place in refrigerator for at least a week. For the spring roll: soak glass noodles until soft. Drain and add the smoked chicken, carrots and snow peas. Mix the soy sauce and peanuts well. Then place a small amount of product in center of the spring roll. Fold in the two sides first and then fold in the side toward you and start rolling. Make sure you roll tightly. Brush the end with egg yolk to seal, deep fry until crispy brown. **For the vinaigrette:** mix all the ingredients and whisk by hand. Season to taste. **Presentation:** Place the mashed potatoes in the center of plate, fan the rare tuna on top of the potatoes. Place the spring roll that has been cut at an angle on the side of the plate. Drizzle the vinaigrette around and place the rouille near the tuna.

Serves 8 people.

LOBSTER PROVENCALE

8	pieces 1½-pound lobsters	2	ounces Parmesan cheese

FOR THE SAUCE:

3	ounces white wine	¼	ounce pureed garlic
½	ounce chopped thyme	2	tablespoons olive oil
½	ounce chopped basil	5	ounces heavy cream

FOR THE SALAD:

6	pieces Belgian endive	3	tablespoons champagne vinegar
8	ounces Mesclun greens		Salt & pepper to taste
3	tablespoons olive oil		

FOR THE RATATOUILLE:

3	ounces zucchini	½	ounce pureed garlic
3	ounces eggplant		
3	ounces red bell pepper	3	ounces tomato
		2	tablespoons olive oil
3	ounces yellow onion		
		3	tablespoons thyme
1	ounce black olive	½	ounce basil

Preparation for the lobster: Boil in Court Bouillon for four minutes. Cut in half; remove the contents of the head. Remove the tail, dice and put back into shell. Remove the meat from the claw and place it in the head cavity. Cover with sauce and sprinkle Parmesan cheese. Bake at 400 degrees for 8 minutes.

Preparation for the sauce: Reduce white wine and garlic puree. Add the cream, thyme, basil, salt and pepper to taste. Whisk the olive oil into it until smooth. Set aside.

Preparation for the ratatouille: Sauté the vegetables in olive oil separately until soft. Then mix together with garlic, thyme and fresh chopped basil and black olives. Cook for 20 minutes over low flame. Keep warm until ready to serve.

Presentation: Mix the greens in a bowl with the chopped endive. Keep some nice leaves for garnish. Drizzle olive oil, vinegar and salt and pepper over salad. Place the salad in the center of plate. Then place the lobster on top of salad. Place a bit of ratatouille on all four sides of plate. Garnish with chopped black olives and drizzle with sauce. For 8 people.

Continued Page 61

ALLIGATOR RAGOUT WITH CHIPOLTE CREOLE TOMATO SAUCE

2	pounds alligator meat (tenderized) and diced to ¼ inch cubes	¼	cup onion, diced
		1	ounce garlic, chopped
1	ounce chipolte pepper, roasted	1	cup white wine
		1	ounce olive oil
6	ounces tomato, peeled and diced	2	cups chicken stock
		¼	cup Andouille sausage, diced
4	ounces leeks (white and green parts)	1	ounce roux (made with ½ ounce each of flour and butter)
2	oranges – zested		
1	cup corn		

In a medium-size stock pot heat olive oil. When hot brown leeks and onions. Add the alligator meat, season to taste with salt and pepper. Then add garlic, diced tomatoes and orange zest. After 3 minutes, add the sausage and chipolte peppers. De-glaze with white wine and chicken stock; let boil. Add roux little by little and whisk. When thick add rest of ingredients. Let stew for 1 hour. Can be served with pasta or rice.

For 8 people.

SEARED WILD STRIPED BASS, POTATO PORCINI RISOTTO FRIED LEEKS, TOMATO, COGNAC FUME

4	pounds bass or snapper fillets – deboned	2	cups chicken stock
		½	ounce butter
4	cups potatoes, finely diced	¼	cup shallots
		2	diced tomatoes
2	pieces of leeks	1	cup fish stock
6	ounces dried porcini mushrooms – soaked in water (can also use fresh)	1½	ounces cognac
		2	ounces cream

Wash and dry the potatoes. In a saucepan place the olive oil and the white parts of the leeks. Let these sweat for a few minutes. Add the diced porcini mushrooms and potatoes. Sauté very gently, add the chicken stock little by little. Cook for about eight minutes or until tender. Set aside until ready to use. Portion and season the fish. Sear in a very hot pan about 4 minutes on each side or until desired doneness is reached. For the sauce: In a sauce pan place the butter, shallots, diced tomatoes, fish stock, cream. Cook over low flame for 15 minutes. Add cognac. Strain through fine sieve. Then keep warm until ready to use. Next julienne the green parts of the leeks. Deep fry them for two minutes. Place on paper towel to drain oil. To assemble: Place the risotto one side of the plate, fish in center, sauce around and leeks on top for garnish.

For 8 people.

PASSION FRUIT CRÈME BRÛLÉE

2	cups cream	11	ounces egg yolks
2	cups milk	2	tablespoons passion fruit compound
1	vanilla bean, split and scraped		
7	ounces sugar		

Boil cream, milk and vanilla bean. Temper into beaten yolks and sugar. Add passion fruit compound. Strain through fine strainer. Pour into crème brûlée dishes. Bake at 200 degrees to 225 degrees 1 hour or until set. Cool.

RESTAURANT CUVEE

322 Rue Magazine
New Orleans, LA 70130
(504) 587-9001

Richard "Bingo" Starr, Executive Chef

*"The boom that brought a host of new restaurants to New York in the last three years did the same for New Orleans" "It took a graduate of Emeril's and Nola's to help get things rolling. Richard Starr, better known as Bingo, took his robust, lapel-grabbing culinary style to Cuvee, a bistro in the central business district" said William Grimes in **The New York Times** News Service. In addition to fabulous food, the restaurant has a large wine selection – over 500!*

PAN ROASTED SEAFOOD BOUILLABAISSE
WITH A TOMATO-SAFFRON BROTH AND GARLIC CREAMER POTATOES

THE BROTH:

2	tablespoons olive	1	teaspoon minced garlic
¼	cup diced onions	1	pinch saffron
1-2	tablespoons tomato paste	⅓	cup white wine
¼	cup diced pepper	1	quart seafood stock
2	tablespoons diced fennel	1	teaspoon fresh thyme
2	tablespoons diced celery		To taste salt, pepper, Crystal hot sauce and Worcestershire
2	tablespoons diced carrots		

THE DISH:

3	each shrimp	Roasted garlic
2	each scallops	mashed potatoes
2	tablespoons crawfish tails	French bread croutons
2-3	ounces fish pieces	Red pepper rouille
½	cup tomatoes dice Salt & pepper to taste	Green onions for garnish

Method: For broth sauté onions, peppers, fennel, celery, carrots and saffron in olive oil. Add tomato paste, garlic, Worcestershire and hot sauce. De-glaze with white wine and add fish stock. Season with salt, pepper and thyme. Simmer for about 10 minutes. Season all of the seafood with salt and pepper. In a hot sauté pan sear the scallops, fish and shrimp. Add diced tomatoes and crawfish. Add desired amount of broth. Add green onions and season with salt and pepper. Place mashed potatoes in center of the bowl. Ladle stew around the potatoes. Garnish with the croutons and rouille.

One serving

DUCK CONFIT WILD MUSHROOM POTATO HASH

1	each medium bag Zapps potato chips	¼	cup grated Parmesan cheese
1	cup pulled duck confit	½	bunch green onions sliced
1½	cups sautéed wild mushrooms		To taste salt and pepper
1-2	tablespoons white truffle oil	2	ounces demi-glace

In a large bowl toss potato chips with duck, mushrooms, truffle oil, green onions and ½ the cheese. Season with salt and pepper and top with the rest of the cheese. Place in a 300 degree oven for 1-2 minutes. Drizzle with the demi-glace.

Serves 4.

CAJUN FRITATA WITH TOMATO HORSERADISH AND BOILED SHRIMP

2	ounces sausage	1	ounce pepperjack cheese
1	tablespoons red/yellow/green bell pepper	4	each whole eggs whipped
1	tablespoons green onion	2	each jumbo shrimp boiled
1	tablespoons chopped onion	2	ounces traditional cocktail sauce
3	each new potatoes diced and blanched		

Sauté sausage and vegetables in omelet pan till golden brown. Add eggs stirring constantly until medium firmness. Fold in pepperjack cheese. Bake in oven at 350 degrees until eggs are firm. Serve on pool of cocktail sauce. Garnish with boiled shrimp.

Serves one.

RESTAURANT AUGUST

301 Tchoupitoulas Street
New Orleans, LA 70130
(504) 299-9777

John Besh, Executive Chef

Acclaimed chef John Besh grew up hunting and fishing in Southern Louisiana, learning at an early age the essentials of Louisiana's rich culinary traditions. As a teenager he began working in commercial kitchens, where his knowledge of food and dining truly began to blossom. "With the many cultural influences in Louisiana," he says, "it's an exciting place to learn about food." John has traveled the world over, concentrating on southern Europe, searching out the roots of those far-flung influences. John had an internship at the Michelin-starred Romantik Hotel Spielweg, under the direction of famed German chef Karl Josef Fuchs. He also trained in France under Chef Alain Assaud, at the Eponymous bistro in St-Remy, Provence. In the fall of 2001, John returned to New Orleans at the helm of the much-anticipated Restaurant August.

*Besh brings to the table such accolades as "Best New Chef of 1998" according to **New Orleans Magazine**, and listing among **Food & Wine's** "Top 10 Best New Chefs in America." He defined his engaging Contemporary French cuisine most recently as Executive Chef at Artesia, in Abita Springs, Louisiana, which was honored by **Gourmet** as one of its "Top Restaurants of America." After his formal training at the Culinary Institute of America, Besh furthered his education in the kitchens of such renowned establishments as Maxim's in New York, The Windsor Court's Grill Room, in New Orleans, and a number of others throughout Europe.*

Chef Besh returns to France annually, to the Chateau de Montcaud in Bagnols-sur-Ceze, as a chef consultant, training fellow chefs in the fine points of Creole cuisine. "The correlation between our cuisine of Nouvelle Orleans and that of southern France is intriguing," he say, "Our Creole food and culture are quite exotic to the French, yet familiar enough for them to enjoy."

CHILLED FAVA BEAN SOUP WITH CRABMEAT AND CREAM

1 pound fava beans, shelled
2 quarts crab stock
½ pound potatoes, peeled and diced
¼ pound butter
1 leek, sliced
1 tablespoon fresh tarragon
1 teaspoon garlic, minced
½ cup whipped cream
¼ pound jumbo lump crabmeat
3 tablespoons chive oil
¼ cup chives, chopped
Salt & pepper

In a saucepan, heat the butter and sauté the leeks and garlic over medium heat until translucent. Add the crab stock and bring to a boil. Add the diced potatoes and simmer until tender. Add the fava beans and tarragon. Cook for several minutes over high heat and puree. Once pureed, pass the liquid through a sieve and season with salt and pepper. Chill.

Assembly: Pour soup into individual bowls. Garnish with a spoonful of crabmeat, whipped cream and a splash each of chive oil and olive oil.

Serves 8.

Continued Page 64

SALAD OF DANDELIONS, CRISPY SEARED FOIE GRAS AND TEMPURA CEPES

¼	cup cornstarch	4	6-ounce young dandelions (or baby arugula)*, well-cleaned
½	cup flour		
½	teaspoon onion powder		
½	teaspoon garlic powder	6	tablespoons dried cherries, minced
¼	teaspoon salt	2	tablespoon nice wine vinegar
2	dashes cayenne pepper	3	tablespoons walnut oil
1	cup ice water		
12	slices fresh cepe mushrooms, cleaned	1	dash pumpkin seed oil
	Peanut or canola oil for frying	1	pinch sugar
		1	teaspoon minced shallot
6	ounces fresh foie gras, divided into four equal portions	1	teaspoon minced black truffle
	Salt and freshly cracked black pepper to taste		Salt and freshly cracked black pepper to taste

*John Besh likes to use a mixture of 3-inch greens, all of which are quite spicy, such as arugula, pepper cress, or any of the baby mustards.

VINAIGRETTE:

Combine cherries, shallots and wine vinegar in a food processor. While processing slowly add walnut and pumpkin seed oils until well combined. Season with salt and pepper to taste. Add minced truffle.

TEMPURA OF CEPES:

Blend the flour, cornstarch, onion powder, garlic powder, cayenne pepper and salt. Add the ice water to the dry ingredients. Do not over-mix the batter – add water until just combined and reserve in the refrigerator until ready for use. Coat each slice of cepe with tempura batter and carefully turn each cepe at least once until they become a uniform golden brown. Remove and reserve each slice on an absorbent paper towel.

FOIE GRAS:

Season each slice of foie gras and sear in a very hot nonstick skillet for one minute before removing from heat.

Assembly:

Toss the young dandelion greens in a bowl with the dried cherry vinaigrette and place in a bed in the center of each plate. Around the greens, place 3 slices of tempura cepe. Place a seared medallion of foie gras on the bed of greens.

Serves 4.

Note: Any fresh wild mushroom will do if cepes are out of season. Cepes also go by the name porcini and steinpilzen. John Besh loves using chanterelles, black trumpets and hedgehog mushrooms in this recipe as well. He often garnishes this salad with delicate chervil leaves and chive blossoms.

GNOCCHI WITH CRAB AND TRUFFLE

2½	pounds Yukon gold potatoes		Salt and white pepper to taste
3.4	ounces butter	2	cups dry vermouth
	Dash fresh grated nutmeg	2	sprigs marigold mint
5	egg yolks	3	shallots, minced
7	ounces all-purpose flour	½	pound unsalted butter
1½	teaspoons salt	1	pound lump crabmeat
1	quart crab stock	¾	pound regiano parmesano, shaved
2	cups heavy cream		
½	teaspoon cayenne pepper	1	medium-size black truffle

For gnocchi (small dumplings), place potatoes in small pot covered with water. Cook over high heat until fork tender. Strain and return to pot. Place in 250-degree oven for 15 minutes. Force potatoes through ricer into a fine mesh drum sieve. Use spatula to press all potatoes through into clean bowl. Add butter and egg yolks. Mix well. Fold in flour, salt, nutmeg until dough forms. Roll into six logs, about one inch in diameter. Cut dough in inch-size pieces. With a gnocchi board (a grooved wooden board) roll cut dough using thumb so dough curls around thumb and grooved edges form on outside of dumpling. Drop into boiling water and poach for 30 seconds. Remove.

For sauce, combine vermouth, cream and stock with shallots, cayenne and mint in a sauce pot and bring to boil. Reduce by two thirds and add butter. Add

Continued Page 65

gnocchi and crabmeat. Season and reserve. To assemble, spoon gnocchi and crabmeat into bowl. Shave truffle over mixture and top with cheese.

Serves 6.

WARM STRAWBERRY COBBLER WITH VANILLA ICE CREAM

2	pints fresh Louisiana strawberries	6	tablespoons heavy cream
4	tablespoons unsalted butter, diced	4	sprigs fresh mint, chiffonade
¼	cup flour, sifted	4	tablespoons powdered sugar
¼	cup sugar Zest of 1 lemon	2	whole eggs
1	teaspoon vanilla	2	teaspoons baking powder

Liberally butter a 2-quart earthenware dish. Add a layer of berries. In a mixing bowl, cream together the remaining butter, sugar, eggs, lemon zest and vanilla. Then add the flour and slowly add the cream until well combined and without lumps. Pour the mixture over the berries and bake for 25 minutes in a 400-degree oven. Remove from oven and dust with powdered sugar and chiffonade of fresh mint. Serving ideas: Can be served hot or cold, with or without ice cream. Note: You may substitute any type of seasonal berries or fruit.

Serves 4.

STELLA!

1032 Rue Chartres
New Orleans, LA 70116
(504) 587-0091
www.restaurantstella.com

Scott Boswell, Chef/Owner

Louisiana native, Scott Boswell, attended The Culinary Institute of America in Hyde Park, New York where he graduated with high honors. One of his first mentors was Chef Kevin Graham at New Orleans' Grill Room at the Windsor Court Hotel. He continued his quest for culinary excellence by working in two great kitchens of Europe. He credits Chef Pascal Morel at L'Abbaye de Ste Croix (one Michelin star) in Salon de Provence, France, with teaching him many of the techniques and nuances, which prevail in his food today.

His year in Provence was followed by another 6 months in Italy's famed Enoteca Pinchiorri (two Michelin stars) in Florence. It was in this wonderful restaurant that Scott learned to make the pasta he is quickly becoming known for. It was also in this kitchen where Boswell worked at the side of and befriended Masahiko Kobe, now better known as "The Italian Iron Chef."

On April 4, 2001, Stella! was opened. His lovely French Quarter restaurant is located just 2½ blocks from historic Jackson Square. He serves up polished European fare with Asian accents and bold Creole flavors, using the freshest local ingredients available. In its short time on the scene, Stella! has quickly become a favorite for locals. The small, intimate restaurant has the ambiance of a French country inn. The two dining rooms seat a total of 60 persons, and there is another lovely room for private parties. A courtyard adjoins one dining room, while the other overlooks carriages going by on Chartres Street.

Continued Page 66

MY GOOD FRIEND BOB'S TOMATO CURRY PUREE WITH CUMIN GRILLED SHRIMP
(NEW IMPROVED VERSION)

GARAM MARSALA:
(MIXTURE OF GROUND SPICES)

1	tablespoon cumin	3	whole cloves
1	tablespoon coriander seed	3	whole green cardamom
1	tablespoon mustard seed	3	bay leaves
1	cinnamon stick	1	teaspoon whole black peppercorns

Lightly toast all ingredients in 350 degree oven adding the bay leaves toward the end. Cool spices and grind in a spice grinder and reserve for soup.

SOUP PUREE:

⅓	cup chopped garlic	3	tablespoons finely chopped Methi leaves (Fenu Greek Leaves)
⅓	cup chopped ginger		
3	tablespoons olive oil	2	tablespoons Vietnamese Chile Paste
6	pounds diced pear tomatoes		
2	cups ketchup		Salt & pepper to taste
2	cups chicken stock		
2	cups heavy cream		Sugar to taste

Sauté garlic and ginger until lightly brown. Add tomatoes, ketchup and chicken stock. Slowly bring to simmer and cook for 15 minutes. Add chili paste and Garam Marsala to taste. Add heavy cream, methi leaves and chili powder. Puree soup and adjust salt, pepper and sugar. More garam marsala can be added for stronger curry flavor.

Note: Garnish with a grilled shrimp dusted with cumin and fresh chopped chives.

FRESH RICOTTA AND MAINE LOBSTER RAVIOLI

FOR THE DOUGH:

½	pound of all-purpose flour	⅛	teaspoon of salt
2	whole eggs	½	teaspoon of extra virgin olive oil

Place all ingredients in food processor and pulse until it forms a ball. You may have to add a little more flour or a touch of water if too dry or wet. Wrap dough in plastic wrap and rest for about an hour.

FOR THE FILLING:

3	cups of ricotta cheese	1	cup of grated Parmesan cheese
1	whole egg	1	steamed Maine lobster cut into small medallions
	Salt & pepper to taste		

Place ricotta cheese, whole egg, egg white and Parmesan cheese into bowl and mix well. Salt and pepper to taste. Steam lobster about 4-5 minutes and set aside to cool. Cut into small medallions to fill ravioli.

FOR THE RAVIOLI:

Flour counter top area that you will roll out your pasta dough. Set pasta machine to the highest number to start. Flatten out ball of pasta dough and flour both sides moderately. Roll through on highest setting and fold in half. Repeat this process four to five times to knead the dough. Lower your setting one number at a time and roll out dough to desired thickness. Take top section of ravioli press and measure rolled out dough into sections. Flour base of ravioli press generously. Place one section with of dough over ravioli base. Fill each section with ricotta filling (a pastry bag will make this easier). Place one medallion of lobster over each filling. Place another sheet of pasta over this and lightly press with hands to remove air. Use a rolling pin to roll over the ravioli press and cut the ravioli. Yield: 10 portions of three ravioli.

VICTOR'S

The Ritz Carlton
921 Canal Street
New Orleans, LA 70112
(504) 524-1331

Victor's is located in the elegant and beautiful Ritz Carlton Hotel at 921 Canal Street. The restaurant has only been open a little more that a year, but in that year, it has received "rave reviews" from the critics. **New Orleans Magazine** *(September 2001) named it "Best New Restaurant" and voted Chef Frank Brunacci as "Best New Chef." These accolades came from ballots cast by the City's top food critics and restaurant reviewers.*

John Mariani, the nation's most renowned food critic, recently touted Victor's cuisine and its chef. He said, "Certainly the most impressive chef to hit town in a long while is Frank Brunacci at Victor's in the beautiful new Ritz-Carlton Hotel." William Grimes of the New York Times wrote that Chef Brunacci is "doing it with a lot of style. In a city that loves to be entertained, he may be the best show around." Victor's has also been featured in **Wine Spectator, Town & Country, Departures, Diversions, Food Arts, Food and Wine, New Yorker** *Magazine,* **The National Culinary Review, The Times-Picayune, Gambit** *Magazine,* **New Orleans City Business,** *and WHERE.*

GULF SHRIMP WITH BLOOD ORANGE & OLIVE OIL ICE CREAM

1	portion – 6 shrimp peeled and de-veined	1	teaspoon chopped chives
1	blood orange segmented	8	picked cilantro leaves
2	tablespoons virgin olive oil	1	teaspoon chopped shallots
			Salt & pepper

OLIVE OIL ICE CREAM:

1	quart milk	4	ounces sugar
1	vanilla bean	7	ounces olive oil
20	leaves basil	7	ounces whipped cream
8	egg yolks		

Directions: Boil milk with vanilla bean, basil and infuse for 30 minutes, strain. Make anglaise with sugar and yolks, strain. Incorporate olive oil and churn in ice cream machine. When almost ready, add cream. Garnish with fried ginger, micro cilantro, slice truffles and olive oil.

CRAB WITH CAULIFLOWER REMOULADE TOMATO SORBET

4	ounces lump crab	1	teaspoon lemon oil
1	teaspoon chopped, chives, tarragon, chervil		Salt & pepper
		½	teaspoon, lemon confit chopped

Mix together and season with salt and pepper.

CAULIFLOWER REMOULADE:

One head cauliflower cooked in milk well done, strain. Add to saucepan with 300ml cream and cook until thick. Blend to puree with 1 tablespoon of horseradish. Salt and pepper. To order add 1 tablespoon seeded mustard.

TOMATO WATER:

10	tomato wedges	4	ounces horseradish
10	leaves basil		

Season. Combine everything in a large mixing bowl. Cook over a pan of boiling water for 1 hour, strain.

TOMATO SORBET:

1	quart tomato juice	1	tablespoon sherry vinegar
1	tablespoon celery salt	4	ounces olive oil
4	ounces glucose		

Mix and churn in an ice cream machine until set.

To assemble: Place some of the lump crab in a soup cup. Spread a thin layer of the cauliflower remoulade on top of the crab. Spoon a thin layer of the tomato water on top. Place a scoop of tomato sorbet in the middle. Garnish with vanilla oil, micro celery and caviar.

Continued Page 68

TRIBUTE TO BANANA FOSTER

Banana cut into 2-inch length and into halves. Caramelize in brown sugar and butter and flambé with dark rum.

MILK JAM:

1	quart milk	1	teaspoon salt
8	ounces sugar	2	vanilla beans

Boil to condensed milk consistency

ICE CREAM:

1	teaspoon stabilizer	2	vanilla beans
1	quart milk	1	cup softly whipped
	Milk jam		cream

Directions: Bring everything but the cream almost to boil Strain and chill. Place in the ice cream machine and churn. When almost set, add the cream. Remove and freeze.

WAFFLE:

½	quart milk	2	ounces sugar
3	ounces butter	10	ounces flour
1	vanilla bean	7	egg whites
7	egg yolks	3	ounces sugar

Directions: Bring milk, butter, vanilla bean and half the sugar to a boil. Whisk the egg yolks, flour and the remaining sugar together. Add a little of the milk and slowly whisk in the remaining milk. Bring the whites and sugar together and whisk to a soft peak. Fold into the milk mixture.

THE RITZ-CARLTON®
NEW ORLEANS

TRADITIONAL LOUISIANA RECIPES

BEIGNETS
(NEW ORLEANS STYLE DOUGHNUTS)

1	cup boiling water	2	eggs, beaten
¼	cup shortening	½	cup warm water
½	cup sugar	4	cups flour
1	tablespoon salt	3	cups flour
1	cup evaporated milk		Confectioners' sugar
1	package dry yeast		Oil for frying

In a small bowl, dissolve the yeast in the warm water and set aside. In a large bowl pour the boiling water over the shortening, sugar and salt. Add milk, yeast mixture and eggs. Stir in 4 cups flour and beat. Add remainder of flour to make a soft dough. Place the dough in a greased bowl turning to grease the top. Cover and refrigerate until needed. Roll out dough to ¼-inch thickness and cut into 2 x 3-inch rectangles. Deep fry at 350 degrees. Brown on one side, turn and brown on the other. Sprinkle with confectioners' sugar and serve hot.

Yield: 4 dozen

Ann Bailey

PRALINES

2	cups sugar	2	teaspoons vanilla
1	teaspoon soda	2	cups pecans
1	cup buttermilk		

Mix sugar and soda and add buttermilk. Cook until this forms soft balls in water. Remove from heat when done and let stand for 5 minutes. Add vanilla and pecans. Stir slowly until candy begins to thicken. Drop by spoon onto foil and let cool.

Makes 1 dozen.

Author's Note: The praline recipe is a recipe that my Aunt Nell Pollard used for years. It's delicious! A Louisiana cookbook would not be complete without recipes for pralines and beignets!

NORTH SHORE AREA – Once a resort region for wealthy New Orleanians known as *l'autre cote du lac* (the other side of the lake), the North Shore area is connected to New Orleans by a causeway across Lake Pontchartrain—also by its cultural and historical ties. Here you'll find beautiful countryside, winding waterways, gently rolling hills, piney forests and small-town charm blending in a delightful way with many of the flavors and joys of New Orleans culture.

MANDEVILLE, on the shores of the lake, is a blossoming community of pretty Victorian cottages and other beautiful homes, trendy shops, art galleries, theatres, and restaurants.

COVINGTON – Historic downtown Covington has an eclectic array of shops, galleries, restaurants and day spas. Unique gifts, antiques, fine art and great food can be found in the charming historic district. For a unique experience visit the Insta-Gator Alligator Ranch & Hatchery. Touch, hold, feed a gator! Experience the industry from hatchling to handbag. The only licensed alligator ranch in Louisiana.

ABITA SPRINGS – The lovely little village of Abita Springs is along the Tammany Trace, and rental bikes are available for long rides or a quick spin. Be sure to stop at the UCM Museum, one of the most delightful attractions around. It's a whimsical compound of buildings fronted by an ancient gas station, and displays an eclectic collection of artistic creations as well as found and recycled objects.

SLIDELL is the largest city on the North Shore, and its Olde Towne area (Slidell Cultural Center) is a haven for arts and culture. You can take a real-life adventure through the Honey Island Swamp, one of America's least altered, most beautiful cypress-river swamps.

HAMMOND – This quaint college town is dotted with coffeehouses and interesting shops, and the renovated Annie Eastman School is a haven for artists. Also nearby is Zemurray Gardens in Loranger, a hidden paradise of azalea, camellia and dogwood created by a wealthy banana tycoon in the 1920's. Zemurray Gardens is a 150-acre azalea garden that includes a 20-acre lake.

PONCHATOULA is "America's Antique City." The Historic District was renovated in the 1920-1930's and features over 40 antique stores representing 200 dealers. Nearby is Camp Moore Confederate Museum, housing artifacts and documents giving insight into the lives of Civil War soldiers.

BOGALUSA is located near the beautiful and scenic Bogue Chitto River. This is a great river for canoeing and tubing.

FRANKLINTON – The Mile Branch Settlement is an historic pioneer village representing early life in Washington Parish. Over 20 authentic structures dating to the mid-1800s include a gristmill, general store, school & church.

MICHABELLE INN & RESTAURANT

1106 South Holly Street Hammond, LA 70403 (985) 419-0550

Michel Marcais, Chef/Owner
Isabel Marcais. Manager

Micahabelle Inn & Restaurant is located in the historic MacGehee home built in 1907. It is the only home in Hammond, Louisiana on the National Historic Register. Chef Michel and his wife bought the home from the MacGehee family in 1998 and turned it into a "French style country inn." The inn features seven bedrooms, three dining rooms, a library and a bar. The Greek Revival home is situated on three acres of land which provide room for the extensive gardens and an atrium style banquet hall, called the Glass Pavilion. Since 1998 Michabelle has been the scene of many of Hammond's cultural and social events. Michabelle has become one of the premier spots for weddings in the North Shore Area of Louisiana.

Chef Michel is a classically trained French Chef from Angers, France. He has worked extensively all over Europe, the United States and the Caribbean. He is a Maitre Cuisiner de France and was also awarded the New Orleans Chef of the Year Award in 1981. He has prepared banquets for Presidents Gerald Ford, Ronald Reagan and George H. Bush. He participated in the original Great Chefs of New Orleans and was the President and one of the founding members of the Chef Association in New Orleans.

ILE FLOTTANTE AU CHOCOLATE ET AU RHUM

(FLOATING ISLAND OF CHOCOLATE AND RUM)

6	eggs	1	tablespoon cornstarch
3	cups milk		
1	cup cream	1	tablespoon chocolate powder
2	tablespoons sugar		
		1	tablespoon rum

Separate egg yolks and whites. Whip egg whites until stiff and add sugar. Boil milk in a pan and scoop on egg white in 6 large balls. Cook them on the milk. Mix egg yolks, sugar, chocolate, milk and cream. Cook until thick. Flavor with rum. Pour cream custard into 6 cups and place egg white on top.

(6 servings)

RABBIT A LA CREOLE

1	rabbit	1	carrot diced
1	cup tomato puree	2	celery sticks diced
1	onion chopped	1	cup white wine
2	tablespoons flour		Seasoning
2	tablespoon oil		

Cut rabbit into pieces and sauté with onion in butter until brown. Add flour, tomato puree, white wine, diced carrot and celery. Cover with water and season to taste. Cook until tender

(6 servings).

ESCARGOTS CASSEROLE

36	snails (cooked)	1	cup white wine
1	tablespoon garlic, chopped	1	teaspoon flour
		2	tablespoons bacon diced
1	green onion, chopped		
1	tomato, diced		Butter and seasoning

Sauté snail in butter. Add garlic, green onion, bacon and sprinkle with flour. Add white wine and a little snail bouillon. Add diced tomato and season to taste.

(6 servings)

RISTORANTE DA PIERO

116 West Pine Street
Ponchatoula, LA 70454
(985) 370-6221

IL PASSATORE
"Delivers the Best of Italy"
Extraordinary Regional Italian Cuisine
from Emilia Romagna

Genuine, Fresh, Homemade, Italian!
Come home to Italy for your Anniversary,
Baptism Party, Divorce, Meeting, Communion,
Wedding, Birthday, Reunion or Confirmation
and Funeral Party. Thank you!

Ristorante Da Piero is rated the top restaurant
for authentic Italian cuisine in the New Orleans
area by Tom Fitzmorris.

ORTOLANA SALAD

2	handfuls of baby spinach leaves	2	tablespoons extra virgin olive oil
6	mushrooms	1	tablespoon white wine vinegar
1	ounce Gorgonzola cheese		Salt to taste
1	red onion – 3 slices	1	pinch of thyme
1	clove of garlic		

Place baby spinach leaves in a big bowl. Add sliced mushrooms in a side bowl, mix olive oil, white wine vinegar, smashed garlic, thyme and salt. Pour this mixture over the baby spinach. Mix well. When finished, add the red onion slices on top and serve.

ITALIAN APPETIZER FROM EMILIA ROMAGNA,
ITALY BY THE MEDITERRANEAN SEA

12	jumbo shrimp (heads on)	¼	tablespoon lemon juice
2	tablespoons extra virgin olive oil		Arugula lettuce
	Parmesan cheese thinly sliced wedges	1	cup Parmesan cheese grated
		1	clove of garlic crushed

Boil the jumbo shrimp. Prepare a cup of extra virgin oil and one cup of grated Parmesan cheese. When shrimp are cooked (with heads on) dip first in the olive oil with a clove of crushed garlic to season oil, then cover your dipped shrimp in Parmesan cheese. Prepare a bowl of arugula lettuce. Season with olive oil and lemon juice. Salt to taste. Plate your arugula lettuce and put the jumbo shrimp on top of your lettuce, cover the shrimp with the thin wedges of Parmesan cheese.

Serves 4.

FILETTO AL PEPE VERDE (ENTRÉE)

(Medallion of beef tenderloin served with cream sauce flavored with fresh peppercorns)

1	tablespoon cognac	3	drops Worcestershire sauce
8	ounce tenderloin beef		
	Flour	1	drop Tabasco sauce
1	sprig rosemary	1	teaspoon of green pepper corns
1	tablespoon extra virgin olive oil	½	cup of heavy whipping cream

Flour the 8-ounce beef tenderloin, place in a hot skillet and cook to the desired temperature with the rosemary and olive oil. Add the cognac and let evaporate, then add the Worcestershire sauce, Tabasco sauce, green peppercorns and cream. Let the cream reduce and it's ready to serve.

Single serving.

Continued Page 73

HOMEMADE PASTA STROZZAPRETI

½	pound of flour		Warm water
2	egg whites		enough to make
1	tablespoon		dough kneadable
	Parmesan cheese	1	tablespoon olive oil
1	pinch of salt		

Place flour on flat surface. Make a hole in the center of the flour and add all of the above ingredients and mix with a fork from the center of the flour, until all ingredients are incorporated very well into the flour. If mixture (dough) is hard, add warm water a little at a time until dough is kneadable. Once you have reached this point, roll your dough out on a flat surface until you have a very thin well rolled out dough. Cut your thin dough into stripes and roll these stripes between your two hands forming twists around 2 inches long in length. These stripes of dough are called strozzapreti in Italian. It's a very well known type of pasta in Tuscany and throughout Emilia Romagna, Italy. Pasta is cooked when it floats to the surface of boiling water.

THE CERVESE SAUCE:

	Jumbo shrimp		Extra virgin olive
	Garlic		oil
	Cherry tomatoes	¼	cup of tomato
	Basil		sauce
	Salt to taste		Oregano
	Fried eggplant cut		Crushed red
	into small cubes		pepper to taste

Sauté jumbo shrimp, oregano, crushed red pepper, chopped garlic (two pinches) and fried eggplant cubes. Add ¼ cup tomato sauce, cherry tomatoes and basil until shrimp are cooked. Add cooked pasta (strozzapreti). Toss and serve.

POOLES' BLUFF CATFISH RESTAURANT

62249 Pooles' Bluff Road
Bogalusa, LA 70427
(985) 735-8446

Pam Penton, Owner/Manager

Located on the serene Pearl River, Pooles' Bluff Catfish Restaurant has been a family tradition since 1976. Originally owned and operated by Bill and Mary Penton, the restaurant's daily operation and management remain in the family today and are carried out by Bill and Mary's daughter, Pam. This restaurant continues to attract customers who are both new to the area and those who have for many years made Pooles' Bluff Restaurant their choice for a delicious weekend dinner. Pooles' Bluff is known locally for its homemade tartar, hushpuppies and great tasting fried catfish, in addition to its personable staff and beautiful riverfront location.

SOUTHERN GRILLED FISH

Pat dry your catfish fillets. Spray the grill with a nonstick spray. Season fillet with lemon pepper or for a less salty taste, squeeze fresh lemon on fish and then lightly sprinkle with pepper. You may also spray the fish with non-stick spray before laying it on the grill. Lay your seasoned fish on a preheated grill (medium heat). Cook the fish ribbed side down for approximately 10 minutes. Only turn the fish once, so be sure that it is done on the first side before turning. Fish will have a firm texture if it's done.

FRIED OYSTERS

Season corn flour with Creole seasoning to taste. Drain oysters and toss them in seasoned corn flour. Deep fry at 350 degrees. Oysters are done when they float to the top. Fry to desired crispness.

TOPE LA!

104 North Cate Street
Hammond, LA 70401
(985) 542-7600

Nestled in the downtown area of historic Hammond, LA, Tope La Restaurant provides an overwhelming atmosphere with the professionalism of the finest restaurants, mixed with the friendliness of a small town café. Owned by Jim Hebert, Troy Tallo, Tracy Barringer and Executive Chef Tommy Masaracchia, Tope La graces Hammond with the finest food in the area. The name Tope La means the joining or clasping of hands, symbolizing the perfect union of French and Louisiana culinary cultures. With excellent service and exquisite food, Tope La provides all with an enchanting dining experience.

CRAWFISH AND ANDOUILLE STUFFED PORK LOIN WITH HOT PEPPER JELLY DEMI-GLACE

4	pound boneless pork loin	4	cups – cornbread
	Salt	⅓	cup fresh parsley, minced
	Black pepper	⅓	cup – green onion tops, sliced
3	ounces butter	¾ - 1	pound smoked gouda cheese, grated
1	pound – Andouille sausage, small dice		
1	cup onion, diced		Salt, black pepper, cayenne pepper to taste
1	cup green bell pepper, diced		
⅓	cup celery, sliced		Chicken stock as needed
1¼	tablespoons – garlic, minced		
1	Granny Smith apple, peeled, cored and small dice	1	pound – applewood smoked bacon or regular smoked bacon

To prepare the pork loin, make an incision lengthwise in the top one third of the loin so that the loin is butterflied. There will be a thick side and a thin side. Butterfly the thick side so that loin lays flat and is ready for stuffing. Season with salt and black pepper. Reserve.

To make the stuffing, melt butter and sauté the Andouille sausage until browned. Add the onions, bell peppers, celery, garlic and sauté until vegetables are wilted. Add the cornbread, parsley, green onions and crawfish tails. Mix well and allow to cool. When the mixture has cooled, add the smoked gouda cheese and mix. Season with salt and both peppers. If mixture is too dry, add chicken stock to achieve desired stuffing consistency.

Fill pork loin with stuffing and roll up to achieve a pinwheel effect. If desired, wrap pork with applewood smoked bacon and secure with butcher's twine. Sear meat on all sides so that bacon is crisp. Place in a 350-degree oven for 45 minutes until internal temperature is 160 degrees. Allow to cool before slicing.

HOT PEPPER DEMI-GLACE:

3	cups – demi-glace or beef gravy	1	cup – hot pepper jelly (red colored)

Heat demi-glace and hot pepper jelly in a saucepot until hot and blended. Serve over stuffed pork loin.

Serves 10-12 people.

LOUISIANA OYSTERS AND ASSORTED MUSHROOM BIENVILLE IN PASTRY WITH A LEEK CREAM

BIENVILLE STUFFING:

½	cup butter	½	teaspoon cayenne pepper
1	cup onion, diced		
1	cup green onions, finely chopped	2½	dozen oysters, poached
½	pound baby shrimp, peeled and deveined	½	cup all-purpose flour
1	tablespoon garlic, minced	1	cup heavy whipping cream
4	cups assorted mushrooms (chanterelle, shiitake, portabella, button, etc.)	1	cup milk
		½	cup grated Romano cheese
		4	egg yolks
		1	teaspoon salt
¼	cup cream sherry	1	teaspoon white pepper

Continued Page 75

Melt butter in a saucepot over medium heat and sauté onions, green onions, shrimp, garlic and mushrooms until soft ad onions are translucent. Flame vegetables with cream sherry. Add flour and mix well to incorporate. To the pot add both the cream and the milk. Stir mixture until hot and thickened. Add the egg yolks and stir vigorously to incorporate. Add Romano cheese and seasonings. Cook for 5 minutes longer and remove from heat. Chop oysters and fold into the bienville stuffing. Chill.

PASTRY DOUGH:

1	pound, 9 ounces all-purpose flour	1	pound unsalted butter, softened
1	tablespoon salt	5	ounces lard
		⅔	cup ice water

Place ingredients in a bowl except for water. Work the butter and the lard into the flour until small pea sized butter remains. Add water and incorporate. Cover dough and refrigerate for 1 hour.

Roll dough out to ⅛ inch. Cut into 6-inch circles. Place bienville stuffing in center of dough. Paint the edges of the dough with an egg wash and cover the stuffing with another circle of dough. Seal the edges so that all the air is removed and the ends of the pastry are sealed. Repeat with remaining dough and stuffing. Paint each pastry with remaining eggwash making sure to not miss any of the pastry. Line baking sheet with parchment paper and brush with butter. Place pastries on parchment paper and bake at 425 degrees until pastry is golden. Serve over leek cream.

Serves 10-12 people.

LEEK CREAM:

1	large leek	2	tablespoons – all purpose flour
2	ounces – salted butter	1	quart heavy whipping cream
2	ounces – dry vermouth or white wine		Salt, white pepper to taste

Remove root from leek and separate the white and green parts of the leek. Clean the leek thoroughly to remove all dirt. Slice the white of the leek into thin slices. Heat butter in a saucepot and sauté the whites of the leek until soft. Deglaze with vermouth. Add flour and incorporate. Add cream and cook until thick consistency. Season to taste with salt and white pepper. When sauce is finished, slice the green of the leek into thin slices and add to sauce. Cook until the green of the leek is soft but has not lost its vibrant green color.

MAIN STREET RESTAURANT
1102 Main Street Franklinton, LA 70438

Jeanette Sumrall
Chef/Owner

This casual country restaurant features home-cooked meals daily, babyback ribs, steaks seafood and sandwiches. Chef Jeanette has been in business for 22 years and learned her wonderful cooking skills from her mother.

CORNBREAD DRESSING – LOUISIANA STYLE

4 to 5 pounds Turkey meat (for broth)

Boil until tender – Debone and set aside with broth. (Should have 2 to 3 quarts of broth). Boil 6 eggs – dice.

CORN BREAD:

2	cups of yellow corn meal	¾	teaspoon of baking soda
1	cup of self-rising flour	2	teaspoons of salt
4	tablespoons of baking powder (heaping)	2	eggs
		4	tablespoons of cooking oil Milk to Mix

Mix all ingredients well with milk and cook in a greased pan at 350 degrees until golden brown.

In a skillet with 2 tablespoons of butter:

Sauté 1 celery heart, diced - 1 medium bell pepper, diced - 1 medium onion, diced and 1 bunch of green onions, diced.

Crumble cornbread, mix diced eggs, add sautéed greens, add 4 tablespoons mayonnaise, add deboned turkey, pour broth over all until well mixed (should be loose and not stiff). Pour in a buttered pan – 9"x13"x½". Drizzle butter on top and bake at 350 degrees until golden brown.

Continued Page 76

PEACH COBBLER

2	cups of self-rising flour	2	large cans of sliced peaches
2	cups of sugar	1½	sticks of butter or margarine
2½	cups of milk		

Melt butter in a 9"x13"x½" pan. Mix together flour, sugar and milk. Whisk to get any lumps out. Pour over butter, drain peaches and place over butter. Bake at 350 degrees until golden brown. Crust will rise to the top.

Serves 10 people.

STRAWBERRY PIE

2	graham cracker pie crusts	3	heaping tablespoons of cornstarch
3	pints of Louisiana strawberries	1	box of strawberry gelatin
2½	cups water	1	large container of Cool Whip topping.

Wash & drain berries – slice and place in pie crust. The crust should be full. In a 2-quart saucepan, mix sugar, cornstarch and water. Boil until thick. Add large box of gelatin. Pour over berries in crust. Cool until set and cover. Top with Cool Whip topping. Makes 2 pies.

THE BROKEN EGG CAFÉ

200 Gerard Street Mandeville, LA 70448

ANOTHER BROKEN EGG CAFÉ

Covington, LA

Ron E. Green, CEO/Founder

The Another Broken Egg of America, Inc. since its inception in 1996 as had remarkable growth and stability in the large scale sector of the small restaurant/café venue. The original site in Old Mandeville, Louisiana called "The Broken Egg" opened in the fastest growing community in Louisiana in November 1996. Tremendous success followed for the small Café, so much that it prompted the founder to seek his brother's assistance in opening up Another Broken Egg in Destin, Florida. Subsequently with that opening, and the fine tuning of the concept, additional sites have been opened in the last year and half in Tallahassee, Florida and Covington, Louisiana. Articles have been written in **Southern Living** *Magazine and other publications about the success of this restaurant concept.*
Sid Cavallo, Chef

Continued Page 77

APPETIZER:

BAKED BRIE WITH APPLE, PECAN & RAISIN TOPPING

Purchase small brie wheel and slice open (to breathe). Put in oven at 250 degrees or microwave for 1 minute to soften.

Sauté the following:

3	ounces apples (Granny Smith finely chopped)		Powdered sugar (sprinkle on)
3	ounces pecans (chopped)	½	ounce Grand Marnier
1½	ounces raisins		Butter

Sauté all three of the items in a small pan with butter. Add a large pinch of powdered sugar, continue sautéing. Squeeze ½ ounce of Grand Marnier to glaze, sauté for 30-60 seconds, add small amount of butter to finish off, fold onto half of baked brie wheel.

THE BROKEN EGG RECIPE CRABCAKE CAVALLO

1	pound claw crabmeat	1	cup breadcrumbs
¼	red bell pepper (⅛" diced)	3	ounces Florentine sauce
½	bunch green onion (⅛" diced)	¼	ounce garlic (granulated ok) Salt & pepper to taste
¼	red onion (⅛" diced)		
1	egg yolk	¼	ounce parsley (dry) Tony C's seasoning to taste
1	tablespoon mayonnaise		

Open crab meat and line a metal mixing bowl with paper towels. Lay one pound of crab meat on paper towels evenly. Let this sit until you finish dicing the other ingredients and are ready to incorporate them all. Fold ingredients 1 through 10 evenly. Form into 1.5 ounce patties; lay on patty paper and allow to set for a few hours. (Freeze if desired to make them easier to flour). Flour, egg wash & breadcrumb cover it! Lay on patty paper.

SEASONINGS:

Flour with Tony C's
Egg wash with garlic, salt & pepper
Breadcrumbs with garlic, parsley & Tony C's

(Take old French bread, thin slice it and let it sit out overnight to stale and harden, sprinkle with above items and/or bake till crispy; run in food process or make crumbs).

ANDOUILLE HOLLANDAISE:

4	ounces Andouille sausage (smoked ok) chopped VERY fine	⅛	cup green onions (finely sliced)

Sauté sausage till browned. Take off heat and add green onions. Let sit for ten minutes to absorb flavors and for green onions to begin to release flavor. Pour into a metal mixing bowl add and fold hollandaise until the desired consistency is reached.

Building the dish: Toasted English muffin, 2 1½-ounce grilled crabcakes, 2 medium poach eggs, Andouille hollandaise (lightly cover) and green onion garnish.

THE BROKEN EGG'S BANANA'S FOSTER SAUCE

½	pound of butter	½	box light brown sugar
⅛	cup Gran Gala Orange Liqueur	2	tablespoons vanilla
⅛	cup banana liqueur		

Melt butter then mix with brown sugar thoroughly. Add liqueurs and vanilla and whisk thoroughly.

BANANA'S FOSTER PANCAKE/FRENCH TOAST

Prepare one large banana pancake/French Toast

Pour 4 ounces ladle of prepared Banana's Foster sauce. Add large dollop of whip cream to center. Sprinkle with chopped pecans. Add sliced bananas on top.

TREY YUEN

Cuisine of China
2100 N. Morrison Blvd.
Hammond, LA 70401
(985) 345-6789

600 N. Causeway
Mandeville, LA 70448
(985) 626-4476

"An American Dream"

James, Frank, John, Tommy and Joe Wong were all born in Hong Kong after their parents fled the Communist revolution. The Wong brothers came to America in 1967 with their mother and settled in Amarillo, Texas where their grandfather had a small Chinese restaurant. After his death, the Wong brothers went their separate ways seeking employment in different states from California to Louisiana.

In 1971, the brothers were reunited in Hammond, Louisiana where they opened their first restaurant. It was the town's first introduction to Chinese cuisine. The brothers had brought with them new ideas on traditional Chinese cooking. They began creating new and special dishes offering them to regular customers. They found that the people in south Louisiana were use to highly seasoned foods, so they started experimenting with more spices. They held regular meetings continually evaluating the food and planning innovations based on customer response. The result of this close attention to quality control and consistency was that folks flocked from all over to taste the real thing.

The brothers have become world renowned, being featured on national and local television as well as in books, magazines and newspapers. The brothers now operate three beautiful restaurants: Hammond, Mandeville and New Orleans. Authentic Chinese décor, consistently great food and attentive service, generous portions and the Wong brothers personal touch all combine to make Trey Yuen "an aesthetic and gastronomic delight".

HOT AND SOUR SOUP

¼	pound pork
4	dried Chinese black mushrooms
1	teaspoon dried mo-er mushrooms
14	tiger lily buds
¼	cup bamboo shoots
1	square fresh bean curd
2	tablespoons cornstarch (mixed with 3 teaspoons of water)
1	egg beaten
5	cups soup stock
1	small green onion (finely chopped

SEASONING:

1½	tablespoon light soy sauce
2½	tablespoons red wine vinegar
½	teaspoon black pepper
	Salt to taste
1	teaspoon chili oil or 1 teaspoon red hot pepper flakes
1	teaspoon sesame seed oil

To Prepare: Cut pork into matchstick-sized shreds. Marinate with 1 teaspoon of soy sauce and 1 teaspoon of cornstarch. Soak Chinese mushrooms and lily buds in l cup of hot water for 20 minutes. Then rinse, drain and shred mushrooms. Cut tiger lily buds to 1-inch lengths. The bean curds are to be cut into shreds. Beat egg thoroughly.

To Cook: Heat soup stock until boiling and add pork and mix with chopsticks. While soup is boiling add the dry ingredients. Add the seasoning and boil for 2 more minutes stirring a few times.

POT STICKERS

FILLING:

2	cups ground turkey (or 1 cup ground turkey and 1 cup small bay shrimp)
2	cups finely chopped bok choy (blanch whole stock, white and green parts; finely chop; then squeeze out excess water in cheese cloth)

1	tablespoon minced ginger
1	tablespoon minced white part of green onion (save green part)
1	tablespoon sesame seed oil
2	egg whites
½	teaspoon white pepper

WRAPPERS:

1	package of pot sticker wrappers or Gyoea skins
1	whipped egg white

Continued Page 79

SAUCE:

½ cup low sodium soy sauce and
½ cup vinegar (mixed together)
Crushed chili pepper with oil, to taste

Garnish with chopped green onions (green part)

To Prepare and Cook: Mix all filling ingredients in bowl. Cover and place in refrigerator for 1 hour.

To Stuff Pot Stickers: Place one teaspoon of stuffing mix in center of wrapper. Brush egg white around outer edge. Fold in half and tuck. This is a foolproof way to cook pot stickers. Place the desired number of pot stickers on plate and steam for 8-10 minutes. When done place flat side in a Teflon-coated skillet with a little poly-unsaturated oil. (No olive oil – too strong of a taste). Cook over medium-high heat until crispy golden brown. Remove and serve with soy-vinegar sauce for dipping.

SZECHUAN SPICY ALLIGATOR

¾ pound alligator meat (use fresh alligator for best results)
⅓ cup celery
⅓ cup carrot
⅓ cup onion
⅓ cup red or green bellpeppers
2 green onions (cut in 2-inch slices)
3 dried hot peppers

½ teaspoon garlic (finely chopped)
½ teaspoon salt
1 teaspoon sesame seed oil
½ teaspoon crushed Szechuan peppercorn (optional)
2 tablespoons sugar
1 tablespoons vinegar
1 tablespoon sherry

MARINADE:

1 tablespoon soy sauce
1 teaspoon cornstarch

1 tablespoon oil
¼ teaspoon salt & white pepper
½ egg white

To prepare: Slice alligator ⅛ inch thick and 2 inches long, removing fat and gristle. Sprinkle with cornstarch, soy sauce, oil and salt & pepper. Mix thoroughly. Coat with egg white and let marinade ingredients set for 20 minutes. Cut all vegetables julienne style 2 to 2½ inches long.

To cook: Heat wok or heavy skillet until very hot, adding ½ cup oil for 45 seconds over high heat. Drop alligator in hot oil. Stir gently to separate and cook until 70% done. Remove meat from pan and drain oil. Reheat pan with 3 tablespoons of oil. Break dry hot pepper in half into the oil until it turns brown. Add garlic, then add vegetables. Stir-fry for 1 to 2 minutes. Add alligator back into wok. Add sherry, vinegar, soy sauce, salt, peppercorn, sugar and sesame seed oil. Stir for 30 seconds. Remove from wok to serving platter.

CRAWFISH WITH SPICY LOBSTER SAUCE

½ pound crawfish tails
4 ounces pork (finely chopped)
1 tablespoon peanut oil
3 green onions (white-cut in 2 inch slices, green fine cut for garnish)
2 white onions (cut in2-inch stripes)
½ tablespoon light soy sauce
1 egg (beaten)

3 tablespoons sherry or rice wine
½ teaspoon chopped ginger
½ teaspoon chopped garlic
1 teaspoon black beans (rinse off before crushing)
½ teaspoon sugar
2-3 chili peppers (Crush these last five ingredients together)
½ cup chicken stock

SEASONINGS:

½ teaspoon sesame seed oil
½ teaspoon dark soy sauce

¾ tablespoon cornstarch
½ teaspoon peanut oil
Salt to taste

(Mix Seasoning ingredients together)

To Prepare: Heat work or heavy skillet until hot. Add peanut oil and pork. Sauté both sides until slightly brown. Add garlic, ginger, chili peppers and black beans to oil. Add onions and stir for 10 seconds. Add crawfish; sauté with wine and light soy sauce. Add chicken stock and cover. When mixture comes to a boil, add seasonings and cornstarch, stir till thickens. Spread beaten egg over mixture. Reduce heat and cover for 10 seconds more. Remove to serving platter and garnish with green onions.

Serves 1-2.

A TASTE OF BAVARIA
BAKERY – RESTAURANT – DELI

14476 Highway 22 West
Ponchatoula, LA 70454
(985) 386-3634

A Taste of Bavaria was established in 1985 by Larry & Mary Alice Larrieu who although were not German, they both had a passion for Germany. After 15 years of a hugely successful business, they sold their dream to Justine Hedrick & Lori Reed who intend to carry on the tradition. Justine was born in Bayreuth, located in Bavaria and lived there 27 years. She brings forth with her, her true heritage and knowledge of authentic German cuisine, traditions and, of course, the language. Lori, originally from Chicago, spent 20 years in the restaurant industry and always dreamed of having her own restaurant. The new owners, friends for 15 years, are living their dream together along with their families. Working daily to prepare the freshest baked breads, European pastries and homemade authentic German cuisine. A trip to Taste of Bavaria is worth remembering!

GERMAN POTATO SALAD

5	pounds sliced red potatoes	1	cup balsamic vinegar
1½	pounds bacon, chopped	½	cup white vinegar
1	onion, sliced	½	cup prepared mustard
1	large or 2 small cucumbers, peeled & sliced	¼	cup Worcestershire sauce
2	bay leaves		Salt & pepper

Boil sliced potatoes until soft and drain. Sauté bacon, onion, bay leaves and cucumber until onion is soft. Add balsamic vinegar and simmer. Remove from heat, add remaining ingredients, mix well and add salt & pepper to taste.

Serves 4-6.

BAVARIAN POTATO SOUP

4	carrots, sliced	1⅔	gallon chicken stock
8	ribs celery, chopped	4	pounds new potatoes, sliced
1	onion, chopped		White wine
1	pound bacon, chopped		Salt & pepper
2	bay leaves		

Sauté bacon in heavy gauge pot until almost crisp, and then add all remaining ingredients except stock and potatoes. When vegetables begin to soften, add a little white wine to deglaze the bottom of the pot. Add stock and potatoes, bring to a rolling boil, turn down to a simmer. Cook until potatoes are soft. Salt & pepper to taste.

Makes 2 gallons.

THE DAKOTA RESTAURANT

629 North Highway 190
Covington, Louisiana 70433
(985) 892-3712

Since the opening of The Dakota Restaurant in 1990, with partner Kenneth LaCour, Chef Kim Kringlie has created an eclectic menu that marries global flavors with the zing of Louisiana accents. The food takes on characteristics from French, Asian, Southwestern and other ethnic cuisine. The restaurant is located in Covington, across Lake Ponchartrain from New Orleans. Kim Kringlie was named "Chef of the Year" by **New Orleans Magazine**, *October 2000. The New Orleans* **Times-Picayune** *awarded Dakota its "4 Beans" designation for outstanding food. The restaurant received the "5 Stars" award as one of the Top 5 New Orleans Restaurants by* **Tom Fitzmorris, New Orleans City Business**. *Dakota has received the Wine Spectator's "Award of Excellence" for 10 years running!*

THE DAKOTA'S
LUMP CRABMEAT & BRIE SOUP

2	pounds fresh Louisiana blue crabs	½	cup unsalted butter
2	ounces olive oil	¾	cup flour
2	medium yellow onions (chopped)	1	quart heavy whipping cream
1	medium carrot (chopped)	8	ounces Brie cheese
3	ribs celery (chopped)	1	teaspoon white pepper
1	pod fresh garlic (chopped)	1	teaspoon white pepper
2	bay leaves	1	teaspoon cayenne pepper
¼	cup brandy	1	teaspoon salt
1	cup white wine	½	pound picked jumbo lump crabmeat
2	quarts water		

Using a meat mallet or hammer, crack open blue crab shells until meat is exposed. In a 1 gallon stock pot, heat olive oil, add cracked crabs and sauté for 5

minutes. Add chopped vegetables and bay leaves, continue to sauté for an additional 5 minutes. Add brandy, white wine and water, bring to a simmer over medium heat and cook for 30 minutes. Using a skimmer remove crabs and vegetables from stock. In a separate small sauté skillet melt butter, add flour and blend with a wire whisk until smooth and creamy, simmer over low heat for one minute. Add flour and butter mixture to stock using a wire whisk until all the roux is dissolved. Add heavy cream and simmer for 10 minutes. Remove outside rind from Brie and discard, cut Brie into 1" cubes, add to stock while constantly stirring until all the cheese is completely dissolved. Season soup with salt, white pepper and cayenne pepper. Strain soup through a fine strainer, add jumbo lump crabmeat and serve.

Yields 3 quarts.

POTATO AND PARMESAN CRUSTED OYSTERS WITH SAFFRON BARBECUE SAUCE
INGREDIENTS FOR CRUSTED OYSTERS:

20	large select oysters	2	cups flour
3	cups instant potato flakes	1	egg
1	cup grated Parmesan cheese	1	cup milk
2	tablespoons cracked black pepper	4	tablespoons olive oil

In a small pan, mix potato flakes, Parmesan and cracked black pepper. In a separate pan mix egg and milk. Lightly dust oysters in flour, then dip in eggwash, and coat with Parmesan cracker mix. Heat oil in skillet until hot. Sauté oysters on both sides until golden brown. Place on napkin to drain excess oil. Prepare sauce.

INGREDIENTS FOR SAUCE:

2	tablespoons olive oil	1	teaspoon fresh rosemary
2	tablespoons minced garlic	1	teaspoon fresh basil
½	cup diced tomatoes	1	tram saffron threads
½	cup sliced mushrooms	½	cup seafood stock
½	cup chopped sweet peppers	2	tablespoons lemon juice
¼	cup beer	2	ounces unsalted butter
4	dashes Worcestershire sauce	¼	cup chopped green onions

Continued Page 82

Sauce Method: Heat olive oil in a skillet and sauté garlic, tomatoes, mushrooms and sweet peppers until tender. Deglaze sauce pan with beer, add Worcestershire, rosemary, basil, saffron, seafood stock and lemon juice and simmer until sauce is reduced by half. Slowly add butter and swirl into sauce until dissolved, do not boil. Add green onion, serve sauce on base of plate and garnish with crusted oysters. Serve with your favorite rice or pasta dish.

Serves 4 portions.

SESAME CRUSTED YELLOW-FIN WITH ASIAN VINAIGRETTE

INGREDIENTS FOR TUNA:

16 ounces fresh #1 grade yellow-fin tuna loin	¼ cup black sesame seeds
¼ cup sesame seeds	3 tablespoons sesame oil

Method for Tuna: Heat oil in sauté pan until hot. Mix together sesame seeds and coat tuna. Place tuna in hot oil and sear on all sides. Slice thin for salad.

ASIAN VINAIGRETTE:

1 tablespoon sesame oil	¼ cup lite (low sodium) soy sauce
1 tablespoon minced garlic	½ cup rice wine vinegar
1 tablespoon minced fresh ginger	½ cup vegetable oil
3 tablespoons pepper jelly	1 pinch cayenne pepper

Method for Dressing: Heat sesame oil in skillet and sauté ginger and garlic until tender. Add pepper jelly and heat to dissolve. Place mixture into small bowl blend with remaining ingredients. Serve with sliced yellow-fin tuna and your favorite greens and vegetables.

Yield: 4 portions

LOUISIANA STRAWBERRY SABAYON

2 pints fresh strawberries, washed and sliced	1 teaspoon balsamic vinegar
	2 tablespoons sugar Sabayon

Toss strawberries in a stainless steel bowl with balsamic vinegar and sugar, let set in refrigerator for 1 hour before serving to macerate (steep in liquids).

SABAYON:

8 egg yolks	1 cup fresh cream, 40% whipped and kept chilled
¼ cup sugar	
¼ cup Muscat Beaumes de Venise (dessert wine)	

In a large stainless steel bowl, whisk egg yolks and sugar until a light lemon color. Place bowl over double broiler and whisk continuously until mixture

Continued Page 83

has doubled in volume and becomes thick. Remove from heat and place bowl over a bowl of ice, continue whisking until mixture is cool. Fold in whip cream with a rubber spatula until well incorporated but still light and airy. To serve, spoon 2 tablespoons sabayon into a small glass bowl or martini glass. Add strawberries, top again with sabayon. Serve as is or with a delicate sugar cookie or tuile.

Serves 2-4.

SALMON MUSCAT WITH ROASTED POTATOES AND SWISS CHARD

7	ounces fillet of salmon	1	tarragon leaf – julienne
2	ounces Muscat Beaumes de Venise (dessert wine)	2	teaspoons cold, unsalted butter
1	teaspoon veal glace		Salt & pepper to taste.

In a Teflon (8 inch) sauté pan, sprinkle a ¼ teaspoon Kosher salt. Place on high heat. When very hot, place salmon fillet lightly seasoned with salt and pepper in pan. Sear each side approximately two minutes and cook to medium rare. Remove to a warm plate. Drain rendered oil from the pan, add The Muscate and veal glace. Reduce by ⅔. Add butter, tarragon, salt and pepper. When butter is incorporated, remove from heat and glaze, top of fish. Serve with roasted new potatoes and Swiss chard. The accompaniment of Swiss Chard with the salmon, offers a wonderful tart contrast to the salmon, with its somewhat sweet glaze.

SWISS CHARD

1½	cups Swiss Chard, remove heavy stems and cut into 1 to 2-inch pieces	1	teaspoon rice vinegar
¼	teaspoon sugar	½	teaspoon butter
1	tablespoon water	1	teaspoon virgin olive oil
			Salt & pepper to taste

In a medium skillet, add all ingredients setting pan on high flame and bring to a boil. Reduce heat, stirring chard in pan. Cook for five minutes. Taste to correct seasoning. Drain off excess liquid and serve immediately.

Serves 1.

CORN & CRABMEAT BISQUE

½	pound of unsalted butter (s sticks)	1	pound lump crabmeat
1	cup all purpose flour		Salt and pepper to taste
1	teaspoon liquid crab boil	1½	cups chopped green onions
	Kernels from 4 ears of sweet corn	1½	cups heavy whipping cream

CRAB STOCK:
(Makes 1 quart)

	Shells from 6 medium hard shell crabs	2	quarts of water
		2	medium onions, quartered

To make stock, drop shells into water and add onions. Bring to a boil and simmer over low heat until liquid is reduced to 1 quart. Strain and set aside.

Melt butter in a 5-quart saucepan. Add flour and cook, stirring until flour begins to stick to the pan. Add stock and crab boil. Bring to a boil, stirring constantly and simmer for 15 minutes. Add corn and simmer for 15 additional minutes. Pour in cream and

Continued Page 84

stir well. Gently add crabmeat. Remove from heat and let stand for 15 minutes so that the flavors may blend. Reheat gently to serving temperature. Add salt and pepper to taste. Before serving add green onions.

Serves 8.

NOTE: To hold for serving or to reheat use a double boiler to prevent scorching.

TURTLE SOUP

1¼ cups unsalted butter	½ teaspoon thyme
¾ cup all purpose flour	½ teaspoon ground black pepper
1 pound turtle meat, large grind	1½ cups tomato puree
1 cup minced celery	1 quart of beef stock
1¼ cups minced onions	½ cup lemon juice
1½ teaspoons minced garlic	5 hard cooked eggs chopped
3 bay leaves	1 tablespoon minced parsley
1 teaspoon oregano	Dry sherry

Melt 1 cup (2 sticks) of butter in a heavy saucepan. Add flour and cook. Stir frequently until roux is light brown (over medium heat). Set aside. In a 5-quart saucepan melt ¼ cup butter and add turtle meat. Cover over high heat until meat is brown. Add celery, onions, garlic and seasonings and cook until vegetables are transparent. Add tomato puree, lower heat and simmer for 10 minutes. Add stock and simmer for 30 minutes. Add roux and cook over low heat, stirring until soup becomes smooth and thickens. Add salt and pepper to taste. Add lemon juice, eggs and parsley. Remove from heat and serve. Serve with sherry to taste.

Serves 6.

BREAD PUDDING WITH BOURBON SAUCE

1½ cups sugar	1 tablespoon vanilla extract
3 tablespoons butter softened	¼ cup raisins
6 eggs, beaten	12 slices, each 1 inch thick of fresh French bread
1 pint heavy cream	
Dash of cinnamon	

Preheat oven to 350 degrees. In a large bowl cream together the sugar and butter. Add eggs, cream, cinnamon, vanilla and raisins, mixing well. Pour into a 9-inch square pan 1¾ inches deep. Arrange bread slices flat in egg mixture and let stand for 5 minutes to soak. Turn bread over and let stand 10 minutes longer. Then push bread down so that most of it is covered. Set pan in a larger pan filled with water ½ inch from the top. Cover with aluminum, foil. Bake for 45-50 minutes. Uncover pudding for the last 10 minutes to brown the top. When done the custard should be soft not firm.

BOURBON SAUCE

1 cup sugar	2 teaspoons cornstarch
1 cup heavy cream	1 tablespoon bourbon
1 dash of cinnamon	¼ cup additional water
1 tablespoon unsalted butter	

Combine sugar, 1 cup cream, cinnamon and butter. Bring to a boil. Add in the cornstarch mixed with ¼ cup water and cook stirring until sauce is clear. Remove from heat and stir in whiskey.

Serves 8-10.

"TWO GUYS FROM HAMMOND"

Keith Curet and Sammy Marten

have not forgotten their Louisiana roots and are now operating the CREOLE CAFÉ at 220 S. Claybrook in Memphis, TN 38104
(901) 276-9722

The Creole Café is the culmination of a lifelong dream for childhood friends Sammy Marten and Keith Curet. Growing up in the New Orleans area, they shared a passion for Louisiana cooking and the Cajun "joi de vivre" (joy of living). They hope you enjoy their eclectic mix of Po-Boy sandwiches, Creole dishes, fresh vegetables and other home-cooked delights. "laissez les bon temps rouler!" (Let the good times roll!)

GUMBO YA-YA

2½	cups dark brown roux	1½	handfuls of bay leaves
2	cups chopped onions	1	gallon chicken stock
2	cups chopped green onions	1	pound Andouille sausage in bite-size pieces
2	cups celery		Meat from 3 cooked chickens
2	cups red and green peppers		Salt, pepper, hot sauce, Tony's seasoning to taste
¾	cup parsley		
½	cup garlic		

Method: Sauté veggies and bay leaves in roux until soft. Add sausage and brown. Add stock and simmer. Add spices and chicken and simmer until it thickens.

20 servings.

CREOLE SHRIMP

2	cups medium brown roux	3	quarts rich seafood stock
1½	cups chopped onions	5	pounds shrimp, peeled and deveined
1½	cups chopped celery		Salt, pepper, Louisiana hot sauce, chili powder
1½	cups chopped bell pepper		
¼	cup chopped garlic	6	bay leaves and a bit of sugar to taste.
3½	cups tomato sauce		
1½	cups diced tomatoes		

Method: Sauté veggies in roux until soft. Add tomato sauce and tomatoes and sauté for 15-20 minutes. Add water and all seasonings and simmer until lightly thickened. Then add shrimp and cook for 45 minutes. Adjust seasonings.

20 servings.

BATON ROUGE is the state capital of Louisiana and the center of Plantation Country. The Louisiana State Capitol was built by Governor Huey P. Long, who was gunned down in its hallway only two years after its completion. It's the tallest capitol building in the country. Baton Rouge is the nation's fifth largest port. Along the Mississippi River you can see the U.S.S. KIDD, a restored World War II destroyer. Baton Rouge is also home to Louisiana State University and Southern University. If you make your way to the LSU campus, go see the Campus Mounds. These 5000-year-old Native American earthen structures are older than any in North America, MesoAmerica, and South America, and were built before the pyramids in Egypt.

Also in the area is L'aquarium de Louisiane at the Greater Baton Rouge Zoo, the Enchanted Doll Museum, Blue Bayou Water Park, and the Dixie Landin' Amusement Park. If you've come to the area in search of Mother Nature, go on an Alligator Bayou Swamp Tour, where you can learn about alligators and try to wrap your arms around a 500-year-old cypress tree. The Bluebonnet Swamp Nature Center is another great place to see real live alligators in their natural habitat. Visit the LSU Museum of Natural Science to see the Hall of Louisiana birds, habitat dioramas, mammals, reptiles, amphibians of Louisiana and Mike the Tiger I.

CLINTON – The Clinton Courthouse has been called one of the architectural treasures of Louisiana. Check it out. Clinton is also the home of Cajun Injector and nationally known Chef Reese Williams who is a frequent guest on QVC with his world famous marinades.

ENGLISH LOUISIANA – In the mid-1800's, two-thirds of America's millionaires were planters on the Great River Road between Natchez, Mississippi, and New Orleans. Come see the section along the road known as "English Louisiana," where many of their palaces remain as testament to the size of their antebellum bank accounts. Serious plantation devotees never miss the Audubon Pilgrimage scheduled each spring along the Great River Road.

ST. FRANCISVILLE has 140 buildings on the National Register of Historic Places. (Note: The cover of this cookbook features Greenwood Plantation at St. Francisville) At Oakley House at Audubon State Historic Site, you'll learn about naturalist John James Audubon roaming the woods, studying and painting the birds. He produced 32 of his famous bird studies here. If you're a connoisseur of bed & breakfasts, you'll adore St. Francisville. Barrow House Inn, Cottage Plantation, Hemingbough, Green Springs Inn, Butler Greenwood, Greenwood, Lake Rosemound, Shadetree, and St. Francisville Inn all welcome overnight guests.

BLUE FISH GRILL

7560 Corporate Blvd.
Baton Rouge, LA 70809
(225) 928-FISH

Jennifer Poe, Owner

Blue Fish Grill is home to a 107,000 gallon saltwater aquarium. Currently, 3 man-eating sharks reside in the aquarium along with a variety of other local and tropical fish and moray eels. The aquarium sits in the middle of the restaurant and offers a relaxing atmosphere to our customers. It's the perfect place to bring the kids, a business associate or even a first date. The menu is perfect for all palates offering seafood, steaks and chicken dishes.

Some of our favorites include Crispy Fried Catfish, Seared Yellowfin Tuna with Wasabi Cream, Pecan Tilapia and Pepperjelly Chicken. Don't forget about our homemade Crème Brûlée for dessert. The next time you visit Baton Rouge stop by and sip on a cool beverage in the Shark Bar in front of the 13-foot deep aquarium as the fish swim by in unison.

The R/B River Explorer

BUFFALO SHRIMP

12	21/25-count shrimp (peeled and deveined with the tail left on)		Canola Oil for frying
	Buttermilk	1	cup Crystal hot sauce
	Seasoned flour (flour with seasoning salt)	1	cup of melted butter
		1	teaspoon of seasoning salt

After peeling and deveining the shrimp with the tail on, butterfly by gently slicing down the middle of the tail without piercing the tail. Dip the shrimp in buttermilk, then dredge in the seasoned flour. Fry in hot oil (350 degrees) until golden. Remove from oil and drain on paper towel. Combine hot sauce, melted butter and seasoning salt. Dip fried shrimp in buffalo sauce then serve with ranch dressing and celery sticks on the side.

Serves 6-8 people.

HOT SHRIMP

12	21/25-count shrimp, (peeled, deveined and butterflied)	12	strips of raw bacon
		12	slivers of Jalapeño Pepper (fresh or in the jar)
12	strips of Pepperjack Cheese		Toothpicks

After peeling and deveining the shrimp, butterfly by gently slicing down the middle of the tail without piercing the tail. Place a strip of pepperjack cheese and a sliver of jalapeño on the butterflied portion of the shrimp. Wrap shrimp with bacon slice and secure with a toothpick. Place in a broiler (or oven on broil) for approximately 5 minutes or until bacon is crisp. You may also fry in hot oil instead of broiling. Serve with cocktail sauce.

Serves 6-8 people.

FRONT PORCH RESTAURANT

9173 Highway 67 South Clinton, LA 70722 (225) 683-3030

Call 1-800-221-8060 to order Cajun Injector products.

When Jeanne Williams, her late husband Edgar, and son Reece opened the Front Porch Restaurant in 1977, "I was dead set against it!" laughs Miss Jeanne. It's easy to laugh now as diners from all over south Louisiana and Mississippi pile into her and Reece's upscale country restaurant, nestled in the pastoral countryside of East Feliciana Parish south of Clinton, Louisiana. The wide, inviting front porch is made entirely of cypress.

Edgar Williams pioneered the technique of injecting marinades into meats known today as the "Cajun Injector." Cajun Injector, Inc., is now America's leading injectable marinade company with sales topping $20 million. Cajun Injector recipes and technique have been featured on every major television network from The Today Show to Live with Regis & Kelly. Chef Reece Williams is a weekly regular on the national retail show, QVC and The Outdoor Channel's Louisiana Outdoor Adventures.

The following recipes are from Cajun Injector's Cookbook From Our Front Porch ... To Your Kitchen

CRABMEAT AU GRATIN

13	ounces evaporated milk	½	teaspoon ground red pepper
2	egg yolks	¼	teaspoon black pepper
1	stalk celery, chopped	1	pound lump crabmeat
¼	pound butter	½	pound Cheddar cheese
½	cup all-purpose flour		
1	teaspoon salt		

Sauté onions and celery in oleo or butter until onions are wilted. Blend flour in well with this mixture. Pour in the milk gradually, stirring constantly. Add egg yolks, salt, red and black pepper; cook for 5 minutes. Put crabmeat in a mixing bowl and pour the cooked sauce over the crabmeat. Blend well, folding over and over to keep lump crabmeat from breaking up. Transfer into a lightly greased casserole and sprinkle with grated Cheddar cheese. Bake at 375 degrees for 10 to 15 minutes or until light brown.

Serves 6.

RON'S BAR-B-QUE SHRIMP

CAJUN INJECTOR CREOLE GARLIC MARINADE

½	fresh lemon	2	dozen jumbo shrimp in shells
½	stick butter		

Wash shrimp thoroughly. Pinch off portion of head from the eyes forward. Melt butter in a large skillet. Place shrimp in a single layer in the butter. Shake marinade well and pour over shrimp until almost covered. Cover the top with black pepper. Cook for 5 minutes, occasionally shaking skillet in a back and forth motion – do not stir. Just before removing shrimp from heat, squeeze ½ fresh lemon on top of shrimp and sauce. Remove from heat, serve immediately in bowls with hot French bread on the side. If you don't "sop" your bread in the sauce, it's your mistake!

Serves 2.

EDGAR'S CAJUN AU JUS BEEF

This is the technique that made the "Front Porch Prime Rib" famous!

8	pounds boneless beef top round	16	fluid ounces Cajun Injector Beef Marinade (Creole Garlic recipe)

Pour marinade (2 ounces per pound of meat) into separate container and draw into injector. Place roast into 2-3 inch deep pan and inject marinade at points every 1-2 inches apart. After injecting, pour generous amounts of marinade over roast. Cover with foil and bake at 350 degrees until desired temperature is reached. (You can cook this outside on the pit also.) A whole rib-eye or prime rib prepared this way is wonderful!

JOE'S "DREYFUS STORE" RESTAURANT

2731 Highway 77
Livonia, LA 70755

Joseph & Diane Major, Owners

REMOULADE SAUCE

1 cup mayonnaise	½ bunch flat leaf parsley, chopped fine
½ cup horseradish	
½ cup Creole mustard	
3 ribs celery, diced	Salt, black pepper, Tabasco sauce and Lea & Perrin Worcestershire sauce to taste. Lemon juice to taste
1 large white onion, diced	
1 bunch green onions, chopped fine	

Combine all ingredients. Let stand one hour. Mix with any cooked seafood. Serve over shredded lettuce.

JOE'S STUFFED EGGPLANT

2 or 3 young eggplants	¾ pound small shrimp, peeled and deveined
1 large onion, chopped	
1 bell pepper, chopped	¾ pound crabmeat (white or claw)
2 ribs of celery, chopped	½ pound ham, diced
Butter	Red and black pepper, salt and sugar to taste
	Breadcrumbs

Split eggplants lengthwise and oil them. Place split side down in a shallow pan and bake at 350 degrees until tender. Cool. Remove pulp, chop it coarsely and set aside. Reserve skins. Chop onion, bell pepper and celery. Cook in a little butter until tender. Add shrimp, crabmeat, ham and eggplant pulp. Season to taste. Bind mixture with breadcrumbs, stuff into skins, top with breadcrumbs. Bake for 20 minutes at 350 degrees.

Serves 4.

JOE'S "DREYFUS STORE" RESTAURANT BREAD PUDDING WITH RUM SAUCE

PAN DRESSING:

2 ounces soft unsalted butter	4 ounces powdered sugar

PUDDING:

½ teaspoon ground cinnamon	1 cup shredded sweet coconut
2 cups sugar	1 1-pound loaf (1-2 day old) French bread, ends & bottoms crusts removed, cut in ½" slices
Pinch nutmeg	
1 teaspoon vanilla	
4 eggs plus 2 egg yolks	
1 quart whole milk	
½ cup raisins	

RUM SAUCE:

2 ounces unsalted butter	4 ounces heavy whipping cream
4 ounces powdered sugar	1 tablespoon Myers dark rum

In a small bowl, cream the 2 ounces of butter and the 4 ounces of powdered sugar. Generously coat sides and bottom of a 9"x13"x2"cool, dry cake pan with half the butter & powdered sugar mixture. Reserve the remaining portion. Set cake pan (preferably a glass pan) in refrigerator or cool place. In a large bowl, combine sugar, cinnamon, nutmeg, vanilla, eggs and egg yolks with a whip. Add milk, raisins and coconut and stir until thoroughly combined. Add bread slices, gently pushing them down into the milk mixture. Do Not Squeeze! Let soak ½ hour, turning occasionally. Pour into prepared pan. Pat down. Gently push raisins into the mixture so they will not burn. Melt remaining powdered sugar and butter mixture in reserve. Pour on top. Bake 45-50 minutes in top third of 325 degree oven. (Best if pan is placed on cookie sheet prior to placing in oven.)

To prepare rum sauce: Combine butter, powdered sugar and cream in a small sauce pan. Bring to a boil over medium heat while stirring constantly. Remove from heat. Add rum.

Joe's "Dreyfus Store" Restaurant

JUBAN'S RESTAURANT & CATERING

3739 Perkins Rd. Baton Rouge, LA 70808 (225) 346-8422

A Creole restaurant with the ambiance of the Vieux Carré. The "Wine Spectator's Award of Excellence. Private dining, banquet facility & catering.

Miriam Juban, Co-Owner

Carol Juban, Co-Owner

Terry McDonner, Executive Chef

HALLELUJAH CRAB

1	ounce crabmeat, backfin	1	tablespoon butter Seasoned breadcrumbs
1	ounce shrimp		Salt & pepper to
1	ounce crawfish		taste
1	tablespoon onions, diced		Soft-shell crab, cleaned
1	tablespoon green pepper, diced	1	egg water
1	tablespoon celery, diced		Self-rising flour

Mix seafood in a bowl together. Melt butter in skillet over medium heat. Add onion, green pepper and celery. Sweat until tender. Combine seafood and vegetables folding together gently in skillet. Season to taste. Cook until seafood is done. Add breadcrumbs. Cool. Form into two soft balls. Let the points of the crab shell and place seafood ball. Repeat on the other side. Combine egg and milk to make a wash. Place flour in separate container. Dredge stuffed soft-shell crab in flour, egg-milk wash and again in flour. Drop gently into fryer. (Oil should be 350 degrees). Cook 6-8 minutes. Top with Creolaise sauce (combination of Creole mustard with hollandaise sauce). For presentation, place crab with legs reaching up.

One serving.

STUFFED TOMATOES WITH CRAB AND CORN COULIS

4	medium tomatoes	4	slices bacon, cooked and crumbled
3	ears fresh corn, shucked		
1	sweet yellow pepper, split, seeded and cored	2	tablespoons chives, finely chopped
1½	tablespoons olive oil	5	basil leaves, julienne
1	clove garlic, finely chopped		Salt & pepper to taste
14	ounces fresh lump crabmeat	½	cup chicken stock
		½	tablespoon olive oil

Bring 2 quarts water with ½ tablespoon salt to a boil in a medium-size pot over high heat. Plunge in the tomatoes and boil for 15-30 seconds, remove with a mesh skimmer, and cool under cold running water. Peel the tomatoes with a small knife. Cut a ¼ inch cap from the top of the tomatoes. With a small spoon, carefully scoop out and discard the seeds and pulp, leaving the shell intact. Refrigerate the tomato shells with their caps on the side. Return the same water used for the tomatoes to a boil, add the corn, and cook for 3-4 minutes. Drain well and transfer to a plate and let cool. Set aside. Preheat broiler. Place the red and yellow peppers in a broiler pan skin side up. Broil until the skin turns black, about 8-10 minutes. Remove the peppers, cool under cold running water, and peel off the burn skin. Dice the peppers into ¼ inch pieces and set aside.

In a sauté pan, heat 1½ tablespoons olive oil over medium heat. Gently fold in garlic. Add peppers, crabmeat, bacon, chives, basil and salt and pepper to taste. Salt and pepper each tomato shell and fill it with the crab mixture up to just above the rim. Cover with the cap and refrigerate until needed. To make the coulis, cut corn off cob and transfer to a blender or food processor and puree. In a small non-reactive saucepan, heat corn and chicken stock to desired thickness. Just before serving, drizzle ½ tablespoon olive oil over the tomatoes and warm then in the microwave for 2 minutes on high. The tomatoes should not become too soft but the crab mixture should be hot. If you do not have a microwave, cover the tomatoes with foil and warm them in a 375 degree oven for 10 minutes. Evenly divide the coulis among 4 warm plates. Place one hot tomato on top of the sauce and decorate each tomato with a sprig of basil.

Servings: 4

Continued Page 92

BAYOU PEARLS

1	pound crabmeat	3	ounces heavy cream
4	ounces tasso, ground	1	cup Italian breadcrumbs
1	red pepper, diced		Salt & pepper to taste
1	bunch green onions, sliced thin		
1	tablespoon chopped garlic	8	ounces cooked angel hair pasta
2	whole eggs		

In a mixing bowl, combine crabmeat, tasso, diced red pepper, green onions, chopped garlic, eggs and cream. Mix thoroughly. Add breadcrumbs to tighten mixture. Season with salt and pepper to taste. Add pasta and mix well. Roll into 1½ inch balls and fry in 350 degree oil until golden brown, about 2-3 minutes.

ORANGE CHOCOLATE CRÈME BRÛLÉE

5	ounces sugar	4	vanilla pods
10	egg yolks	3½	ounces milk
10	ounces orange-flavored chocolate	1½	pints heavy cream
			Brown sugar

Mix the sugar and egg yolks well together in a bowl. In a small, dry non-reactive bowl, melt chocolate. Add melted chocolate to egg yolk mixture. Split vanilla pods in half and scrape the seeds out into the milk and cream in a pan. Add the pods, too, and heat gently so that the full flavor of the seeds and pods infuses the liquid. Pour the cream and milk onto the egg yolk mixture, mix well, then strain. Divide the mixture between 10 ramekins. Cook in a bain-marie of hot water in the oven preheated to 250 degrees for about 30-40 minutes or until just set. Allow to cool and set, then chill. Sprinkle the tops with brown sugar, and glaze under a hot grill. Allow the sugar to set hard, then serve in the dish.

Serves: 10

MAGNOLIA MOUND PLANTATION

2161 Nicholson Drive Baton Rouge, LA 70802 (225) 343-4955

A French Creole Plantation – on the National Register of Historic Places
Surrounded by 200-year-old live oaks, Magnolia Mound has retained its Creole plan and character for over 200 years. Construction is of cypress beams with bousillage-entre-poteau, and the original cypress flooring runs throughout the house. The original section of the main house, built circa 1791, was expanded to its present size at the beginning of the nineteenth century.

Today the plantation retains 16 of the original 930 acres, and provides the opportunity to study life on early Louisiana plantations. The house is furnished with fine examples of Federal and Louisiana-made artifacts. On the grounds are several outbuildings, including the Overseer's House, Slave Quarters and a Pigeonnier – a structure designed for raising squab. This living history museum is owned and operated by the East Baton Rouge Parish Recreation and Park Commission.

The plantation, with its garden, pigeonnier and smoke house, supplied the basic food items that would be supplemented by large amounts of foodstuffs imported through the port of New Orleans. The steamboat, inaugurating upstream travel in 1812, provided easy transportation of imported goods upriver, thus opening the Baton Rouge market to the world.

The following recipes are from THE Magnolia Mound Plantation KITCHEN BOOK:

Continued Page 93

OYSTER STEW

4	10-ounce jar oysters		Pinch nutmeg	
4	tablespoons butter	1	teaspoon salt	
1	tablespoon flour	2	egg yolks, beaten	
1	cup milk or cream	½	cup breadcrumbs	
	Pinch cayenne pepper (or to taste)			

In a pan melt butter and add flour, stir well. Slowly add milk or cream and cook 3 to 4 minutes, stirring all the while. Add cayenne, nutmeg and salt; then add the oysters. Cover and cook until edges of the oysters curl. Turn off heat and gently stir in egg yolks. Place in a serving bowl that can be placed under a broiler; sprinkle with crumbs. Broil to golden brown. Serve at once.

Serves 6-8.

SHRIMP PIE

4	cups medium shrimp, peeled & deveined	½	teaspoon salt
1½	teaspoons anchovy paste	2	ounces (4 tablespoons) dry vermouth
⅛	teaspoon mace	1	recipe light pastry dough for top crust
⅛	teaspoon ground cloves		

OPTIONAL SEASONINGS:

1	pinch cayenne	1	teaspoon dried parsley
¼	teaspoon thyme		

Measure the anchovy paste in a small bowl and thin with a very small amount of the wine. Gradually add the remainder of the wine; stir in seasonings until salt is dissolved. Pour mixture over shrimp and marinate while you prepare pastry dough. Divide the shrimp equally into 4 au gratin dishes (or put in a pie pan) and cover with crust. Bake at 425 degrees in a preheated oven for 25-30 minutes or until crust is lightly browned.

Serves 4.

A FRENCH CAKE

2½	cups flour	1	cup milk or cream
1½	cups sugar	3	medium eggs
1	teaspoon cinnamon or nutmeg	1	teaspoon baking powder
½	teaspoon salt	½	teaspoon warm water
5	tablespoons butter		

Mix flour, sugar, cinnamon or nutmeg and salt together in a bowl. Cream the butter. Add milk or cream to the butter, alternating with the flour mixture. Beat the eggs until very light in a separate bowl and add to the cake batter and beat for 10 minutes. Dissolve the baking powder in warm water and add to batter; stir only long enough to mix well. Butter a deep pan (bundt or angel food pan). Bake at 350 degrees for 40-45 minutes. Good served with hot tea.

PINEAPPLE SHERBET

2	ripe pineapples, peeled and sliced or cut in segments	2¼	cups sugar (or 1 cup sugar to each cup of juice)
1½	quarts boiling water	4	egg whites, lightly beaten

Pour boiling water over pineapple and let it stand one to two hours. Strain it well and measure the juice. (Be sure to press the pineapple in the strainer to extract all the juice.) Add sugar to the juice, bring it to a boil, stirring until the sugar has dissolved. Boil 5 minutes. Cool and then chill. Just before freezing in an ice cream freezer, add the egg whites. Freeze until firm.

Makes 2-3 quarts.

Magnolia Mound Plantation
Baton Rouge, Louisiana

MANSUR'S RESTAURANT

Fine Dining & Catering
3044 College Drive
Baton Rouge, LA 70808

**Gil Engelhardt III, Tim Kringlie,
Justin McDonald – Owners**

Charles Taucer – Executive Chef

Brandon McDonald – General Manager

Hidden in the corner of an old strip mall in the heart of Baton Rouge lies an experience that one can find in not other restaurant in town. Mansur's since its 1989 opening and through the determined dedication of its staff, has made a name for itself nationwide for providing award-winning Contemporary Creole Cuisine and impeccable service to its beloved clientele. Many professional pianists perform nightly.

*The restaurants atmosphere with the twinkling white lights, gushing water fountain, and mahogany soda fountain bar has an intoxicating affect immediately upon arrival. The spirit offerings are endless and Mansur's boasts its Wine Spectator magazine **Awards of Excellence** honors for the wine list for the past 8 years and counting.*

*The recipe for this Cream of Brie and Lump Crabmeat Soup, proudly served by Mansur's Restaurant, was awarded a Gold medal by Baton Rouge's American Culinary Federation and was even asked to be published in **Bon Appétit Magazine!** Mansur's and Corporate Chef Tim Kringlie proudly present the following recipe for your dining pleasure...*

CREAM OF BRIE CHEESE WITH LUMP CRABMEAT

2 cups of finely diced onion, bell pepper and celery

2 tablespoons crab base (may be purchased at specialty food stores)

6 ounces Brie cheese, out rind removed

8 ounces of fresh crabmeat (Always use fresh, not frozen or thawed crabmeat)

6 cups of half and half cream

¼ teaspoon Tabasco hot sauce

1 tablespoon dry Vermouth

⅛ teaspoon lemon juice

1 teaspoon Creole seasoning (This is a Louisiana developed seasoning. It contains garlic powder, onion, salt, red and black pepper.)

1 teaspoon chopped garlic

2 ounces blonde roux (Equal parts butter and self-rising flour)

3 tablespoons cottonseed oil

Heat the cottonseed oil in a 5 quart pot and sauté the vegetables until tender. Start the roux by melting ½ cup of unsalted butter and whisk in an equal part of flour until smooth and blended. Add the remaining ingredients to the pot with the exception of the Brie cheese and the crabmeat. Bring to a slow boil and thicken with the 2 ounces of the hot blonde roux. Stir continuously until smooth and silky. Add the Brie cheese and the crabmeat when ready to serve. Do not bring to boil after cheese has been added.

Makes 8 cups or 4 bowls.

Continued Page 95

MUSTARD AND CORN MEAL CRUSTED SALMON WITH LUMP CRABMEAT AND LEMON BUTTER

4	8-ounce fillets of Pacific salmon*	1	small shallot, chopped fine
4	ounces olive oil	3	ounces white wine
1	egg		Juice of 1 lemon
4	ounces cold water	3	ounces heavy cream
4	ounces yellow mustard	8	ounces unsalted butter (room temp.)
2	cups yellow corn meal		Salt & pepper to taste
1	tablespoon salt		
1	tablespoon pepper		
½	pound fresh jumbo lump crabmeat		

Whisk together the egg, water and mustard. Season the corn meal with salt and pepper. Heat the olive oil in a 12-inch non-stick sauté pan. Coat the salmon fillets with the mustard-egg wash mixture. Dredge them through the corn meal. Carefully place them in the hot sauté pan. Cook for about 4 minutes on medium heat. Flip the fillets over and continue to cook for another 4 minutes. The fillets should be a nice medium rare and the crust should be golden and crispy. Take the fillets out of the pan and drain on paper towels. Discard the olive oil and return the sauté pan to the heat. Add the shallots and sauté for about 30 seconds. Deglaze the pan with white wine and lemon juice. Add the heavy cream and whisk together until sauce starts to boil and thicken. Add the crabmeat and toss to coat. Start adding the butter one-ounce at a time. Allow the butter to melt into the sauce before adding more. Adjust the seasoning with salt and pepper. Put the salmon fillets on four separate plates and equally divide the crabmeat and sauce right over the top.

*Can substitute any fresh fish fillets for the salmon.

Serves 4.

MAISON LACOUR

*11025 North Harrell's Ferry Road
Baton Rouge, LA 70816
(800) 377-7104*

**Jacqueline Greaud – Chef and
John Greaud – Host (Co-Owners)**

**Michael Jetty – Chef and
Eva Jetty – Hostess/Manager**

We invite you to our cozy place to indulge in French Epicurean delights. We are located in a cottage nestled among Live Oaks and Crape Myrtles on beautifully landscaped grounds. Dedicated to serving the ideal of serving the finest food in a memorable setting, we strive to ensure our customers are comfortable and well served. Our menu offers classic dishes like the Veal Chop and Venison as well as culinary creations like John's Favorite, which consists of a broiled tenderloin medallion with Béarnaise, shrimp with garlic butter and lump crab in puff pastry with Hollandaise. We use the highest quality of ingredients offering a wide selection including veal, game, beef, fowl, lamb and seafood. All are well presented and perfectly cooked.

STUFFED MUSHROOMS WITH CRAWFISH

6	tablespoons butter	1	pound crawfish tail meat, coarsely chopped
½	stalk celery, finely chopped		
½	bell pepper, finely chopped	½	teaspoon salt
4	tablespoons shallots, finely chopped	½	teaspoon cayenne pepper
2	cloves garlic, finely chopped	⅓	cup dry breadcrumbs
2	ounces of tasso or cured ham	2	egg yolks
		24	medium mushrooms
		4	tablespoons olive oil

Continued Page 96

Melt 4 tablespoon butter in a sauté pan. Add the celery, bell pepper, shallots and garlic. Sauté for 1 minute, being careful not to burn the garlic. Add the tasso and crawfish meat. Lower the heat and cook for 5 minutes. Add salt, cayenne and ¼ cup breadcrumbs. Remove from heat and allow to cool to room temperature, about 30 minutes. When mixture has cooled, mix in the egg yolks. Clean the mushrooms and discard the stem. Brush the olive oil on the inside and out side of each mushroom cap. Arrange the caps in a shallow casserole dish. Stuff and mound each mushroom cap with the crawfish mixture, sprinkle with the remaining breadcrumbs and drizzle with 2 tablespoons of melted butter. In preheated oven (375 degrees) bake the stuffed mushrooms for 15 minutes or until brown. Serve immediately.

Serves 6.

SOUP JACQUELINE

2	tablespoons shallots, finely chopped	¼	teaspoon white pepper
2	tablespoons chopped celery stalk	1	cup cream
		3	ounces Brie, trimmed and cubed
2	tablespoons vegetable oil	8	asparagus stalks, blanched and diced
⅓	cup flour	8	ounces lump crabmeat
3½	cups clam juice		

In a medium saucepan, sweat the shallots and celery in oil for about 1 minute. Add the flour and mix well, but do not let it brown. Stir in the clam juice, stirring until smooth, and season with pepper. After the mixture thickens, add the cream and bring to a boil. Lower heat and simmer for 20 minutes. Add the Brie and stir until the cheese is melted. Add the diced asparagus and crabmeat and cook for 3 minutes. Check seasoning. Ladle into 6 heated soup bowls and serve immediately.

Serves 6.

ASSORTED GREEN SALAD

¼	cup arugula	2½	tablespoons hot water
½	cup friseé or curly chicory	½	teaspoon salt
½	cup Boston lettuce	⅛	teaspoon cayenne
½	cup green leaf lettuce	2	tablespoons red wine vinegar
2	tablespoons sugar	⅓	cup light salad oil
¼	teaspoon black pepper		

Wash the greens well, removing any heavy stems, and dry thoroughly. Tear greens into bite-sized pieces and place in a salad bowl. Toss gently to mix the leaves. Prepare the salad dressing by mixing the sugar, pepper, water, salt, cayenne and vinegar until salt and sugar are completely dissolved, then add the salad oil. Let stand for a few hours before serving. Shake well and pour over greens just before serving. Toss gently and divide among 6 salad plates.

SHRIMP BATON ROUGE

4	tablespoons olive oil	½	teaspoon cayenne
1	pound angel hair pasta	½	teaspoon white pepper, ground
¼	pound butter	1	teaspoon dry mustard
⅓	cup salad oil	1	teaspoon prepared horseradish
1	garlic clove, minced	1	teaspoon Worcestershire sauce
1	shallot, minced		
4	tablespoons green onions, minced	1	teaspoon salt
2	cups heavy cream	4	tablespoons Dijon mustard
	Juice of 1 lemon		
1	teaspoon black pepper, ground	30	shrimp, peeled and deveined

Bring 2 quarts of water to a boil. Add 1 tablespoon of olive oil. Separate strands of angel hair pasta and drop into boiling water. Cook for 2 minutes. Drain and rinse with hot water. Toss with 3 tablespoons olive oil and keep warm until ready to serve. In a large sauté pan, heat butter and salad oil until they foam. Add the garlic, shallot and onions. Cook for 1 minute, being careful not to burn the garlic. Add the heavy cream, lemon juice, spices, horseradish, Worcestershire sauce and salt. Simmer for 10 minutes. Whisk in the Dijon mustard. Add the shrimp and cook until they are plump, about 4 to 5 minutes. Arrange shrimp on angel hair pasta and pour sauce over them.

Serves 6.

Continued Page 97

SABAYON GLACÉ

1½	cups medium dry white wine	2	cups heavy cream, well chilled
½	cup raspberry liqueur	1	teaspoon vanilla
6	egg yolks	1	pint raspberries, blackberries, strawberries or blueberries
2	tablespoons water		
½	cup granulated sugar		Mint for garnish
1	tablespoon cornstarch		

Pour the wine and the raspberry liqueur into a saucepan, bring to a boil and lower heat, letting it simmer for 5 minutes. Meanwhile combine the egg yolks, water, sugar and cornstarch in the bowl of a mixer and beat at medium-high speed until the mixture forms a ribbon. Use the low speed of the mixer while pouring in the hot wine and liqueur mixture. Return the mixture to the saucepan and set over low heat, stirring continuously with a whisk until mixture thickens to whipped-cream consistency. Remove the pan from the heat. Pour this custard into a bowl. Place in the refrigerator to chill for about 3 hours, stirring from time to time to prevent a skin from forming. This dessert may be made 1 day ahead, covered and refrigerated. To serve, combine the well-chilled cream with vanilla in a chilled mixing bowl and beat at medium speed for 1 to 2 minutes, then increase the speed and beat for another 3 to 4 minutes, until the cream begins to thicken. It should be a little firmer. Do not over beat or the cream may turn into butter. Still beating, incorporate the cold wine custard and beat for about 3 minutes, until the mixture is homogeneous and very light in texture, like a mousse. Serve in 6 chilled dessert dishes. Garnish with raspberries or berries of choice and with a sprig of mint. Cover and refrigerate.

Serves 6.

Maison Lacour

NINO'S ITALIAN RESTAURANT

7512 Bluebonnet Blvd. Baton Rouge, LA 70810

Nino Giacalone, Chef/Owner

ORANGE SALAD

5	oranges	1	ounce extra virgin olive oil
5	fresh red chili peppers	½	teaspoon of salt
	Greek or Italian black olives		Juice from one orange
¼	teaspoon basil	2	ounces of shredded Pecorino cheese
¼	teaspoon oregano		
½	ounce of water		

Peel and slice oranges. Clean and slice chili peppers. Add olives. Mix in a small bowl oil, basil, oregano, orange juice, salt and water. Add Pecorino cheese. Serve at room temperature.

Serves 2.

LINGUINE AGLIO OLIO & PEPERONCINO

8	ounces of Linguine Pasta	½	chicken bouillon (melt the chicken bouillon in half cup of hot water)
16	large shrimp (cleaned)		
10	cloves of garlic	½	teaspoon of crushed red peppers
2	ounces of extra virgin olive oil		

Cook the pasta "al dente." Heat oil in a large skillet. Add garlic to skillet and sauté till brown. Add the shrimp and sauté till done. Add red pepper. Add chicken stock (bouillon in hot water). Add the pasta to pan and sauté for just a few seconds.

Serves 2.

NOTTOWAY PLANTATION RESTAURANT & INN

LA. Highway 1
White Castle, LA 70788
Toll Free 1-866-4-A-VISIT

"The Largest Plantation Home in the South"

Nottoway was completed in 1859 for Mr. & Mrs. John Hampden Randolph and their eleven children. The Greek Revival and Italianate mansion boasts 53,000 square feet! Randolph acquired over 7,000 acres of land making his fortune in sugarcane.

Savor the excitement, beauty and drama of the old South. Stay in one of Nottoway's thirteen guest rooms, each with its own private bath. Overnight guests receive a tour of the mansion, welcome beverage upon arrival, an early morning wake up call of sweet potato muffins, coffee and juice as well as a full plantation breakfast. The restaurant is also open daily for lunch and dinner. "One of the Top 25 American inns with super chefs" says **Condé Nast Traveler.**

JOHNNY JAMBALAYA'S BEAT THE "SUMMERTIME BLUES" PASTA SALAD

1	cup low-fat mayonnaise	2	large Creole tomatoes, quartered and sliced
1	cup Johnny Jambalaya's Herb Dressing	3	ribs of celery, chopped
12	ounces elbow macaroni, cooked and cooled	1	Vidalia onion, chopped
2	cucumbers, peeled and sliced		Lemon pepper to taste
		2	tablespoons of parsley flakes.

Mix mayonnaise and Chef Johnny's Herb Dressing in a large bowl. Add macaroni and mix. Add cucumbers, tomatoes, celery and onion. Mix all ingredients well. Sprinkle lemon pepper & mix. Refrigerate at least one hour. Serve in chilled lettuce-lined bowl and sprinkle with parsley flakes.

Serves 8.

MANDY'S CHEESE-STUFFED MUSHROOMS

14	large mushrooms	½	cup white wine
2	tablespoons butter	1	tablespoon garlic, minced
2	tablespoons olive oil combined with ⅓ cup Italian breadcrumbs	2	(more) tablespoons J.J.'s Herb Dressing & Marinade
2	tablespoons Johnny Jambalaya's Herb Dressing & Marinade	½	teaspoon parsley flakes
2	tablespoons Parmesan cheese, grated	1	teaspoon lemon pepper
1	cup onion, chopped	½	teaspoon Italian seasoning
		2	tablespoons salsa

Pull stems out of mushroom caps. Set aside caps. Mince stems. Place non-stick skillet over medium-low heat until hot. Add olive oil and 2 tablespoons of Herb Dressing & Marinade mixture and swirl in bottom of pan. Once oil is hot, add onions and sauté five minutes until onions start to brown. Add garlic, chopped mushroom stems, Italian seasoning, lemon pepper, parsley and salsa. Stir and sauté 5 minutes. Melt butter into mixture and stir in Italian breadcrumbs. Add cheese and stir. Remove from heat and allow to cool. Preheat oven to 350 degrees. Spray large glass baking dish with Pam cooking spray. Stuff mushrooms with mixture and place in pan. Mix together wine and Herb Dressing & Marinade and pour into bottom of pan. Cover with foil and bake for 30 minutes. Uncover and bake 15 minutes more until browned.

Continued Page 99

BACON, LETTUCE AND TOMATO SOUP

1	pound bacon, cut into one inch pieces	2	tablespoons Tony's Seasoning
½	pound butter	1	10.5-ounce can cream of asparagus soup
6	large tomatoes, cut into wedges		
2	tablespoons Pickapeppa Sauce	1	quart half & half
2	tablespoons Lea & Perrin's Worcestershire Sauce	1	head of lettuce, cut into one-inch pieces

Cook bacon in large saucepan. Remove bacon before crisp and set aside. Add butter to bacon drippings and tomato wedges. Add Pickapeppa, Worcestershire sauce and Tony's seasoning. Add half & half and heat thoroughly but do not allow to boil. Add bacon back to soup. Serve over lettuce.

JJ'S MEAUX JEAUX PORK MEDALLIONS

6	boneless pork chops (approx. 1½ pounds total)	¼	cup JJ's Herb Dressing & Marinade

SAUCE:

	Juice of 1 lemon	1	cup onion, sliced
	Juice of 1 lime	2	tablespoons dry sherry
½	cup orange juice		
½	cup chicken broth	1	tablespoon garlic, minced
4	tablespoons salsa		
4	tablespoons sweet orange marmalade	¼	cup yellow bell pepper, chopped
2	tablespoons JJ's Herb Dressing & Marinade	1	teaspoon dried parsley
1	tablespoon Worcestershire sauce	1	teaspoon lemon pepper
1	tablespoon dark brown sugar	2	teaspoons cornstarch dissolved in ¼ cup water
2	tablespoons olive oil		
2	tablespoons JJ's Herb Dressing & Marinade	¼	cup green onions, sliced

Rinse pork and place in shallow glass pan. Coat with JJ's Herb Dressing & Marinade. Chill 30 minutes while preparing remaining ingredients. Combine the "Sauce" ingredients in a small glass bowl; set aside. Place a non-stick skillet over medium-high heat until hot. Add 2 tablespoons olive oil and 2 tablespoons JJ's Herb Dressing & Marinade, swirling to coat bottom of pan. Add pork chops and brown for 2 minutes on each side; remove from pan. Add onion and reduce heat to medium. Sauté until onions are brown on edges. Add sherry and swirl to deglaze pan. Sauté 1-2 minutes. Add garlic, bell pepper, parsley and lemon pepper to pan and stir well. Sauté 3 minutes over medium heat. Return pork chops to the pan; reduce heat to low. Pour the sauce over the chops, cover and simmer 20 minutes turning chops once. Uncover skillet and stir in cornstarch solution and green onions. Simmer, uncovered 5-6 minutes turning chops once. Remove pork from skillet and place onto 6 plates. Spoon sauce over medallions and serve.

Serving Suggestions: Place pork medallions on bed of cooked wild rice and top with sauce. Garnish with orange slices.

Serves 6.

BREAD PUDDING

1	loaf sliced white bread, broken in pieces	1	cup milk
		1	cup water, warmed
		1	cup sugar
3	eggs beaten	¼	pound margarine, melted
½	teaspoon vanilla		

Mix in large bowl, the water and margarine. Put broken bread into the mixture and stir. Add milk and stir. Add vanilla, eggs and sugar and stir well. Pour into a 12" by 16" baking pan and bake at 350 degrees for one hour. Serve warm topped with rum sauce. (Recipe follows)

Yield: 20 – 6-ounce servings

RUM SAUCE:

1	stick butter	6	ounces white rum (to taste)
½	cup sugar		
2	16-ounce cans whipped topping		

Melt the butter; add sugar and mix together in a bowl till the sugar is dissolved. Add the whipped topping and whip with a wire whip. Drizzle the rum into the mixture a little at a time. Cover and keep mixture in the freezer until ready for use.

Yield: 20 – 2-ounce servings.

OAK ALLEY PLANTATION RESTAURANT & INN

3645 Highway 18
Vacherie, LA 70090
(225) 265-2151

Oak Alley Plantation begins with its spectacular trees. A quarter-mile alley of twenty-eight sheltering oaks over 250 years old still greets you today. The present day plantation, a National Historic Landmark was built in 1837-39 by Jacques Telesphore Roman, a wealthy French Creole sugar planter. It was built along The Great River Road when Southern aristocracy ruled the land. Oak Alley offers daily guided tours of the antebellum mansion. Luscious grounds, a charming restaurant, gift shop and overnight cottages, plus a calendar of delightful seasonal special events complete the Oak Alley experience. The restaurant serves authentic Creole/Cajun specialties and is located on the grounds of the plantation.

**Recipes Provided by Donna Oliver
Executive Director,
River Parishes Tourist Commission**

PESTO CHEESECAKE

½	tablespoon butter (room temperature)	1	8-ounce package cream cheese
¼	cup fine Italian breadcrumbs	½	cup ricotta cheese
¼	cup plus 1 tablespoon freshly grated Parmesan cheese	⅛	teaspoon salt
		⅛	teaspoon cayenne pepper
		2	large eggs
		¼	cup purchased pesto sauce
		⅛	cup pine nuts

Preheat oven to 325 degrees. Rub 1 tablespoon butter over bottom & sides of 9-inch pan. Mix breadcrumbs with 2 tablespoon grated Parmesan cheese – coat pan with mixture. Using electric mixer, beat cream cheese, ricotta, remaining Parmesan, salt & cayenne pepper in large bowl until light. Add eggs, one at a time, beating well after each addition. Transfer half to medium bowl, mix pesto into remaining half and

pour mixture into prepared 9-inch pan. Smooth top carefully. Spoon plain mixture over top, smooth and sprinkle with pine nuts. Bake until center no longer moves when shaken (about 45 minutes). Transfer from oven and cool completely. Cover tightly with plastic and refrigerate overnight. Run knife around edge to loosen. Garnish with basil.

8 Servings.

BANANAS FOSTER FRENCH TOAST
BANANAS FOSTER SYRUP

1½	cups good quality maple syrup	1	teaspoon rum flavoring (extract) or 1 tablespoon dark rum
2	tablespoons butter		
4	bananas, peeled, halved and sliced lengthwise.		

In a small saucepan, heat syrup over medium heat, add butter and stir until melted and syrup is bubbling. Add bananas and heat thoroughly. Remove from heat and add rum or rum extract. Return to slow heat and keep warm.

FRENCH TOAST:

6	large eggs	8	slices French bread (preferably a few days old)
2	teaspoons vanilla		
½	cup heavy cream		
6	tablespoon butter		

Make batter by first whisking eggs. Add vanilla. Pour in cream and whisk until well blended. Melt 1 to 2 tablespoons of butter over medium high heat. Dip slices of bread into batter and soak thoroughly. Place 2 slices at a time in melted butter and cook each side until golden brown. Repeat with remaining slices. Serve slices with warm syrup and bananas.

SWEET POTATO STUFFED SATSUMA

3	large kiln dried Louisiana sweet potatoes	1	teaspoon ground cinnamon
¼	cup heavy cream or half & half	¼	teaspoon freshly grated nutmeg
½	cup brown sugar, packed firmly	¼	teaspoon ground cloves
½	can whole cranberry sauce	8	satsuma (Louisiana seedless oranges). Note: navel oranges may be substituted

Bake sweet potatoes until soft (45 – 50 minutes at 350 degrees). Wash satsuma well, remove top and hollow

Continued Page 101

the fruit out using a grapefruit spoon or paring knife. Remove enough of the bottom so that orange shells will sit flat, but do not cut through while membrane. Remove white membrane from extracted pulp and chop. Set aside. In a medium sized bowl mash cooked sweet potatoes with butter, cream and spices. Add brown sugar and mix well until sugar is incorporated. Mix in whole cranberry sauce and chopped satsuma pulp. Using a spoon, fill satsuma shells with mixture. Place in rectangular baking dish and bake in a preheated 350-degree oven for 20 minutes.

8 Servings.

PRALINE BREAD PUDDING

2	tablespoons butter, softened	2	tablespoons pure vanilla extract
3	large eggs, well beaten	4	cups heavy cream
1	cup light brown sugar	1	large loaf stale French bread torn in 1" cubes (about 6 cups)
¼	teaspoon cinnamon A pinch of freshly grated nutmeg	½	cup finely chopped & lightly toasted pecans

Generously butter 11" x 3½" x 3" baking dish. In a large mixing bowl combine sugar, beaten eggs, cinnamon, nutmeg, vanilla and heavy cream. Mix with electric mixer for 3-4 minutes. Place torn bread pieces in baking dish, then cover with egg and cream mixture. Push down with the back of a spoon to insure there are no dry pieces. Cover with plastic wrap and refrigerate for 2 hours. Heat oven to 325 degrees. Place bread pudding pan in a larger pan filled with water. Bake for 55-60 minutes until set in center (until it slightly jiggles). Remove bread pudding pan and set on a wire rack to cool for about 45 minutes. Serve with warmed praline sauce (recipe below).

PRALINE SAUCE:

½	cup light brown sugar	1	cup heavy cream
½	cup white sugar	½	cup pecan halves, lightly toasted
¼	cup butter (no substitutes!)	1	teaspoon pure vanilla extract

Place sugars in a heavy saucepan over medium-low heat. When sugar starts to turn color carefully shake and swirl the pan to uniformly brown. Add butter and mix well. Remove from heat and add cream carefully as this will steam. Stir until thoroughly incorporated, then add pecans and vanilla.

12 Servings.

CHICKEN, ANDOUILLE & TASSO GUMBO

BASE:

1	pound Andouille sausage cut in ½" slices	½	cup green onion, chopped
½	pound pork or turkey tasso, chopped in ½" cubes	2	cups onion (yellow or white) chopped
1	3½ to 4-pound fryer, cut up	2	tablespoons parsley, chopped
½	cup green pepper, chopped	8	cloves of garlic, minced
		⅔	cup vegetable oil
		½	cup flour

LIQUID & SPICES:

2	quarts chicken stock	1	teaspoon dried thyme
2	teaspoons sea salt	2	bay leaves, crushed
1	teaspoon black pepper	2	tablespoons Uncle Bill's Filé powder
½	teaspoon cayenne pepper	4	cups cooked long grain white rice

Assemble first 8 ingredients. Brown chicken in heated vegetable oil, turning to insure uniformly browned on all sides. Remove from oil, then sauté Andouille and tasso over medium-high heat for 7 to 8 minutes. Remove from oil and set aside. Begin making roux by gradually adding flour to heated oil, stirring constantly until mixture reaches a medium brown color (it will look like an old penny). Immediately add green pepper, green onions, onions and parsley. Cook for 10 minutes over medium heat while still stirring. Gradually add about a cup of the stock, the chicken, sausage, tasso, the remainder of stock, garlic and all the spices except the filé powder. Raise the heat to bring to a boil, then reduce to a simmer. Cook for an hour, stirring occasionally. Remove from heat. Serve in large bowls over rice. Finish with a generous sprinkle of the filé powder and hot, crisp French bread.

8 Servings.

PAVÉ

711 Jefferson Highway
Baton Rouge, LA
(225) 248-1381

Chip and Susan Strange, Owners
David Resch, Executive Chef/Owner

Pavé is a "unique" dining experience in Baton Rouge. The décor is crisp and inviting with a soothing color scheme and delightfully playful lighting. The menu introduces a masterful blend of new American Cuisine with French and Asian influences from Maine lobster cakes to air dried Peking duck.

RARE TUNA SALAD ASIAN STYLE

FOR THE TUNA ROLLS:

12	ounces fresh tuna loin in 1-inch strips seared medium rare	1	cup rice noodles soaked
1	cucumber julienne	4	rice paper wrappers soaked in hot water
1	avocado julienne		Wasabi to taste
1	carrot julienne		

In the middle of the rice paper, place a small amount of tuna, noodles and vegetables. Spread a little of the wasabi on one end of the rice paper. Roll tightly, then roll tightly in food wrap and twist on both ends. Refrigerate.

FOR THE SALAD:

8	ounces mache lettuce	1	cup julienne carrots
1	cup julienne dikon radish	1	cup julienne green onions

FOR THE VINAIGRETTE:

2	tablespoons sesame oil	2	tablespoons brown sugar
⅔	cup soy sauce	1	teaspoon Thai chili flakes
4	tablespoons lime juice	2	tablespoons fish sauce

Mix well. To assemble, place a mound of salad in the middle of a small dinner plate. Cut spring rolls in half and place against the salad. Garnish with 1 ounce of vinaigrette.

SEARED RED SNAPPER WITH YELLOW TOMATO BLUE CRAB GAZPACHO AND CILANTRO SPROUT SALAD

FOR THE SNAPPER:

4	6-ounce snapper fillets	1	tablespoon chopped fresh chives
1	tablespoon cracked black pepper	1	teaspoon coriander
1	tablespoon Kosher salt	2	tablespoons olive oil

Mix pepper, salt, chives and coriander. Rub snapper with olive oil. Season with spice mixture. Sear on both sides for 3 minutes. Finish in a 400-degree oven for 5 minutes.

FOR THE GAZPACHO SAUCE:

1	cucumber diced	1	ounce rice wine vinegar
1	large yellow tomato diced	1	teaspoon garlic chili paste
1	small onion diced	1	teaspoon sugar
1	red bell pepper diced	½	pound jumbo lump blue crabmeat
1	tablespoon chopped fresh basil		Salt & pepper to taste
1	ounce olive oil		

Mix all ingredients well.

FOR THE SALAD:

6	ounces fresh cilantro washed	½	tablespoon soy sauce
6	ounces dikon or radish sprouts	½	tablespoon rice wine vinegar
1	tablespoon olive oil		Salt, pepper and sugar to taste

Mix well. To assemble, place warm snapper fillet in the center of a large dinner plate. Top with 2 tablespoons crab gazpacho and garnish with sprout salad. Serve at once.

Continued Page 103

CRISPY SOFT SHELL CRAB SANDWICH

FOR THE CRABS:

4	soft-shell crabs, cleaned		Salt, pepper and cayenne pepper to taste
2	cups flour		
2	tablespoons cornstarch	2	cups peanut oil

Mix flour, seasoning and cornstarch. Dredge crabs in flour and pan fry shell on both sides for three minutes in peanut oil. Keep warm.

FOR THE CORN SCALLION CAKES:

2	whole eggs	1	teaspoon chopped garlic
1	cup milk		
1	teaspoon baking powder	2	cups flour
½	cup corn kernels		Salt & pepper to taste
1	bunch chopped scallions		

Mix well. Place three tablespoons in a hot, well-oiled skillet and sauté as you would a pancake.

FOR THE CONFIT:

4	seeded and skinned tomatoes quartered	½	teaspoon Kosher salt
1	tablespoon olive oil	1	teaspoon fresh thyme
1	teaspoon cracked black pepper		

Mix well and roast in a 300-degree oven for 1 hour.

FOR THE AIOLI:

2	egg yolks	1	roasted Habanero chile pepper smashed
2	chopped garlic cloves		
1	teaspoon lemon juice	3	tablespoons heavy cream
1½	cups olive oil		Salt & pepper to taste
1	teaspoon sugar		

Place egg yolks in a medium bowl. Slowly whisk in garlic, lemon juice, sugar and Habanero. Very slowly, drizzle in oil until you reach a mayonnaise consistency. Whip in heavy cream. Season.

To assemble: Place a tablespoon of aioli on a small dinner plate. Place one corn cake over the sauce. Fold crab in half and place on top of cake. Top with tomato confit and arugala. Top with a second corn cake.

PRIMO'S STEAK & LOUISIANA CUISINE

5454 Bluebonnet Blvd. Suite A Baton Rouge, LA 70809 (225) 291-9600

Primo's Steak and Louisiana Cuisine is located in Baton Rouge, the capital and heart of Louisiana. It is casual fine dining at its best with superb service in a warm and relaxed atmosphere. Diners are presented with a dazzling array of Black Angus steaks, Louisiana specialties and the freshest seafood available. In addition to the unique dining experience, Primo's offers the Mahogany Room. An exquisite lounge with a distinctive assortment of fine wines and liquors, hand rolled cigars and exceptional appetizers.

VEAL PRIMO

3	veal medallions (per serving)		3 to 4 ounces crabmeat
3	ounces butter		Salt & pepper to taste
4	thin slices Gruyere cheese		

In a skillet, quickly brown veal medallions in 2 ounces butter and set on paper towels to drain. Sauté crabmeat in 1 ounce butter with lemon juice and seasoning to taste. In a separate skillet or pan layer veal medallion ½ the crabmeat and ½ the cheese, veal medallion, crab cheese, finishing with the last veal medallion. Place pan in a preheated 450 degree oven for three minutes (just long enough to melt the cheese).

SAUCE:

1	tablespoon crushed black peppercorns	2	cups demi-glace
⅓	cup brandy	2	ounces foie gras pate

In a skillet roast peppercorns for approximately 1 minute. Take skillet off heat and carefully add brandy (it will flame). When brandy has finished flaming add demi-glace and reduce to proper consistency. Finish by swirling in 2 ounces foie gras pate.

Continued Page 104

TOP WITH MEUNIERE AND HOLLANDAISE SAUCES
(RECIPES FOLLOW).

MEUNIERE:

2	quarts demi-glace	1½	pounds butter softened (whisk and squeeze in fast)
⅓	cup lemon juice – reduce		
		2	tsp. seasoning salt

HOLLANDAISE

½	cup white wine	½	pound melted butter
4	egg yolks		
2	whole eggs		Salt, pepper,
	Juice of 1 lemon		Tabasco to taste

Bring wine to a simmer in a small saucepan. Whisk eggs with lemon juice then whisk in warm wine. Whisk while cooling in a bain marie until mixture is a smooth custard consistency. Remove from heat. Whisk in melted butter. Season to taste.

STUFFED PORTABELLA MUSHROOMS

4	medium yellow onions	2	eggs
8	shallots	6	cups béchamel
12	cloves of garlic	2	tablespoons Herbsaint
8	ribs of celery		
2	pounds claw crabmeat	15	large portabella mushroom caps (or 30 small ones)
	Italian breadcrumbs		

Sauté all veggies in butter, make sure you don't brown. Sauté in 2 pounds crabmeat, then de-glaze with 2 cups white wine. Cook until there is no liquid at all. Then add to béchamel, Herbsaint, add 2 eggs and add breadcrumbs till desired thickness. Cook down on low heat for about 20 minutes. Season to taste. Preheat oven to 375 degrees. Place a scoop of stuffing on each mushroom cap (where the stem was). Bake for 20 minutes (for large) or 15 minutes (for small).

PRALINE BREAD PUDDING

BREAD PUDDING:

1	pound butter	⅓	cup praline (or hazelnut) liqueur
4	cups sugar		
20	eggs	3	tablespoons vanilla
2	quarts heavy cream	2	loaves bread
		1	cup pecan pieces

Melt butter in microwave and stir into sugar. Add eggs. Heat cream to boiling and slowly beat into egg mixture. Add liqueur and vanilla. Break bread into pieces and put into a larger bowl. Sauté pecans in butter, drain butter and sprinkle pecans over bread. Pour liquid ingredients over bread and mix with hands. Pour into pan and cover with foil. Place pan into bain marie. Bake at 300 degrees for 45-50 minutes. Remove foil and bake for another 10-15 minutes.

SAUCE:

¾	pound butter	3	eggs
3	cups sugar	¾	cup praline liqueur

Cook butter and sugar over double boiler until hot and sugar is dissolved (this will take a while). Remove from heat and allow to cool slightly. Whisking quickly, add eggs. Add liqueur.

Plate Presentation/Preparation: From the pan, cut triangles. Heat the triangles in the microwave until hot (approx. 1½ minutes.) Place a praline Florentine garnish behind bread pudding. Place caramelized pecans and pistachios around bread pudding. Heat sauce in microwave until hot, then pour enough over bread pudding to cover both triangles.

Old State Capitol – Baton Rouge

SHRIMP BUTTER

2	cups cooked shrimp
1	stick butter
8	ounces cream cheese
3	tablespoons mayonnaise
1	tablespoon lemon juice
3	tablespoon onion, grated
½	teaspoon garlic powder
¼	cup parsley, chopped
2	teaspoons Tabasco pepper sauce
½	teaspoon red pepper
1	teaspoon Worcestershire sauce

Mince shrimp or run through food processor. Blend butter and cream cheese together until fluffy. Add to butter and cream cheese mixture, shrimp, mayonnaise, lemon juice, onion, garlic powder, parsley, Tabasco pepper sauce, red pepper and Worcestershire. Mix well. Shape into ball. Refrigerate until firm. Serve with crackers.

RALPH & KACOO'S SEAFOOD GUMBO

3	pounds fresh shrimp	3	(14 ounce) cans whole tomatoes with juice (hand squeezed)
2	pints oysters		
2	pounds lump crabmeat	1	(8 ounce) can tomato sauce
4½	cups flour		
3	cups vegetable oil	3	tablespoons salt
2	cups bell peppers, chopped	3	tablespoons black pepper
8	cups onions, chopped	2	teaspoons red pepper
3	cups celery, chopped	1	gallon water
		¾	cup parsley, chopped
3	tablespoons garlic, chopped	1	cup green onions, chopped

Make a roux by stirring flour and vegetable oil until a well-browned peanut butter color. Not burned! When roux is made, add onions, bell peppers, celery and garlic. Cook, stirring, until vegetables are limp, being careful not to burn. Add hand squeezed tomatoes, tomato sauce, salt and peppers. Cook and stir until well blended. Add water and cook 50 minutes. Turn fire off. Let sit until ready to serve. Just before serving, bring to a light bubble. If too thick, add more water. Add shrimp. Cook 10 minutes. Add parsley, green onions, oysters and crabmeat. Cook 5 minutes more. It is important not to overcook the seafood. Serve immediately.

RALPH & KACOO'S STUFFED CRABS

3	pounds crabmeat, fresh & drained	5	cups stale breadcrumbs
½	cup margarine	2	teaspoons black pepper
2¼	cups onions, chopped		
½	cup green pepper, chopped	½	teaspoon red pepper
		2	teaspoons salt
⅔	cup parsley, chopped	2	eggs
			10 to 12 crab shells

Melt margarine. Add onions and garlic. Simmer until onions are wilted. Remove from heat and add all other ingredients. Mix well. Stuff crab shells and top with a sprinkle of crumbs. Dot with butter. Place stuffed crabs into 450 degree oven until thoroughly heated throughout and crumbs are brown. This is also great for crab balls. Roll in a light batter and deep fat fry.

SAIA'S OAKS PLANTATION

#20 Ave. of Oaks
Destrehan, LA 70047

SAL SAIA'S BEEF ROOM

2645 N. Causeway Blvd.
Metairie, LA 70002

SAIA'S BEEF ROOM

1306 S. Morrison Blvd.
Hammond, LA 70403

No matter where you travel in Louisiana, you can enjoy our perfect atmosphere, delicious food, quality drinks and a professional staff. We serve a variety of entrees from Cajun trout specials to veal dishes to sizzling steaks. The elegance and charm of the plantation located off of historic River Road offers a romantic view of the 160 year old oak trees. A friendly face is always waiting to cater to all your needs at any of our locations.

CRAWFISH, CORN AND POTATO CHOWDER

½	gallon seafood stock	1	teaspoon liquid crab boil
½	gallon chicken stock	1	tablespoon Crystal cayenne seasoning with garlic
2	large yellow onions		
2	green onions	6	ounces half & half
½	stalk celery	16	ounces frozen whole kernel corn
4	garlic cloves		
2	bell peppers	3	ounces sugar
1	bunch curly parsley	1½	pounds red potatoes, diced (skin on)
¾	teaspoon celery seed		
¾	tablespoon dill weed	1½	ounces extra virgin olive oil
¾	tablespoon thyme	2	pounds crawfish tail meat
¾	teaspoon basil		

FOR ROUX:

3	ounces vegetable oil	3	ounces flour

In a braiser, sauté vegetables in the olive oil over medium heat until soft. Whisk in the blonde roux and then add warm seafood and chicken stock, crab boil, diced red potatoes, Crystal cayenne seasoning and sugar. Let simmer for 15 minutes and reduce heat. Add the corn, half & half, and crawfish tails with the fat. Cook over low flame for 10 more minutes.

Yield: 1½ gallons

VEAL DELMONICO

1	ounce butter	½	teaspoon blue cheese dressing
1	ounce white wine		
1	ounce lemon juice		Green onions, chopped
6	shrimp		
4	artichoke quarters		Mushrooms, sliced
1	ounce whipping cream		

Sauté all of the above. Serve on top of panne' veal.

Serves one.

FLAMING ALMONDS AMARETTO FOR TWO

¾	stick butter	½	lemon
1	cup brown sugar	¼	shot 151 rum
3	ounces amaretto		cinnamon
1	cup toasted almonds	4	scoops vanilla ice cream

Melt butter in copper sauce pan. Mix in brown sugar, dissolve, stir in amaretto, then almonds, squeeze lemon, add rum and flame. Throw cinnamon for sparkles. Serve immediately over 2 scoops of vanilla ice cream per person.

Serves 2.

<table>
<tr><td colspan="2">

The Grapevine Market and Café

211 Railroad Avenue Donaldsonville, LA 70536 (225) 473-8463

Dickie and Cynthia Breaux, Owners

</td></tr>
</table>

Crawfish Cornbread

4	eggs	2	cups milk
4	cups yellow corn meal	8	tablespoons melted butter
6	teaspoons baking powder	4	teaspoons sugar
2	teaspoons salt	2½	cups shredded cheddar cheese
4	cups cream style corn	1	pound crawfish tails

Mix all ingredients in a large bowl. Pour into a stainless steel full-size baking pan that has been sprayed with pan spray. Bake at 375 degrees for about 1 hour. Serve as an appetizer plain or topped with crawfish étouffée. Also great served as an entrée topped with fresh grilled fish.

Yield: 1 full size pan = 16 servings. Portion size: 1 slice

Praline Yams

9	cups (about 10-12 potatoes)	1½	cups butter
5	eggs	2½	teaspoons vanilla extract
¾	cup milk	1	teaspoon cinnamon
2½	cups sugar		

Bake potatoes until tender. Cool and peel off skin. Smash potatoes in a large bowl. Add all remaining ingredients and put into a stainless steel full pan. Sprinkle mixture with the following topping:

TOPPING:

1	cup melted butter	1½	cups flour
3	cups light brown sugar	2½	cups chopped pecans

Mix all of the above ingredients and sprinkle on top of potato mixture. Bake at 350 degrees for 30 minutes (or until hot and bubbly).

Peach or Kumquat Sauce

1	cup sugar	¼	cup Peach Schnapps
5	peaches sliced or if Kumquats are used – cut in half	¼	cup Grand Marnier Cornstarch & water blend for thickening
4	cups orange juice		

Caramelize sugar in pot then add remaining ingredients. Thicken with cornstarch to a thin, smooth texture. Serve with roasted quail or glaze over pork tenderloin.

Chocolate Pecan Pie

⅔	cup raw sugar	1	tablespoon flour
1	cup dark Karo syrup	1	cup mini semi-sweet chocolate chips
4	eggs	1½	cups broken pecan pieces
2	tablespoons melted butter	1	pie crust – unbaked pie shell
1	tablespoon vanilla extract		

Beat sugar, syrup, flour, eggs, butter, flour and vanilla in bowl until well blended. Pour semi-sweet chocolate chips in bottom of unbaked pie shell. Pour pecans on to of chocolate chips. Pour liquid mixture over pecans making sure all of the pecans are coated. Bake at 325 degrees for 45 minutes to 1 hour until done.

Yield: 1 pie = 8 slices

Cheesecake

15	sugar cookies	2	tablespoons pure vanilla extract
6	tablespoons melted butter	6	eggs
3	pounds softened cream cheese	2	cups sugar
		1	cup sour cream

Crust: Grind cookies in food processor until fine. Mix with the melted butter. Press mixture in bottom and sides of 8½-inch springform pan that has been sprayed with a pan spray.

Filling: In a bowl, mix cream cheese, sugar, eggs, sour cream & vanilla and beat with electric hand mixer until creamy. Pour over crust. Wrap bottom of pan with aluminum foil – enough to cover the sides so that when baking in the water bath the water does not get into the pan. Bake for 45 minutes to 1 hour at 350 degrees until firm in a water bath. Refrigerate, preferably overnight before serving.

Yield: 1 cheesecake = 12 slices.

MOREL'S

210 Morrison Parkway
New Roads, LA 70760
(225) 638-4057

Georgia and Henry "Buddy" Morel
Owners

The restaurant, located over the lake along the edge of Morrison Parkway, is across the parkway to the rear of Morel Inn, a 10-room inn facing West Main Street in downtown historic New Roads on False River. The Morels also sell antiques, accessories and architectural pieces at the restaurant.

The restaurant is open seven days a week and offers customers a choice of grilled dishes, fried seafood baskets, a variety of salads, a number of freshly made specials each day and several desserts. Some of the most popular specials are an appetizer of fried shrimp on fried eggplant rounds topped with a remoulade sauce; grilled red snapper filet finished with Louisiana jumbo lump crabmeat and a lemon butter sauce on braised spinach and fried or boiled shrimp salad.

SHRIMP-STUFFED BELL PEPPERS

This is a favorite of our customers and is usually prepared by Bettie Nelson, who has worked for Morel's for many years.

4	ounces butter		Dash Tabasco hot
6	ounces onions, minced		sauce
4	ounces celery, minced	1	teaspoon Worcestershire sauce
4	ounces bell pepper, minced	3	ounces green onions, chopped
1	clove garlic, minced	½	cup fresh parsley
1	pound shrimp (or crawfish)	½	cup Italian breadcrumbs
¼	teaspoon pepper	2	cups plain breadcrumbs
1	teaspoon salt		Chicken broth
¼	teaspoon cayenne pepper		

Melt butter. Add onions, celery, bell pepper. Sauté until translucent. Add next 8 ingredients. Cook 10 minutes. Remove from heat. Add breadcrumbs. Add small amount of chicken broth if mixture appears dry. Stuff into blanched bell pepper halves. (Blanched bell peppers are those that have been halved, seeds removed and placed in boiling water for 5 minutes). Warm in microwave before serving.

Stuffs 10 bell pepper halves.

KITTY KIMBALL'S BROCCOLI SOUP

3	tablespoons butter	1	tablespoon salt
5	ounces onions, chopped	2	cloves garlic, minced
4	tablespoons flour	⅛	teaspoon celery salt
10	ounces frozen chopped broccoli	½	cup beef broth
1	teaspoon pepper	1	cup chicken broth
		1¾	cups half & half

Melt butter. Sauté onions in butter until translucent. Slowly add flour until blended. Add next 7 ingredients. Cook for 15 minutes. Process mixture in food processor. Add half & half. Heat. Remove from heat.

Makes 6 cups.

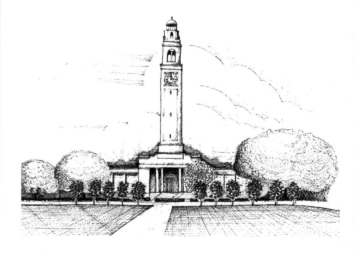

Louisiana State University
Baton Rouge

LAKE CHARLES AREA – Western Louisiana's pinelands attracted many carpenters from the North. These were experienced lumbermen and skilled woodworkers who moved here in the 1880's. The newcomers mirrored mainstream America's penchant for tall, angular Victorian and Queen Anne homes, quite unlike Louisiana's galleried Creole homes. But without the benefit of architects, they developed a unique style that became known as "sawmill Victoriana" and the "Lake Charles style." Today the Historic Charpentier District—French for "carpenter"—invites you to explore this unequaled collection of architectural treasures.

After exploring Lake Charles' enjoyable downtown, relax on any of the sunny beaches west or south of the city. For gaming excitement there are several casinos in Lake Charles and the surrounding area. Take your crew on a canoeing adventure on the Whiskey Chitto estuary in Allen Parish. Or a short drive to the coast will bring you to the Cajun Riviera, which offers sea, sand and sun on the Gulf of Mexico. And you'll find plenty of great surf or freshwater fishing in the area, plus hunting in the marshlands north of the Gulf beaches. Follow the Creole Nature Trail National Scenic Byways as it meanders through four wildlife refuges.

JENNINGS – There are several museums in Jennings. Museums include the Ziglar Museum of European and American fine art, the DeQuincy Railroad Museum, with its vintage 1913 steam locomotive, railcar and caboose, and the W.H.Tupper General Merchandise Museum, a re-created early-1900's general store. The store has a 10,000 piece inventory – most pieces in their original packages and some bearing their original price tags! The Louisiana Telephone Pioneer Museum is located in Jennings. The Telephone Pioneer museum features 10 exhibits, hundreds of pieces of equipment, tools and telephones spanning more than 100 years of service. The Louisiana Oil and Gas Park is located in Jennings. It is a 31-acre park with a replica of Louisiana's first oil derrick.

RAYNE – refers to itself as the "Frog Capitol of the World! The Chamber of Commerce has 30+ frog murals, visitor information, and a live frog pond. Rayne has an annual frog festival. Bullfrogs are celebrated as a true gourmet's delight.

ST. MARTINVILLE – is the home of the world famous Longfellow Evangeline Oak, the Acadian Memorial, Petit Paris Mardi Gras Museum and the Church of the Acadians' the St. Martin de Tours Catholic Church.

BASILE – is the home of the annual Swine Festival! The first weekend in November the partying begins. Pigs and pretty girls are plentiful in the festival featuring a Pork Cookoff, carnival, music and a greased pig chasing contest.

ABBEVILLE has a Giant Omelette Celebration downtown in Magdalen Square. It is a unique celebration of the area's culture – music, food, art show, antique cars and kid's world make up this international event. Cooking of a 5000-egg omelette (French for omelet) will take place in November 2002!

LAFAYETTE – This is the "Capital of French Louisiana". This is the heart and soul of Cajun Country. Experience 19th century Acadian life in South Louisiana at two living history museum villages where you'll come face to face with artisans, blacksmiths, farmers, trappers, hunters, and other residents of a typical Cajun village. Vermilionville, on Bayou Vermilion, contains more than a dozen historic or accurately re-created buildings, plus a Performance Center alive with Cajun music and dance. Included is Beau Bassin, a circa 1840 home built by the son of Louis Arceneaux, whose story inspired Longfellow's *Evangeline*. The National Park Service's adjoining Jean Lafitte Acadian Cultural Center illuminates Cajun history and culture through exhibits and artifacts. Acadian Village contains a quaint chapel, blacksmith's shop and village store, and restored homes and other buildings.

BREAUX BRIDGE calls itself "The Crawfish Capital of the World!" The Breaux Bridge Crawfish Festival is held in late spring each year. Over 35 Cajun, zydeco and swamp pop bands perform on 3 stages. The event features crawfish eating, cooking and dance contests.

OPELOUSAS is the third oldest city in Louisiana. The Opelousas Museum & Interpretive Center preserves and interprets history and culture of the area from prehistoric to present. Opelousas is the Home of the Southwest Louisiana Zydeco Festival archives. It is the "International Capital of Zydeco Music." Renown Chef Paul Prudhomme is from Opelousas.

GRAND COTEAU has more than 70 historic buildings including the Academy of the Sacred Heart, the United States' only Vatican-recognized site of a miracle.

NEW IBERIA is home to the white-column majesty of Shadows-on-the-Teche. It is the only National Trust Historic House Museum and Garden in Louisiana. On nearby Avery Island visit the factory where TABASCO brand pepper sauce is manufactured. A TABASCO country store is nearby. Not far away is Conrad Rice mill, one of the oldest rice mills in the country. Avery Island is also home to Jungle Gardens. Camellias, azaleas and tropical plants, when in season, form a beautiful display.

FRANKLIN - Visit Oaklawn Manor, the residence of Louisiana's current governor, Mike Foster. Come see his collection of Audubon's Birds of America. This is what a lived-in plantation looks like. Also in Franklin is the Grevemberg House Museum, a spectacular 1851 Greek Revival townhouse with a treasure trove of antique toys and Civil War artifacts.

HOUMA has 13 Mardi Gras parades each year, and is second only to New Orleans in its number of parading krewes. Year-round must-sees include the Historic District, Southdown Plantation House/Terrebonne Museum, and the Bayou Terrebonne Waterlife Museum. You can take your pick of swamp tours here—by water, land or air.

THIBODAUX - Visit the Acadian Cultural Center in Jean Lafitte National Historical Park and Preserve. Learn the story of the Acadians who settled along the bayous.

BIENVENUE HOUSE BED & BREAKFAST

421 N. Main Street
St. Martinville, LA 70582
(337) 394-9103

Leslie Leonpacher, Inn Keeper

The Bienvenue House, circa 1830, is listed on the National Register of Historic Places. A truly beautiful antebellum gem, its colorful history has been preserved for you to experience first hand by your hostess, Leslie Leonpacher. The Evangeline Room, the Josephine Room, the Scarlet Room and the balconied Montgomery room all reflect the beauty and history of the era. Bienvenue House cuisine is a delightful gourmet start to the day. The following recipes are a sampling of the delicious meals at the Bienvenue House.

MEDITERRANEAN BLUE BURGER

1 tablespoon olive oil	36 fresh basil leaves
3 pods fresh garlic	Vidalia or sweet onion sliced fine
1 tablespoon fresh or dried rosemary	3 ripe avocados seeded and sliced
1 tablespoon fresh or dried thyme	1 package crumbled blue cheese
1 tablespoon fresh or dried parsley	Garlic infused olive oil
1½ teaspoons salt	Lemon juice
3 boneless skinless chicken breasts cut into three pieces	Salt & pepper to taste
3 boneless skinless chicken thighs cut into three pieces	

Place first six ingredients in food processor to chop herbs fine. Add chicken and process about 60 seconds making sure that herbs are evenly distributed throughout chicken. Oil hands lightly with olive oil and press out to ½-inch thick patties shaped to fit individual French bread rolls. Length and number of patties determined by bread available. Spray patties lightly with cooking spray on each side and grill over coals for 5-6 minutes each side. For each burger: lay a chicken patty in each halved heated French bread roll. Place one layer basil leaves, onions, half an avocado, 2 tablespoons crumbled blue cheese, 1 tablespoon of garlic infused olive oil, 1 teaspoon lemon juice. Salt & pepper to taste. Top with other half of bread and cut and serve.

Serves 5-6.

LESLIE'S BLUEBERRY MUFFINS

3 cups all purpose flour	½ teaspoon salt
4½ teaspoons baking powder	1 cup butter
½ teaspoon baking soda	1¼ cups milk
1½ cups sugar	2 eggs beaten
	2 cups fresh blueberries

Fold dry ingredients together. Put milk in microwave for 1½ minutes. Beat in the eggs. Mix the wet ingredients with the dry and then fold in the blueberries. Scoop into muffin cups with an ice cream scoop. Bake at 400 degrees for 25-30 minutes.

BLUE DOG CAFÉ

1211 West Pinhook Road
Lafayette, LA 70503
(337) 237-0005

Steve Santillo, Owner

Blue Dog Café is a favorite of locals and visitors alike. Offering award winning food, friendly and knowledgeable service, and the world's largest private collection of Blue Dog artwork by world famous artist, George Rodrigue grace the walls. Blue Dog boasts that it "has it all." Many of the dishes on the menu have earned their Chefs prestigious culinary awards. In addition to Cajun favorites such as crawfish etouffe, seafood gumbo and a delicious seafood platter, Blue Dog Café offers fusion cuisine such as crawfish enchiladas with cumin mornay sauce and their signature appetizer of seafood wontons with a plum-ginger sauce. They offer an impressive wine list and homemade desserts such as their popular bread pudding with a pecan praline sauce.

PAN GRILLED GROUPER WITH A CRABMEAT AND CURRY COCONUT CREAM SAUCE

ROASTED GARLIC SEASONED RUB:

4	ounces roasted garlic	2	teaspoons ginger
1¼	tablespoon salt	1	tablespoon white pepper
1	tablespoon black pepper	1	teaspoon tandoori paste
2	teaspoons onion powder		

Place all ingredients into a food processor and puree until pasty. Rub grouper thoroughly and brush with butter. Heat pan to medium heat. Add butter. Cook both sides approximately 2 minutes and finish in a 350-degree oven until done (6 minutes).

CURRY CREAM:

¼	pound butter	13½	ounces coconut milk
1	cup diced onions		
4	ounces Chardonnay wine	1	quart heavy cream Blonde roux as needed
6	ounces yellow curry powder		
1	teaspoon salt	1	pound white lump crabmeat
2	teaspoons rosemary		

Sauté onions in butter till clear, then deglaze with Chardonnay. Add all dry seasonings then cream and coconut milk. Bring to a gentle boil and thicken with blonde roux. Add crabmeat to sauce and keep warm for plate assembly.

CAFÉ DES AMIS

140 East Bridge St.
Breaux Bridge, LA 70517
(337) 332-5273

Dickie and Cynthia Breaux, Owners

VINAIGRETTE DRESSING

4	cups extra virgin olive oil	1	teaspoon black pepper
2	cups olive oil (lesser grade)	1	teaspoon cracked black pepper
1	cup apple cider vinegar	1	teaspoon cayenne pepper
1½	cups red wine vinegar	2	tablespoons Italian seasoning
1	cup Romano cheese	1	tablespoon celery seeds
1	cup minced garlic	1	tablespoon basil
1	cup sugar	1	tablespoon rosemary
4	tablespoons granulated garlic	5	tablespoons salt
1	cup lemon juice		

Mix all of the above ingredients in a bowl and stir well. Best if refrigerated overnight. Great to mix this with blue cheese dressing as a nice dressing combination.

OLIVE CHICKEN

MARINADE:

2	teaspoons soy sauce		Salt, black pepper
1½	teaspoons granulated garlic		& cayenne pepper to taste

Blend the above ingredients together in a bowl and set aside.

4	chicken breasts	24	green Spanish olives with pimento
¼	cup olive oil		
1	teaspoon lemon juice	1	onion cut in thin slices
¼	teaspoon dried basil (or fresh, if possible)	1	teaspoon minced garlic
		¼	cup olive juice
1	teaspoon flour	¼	cup white wine

Tenderize chicken breast with a mallet. Marinate chicken breasts for 1 hour. Dip marinated chicken breast in flour. Panne' chicken breast in olive oil. Melt butter in another pan with basil, lemon juice, onion and minced garlic. Sauté until onion is tender. Add chicken breast, olive juice, olives and wine to mixture

and cook down for about 5 minutes. Serve warm. Note: Makes a very pretty and tasty dish – can be served with rice pilaf or some other type of flavored rice.

Yield: 4 servings

SPINACH AND ANDOUILLE STUFFING

5	cups chopped Andouille (food processor)	¼	pound butter
		2½	tablespoons minced garlic
2½	cups Creole mix (chopped onions & bell peppers)	1	tablespoon lemon juice

Sauté down all of the above ingredients in an iron skillet until onions are tender. Remove from fire and blend in the following ingredients:

1	10-ounce package of frozen chopped spinach	1	teaspoon chicken base
½	cup Romano cheese	¾	cup breadcrumbs

Blend thoroughly by stirring. Try this spicy tasty stuffing with chicken breasts, fish or mushrooms.

GATEAU SIROP (SYRUP CAKE)

1	cup canola oil or peanut oil	2	teaspoons ground cinnamon
1¼	cups cane syrup	2	teaspoons ground cloves
1	cup raw sugar		
⅓	cup dark molasses	2	teaspoons ground ginger
1	cup boiling water		
2	teaspoons baking soda	2	tablespoons vanilla extract
4	eggs	2	cups sifted flour

Mix oil, sugar, cane syrup and molasses in a bowl. In separate container stir baking soda into boiling water. Add to above mixture. Add all other remaining ingredients. Beat well at a medium to high speed with an electric hand mixer. Pour into a large baking pan that has been sprayed with a pan spray. Bake at 350 degrees for about 30 minutes. Test it to see if middle is still wet. Turn pan around in oven to insure even baking. When the middle of the cake begins to firm up, add ¾ cup chopped pecans on top and continue baking until the cake is done throughout. Cake is sliced by cutting cake down the middle and then making 4 cuts horizontally for a total of 8 pieces. Cake is served warm on a plate and garnished with cane syrup drizzles on plate. Great to also garnish with fresh mint leaves when available. Delicious served with vanilla or chocolate ice cream.

Yield: 1 large cake pan = 8 slices.

chicken stock and lemon juice. Sauté 1 minute more. Stir in béchamel and cook 3 minutes more. Serve over angel hair pasta and garnish with a tablespoon of pesto and sprinkle with freshly grated Parmesan cheese.

SMOKED CHICKEN & ANDOUILLE STUFFED MUSHROOM WITH MARSALA CORIANDER VELOUTÉ

STUFFING:

¼	# diced bell pepper	1	cup grated aged Parmesan cheese
¼	# diced celery		
½	# diced onion	2	tablespoons fresh minced garlic
4	ounces Andouille, ½-inch dice	1½	tablespoons Creole seasoning
12	ounces smoked chicken, ½-inch dice	2	cups chicken stock
		½	cup canola oil
2	cups breadcrumbs		

Sauté onion, bell pepper and celery in canola oil until tender, then add garlic and Creole seasoning. Cook two more minutes. Add both meats and cook till heated through. Now pull pan off of heat and add the rest of the ingredients. Blend thoroughly.

MARSALA CORIANDER VELOUTÉ

2	quarts chicken stock	1½	tablespoons Lea & Perrin
6	tablespoons diced roasted red pepper	2⅓	tablespoons Creole seasoning
½	cup chopped green onion	2	tablespoons sugar
5	tablespoons fresh minced garlic	2	teaspoons coriander
1½	tablespoons soy sauce	½	cup Marsala wine Juice of 1 lemon

Combine all in sauce pan and bring to boil. Stir in enough white roux to thicken. Simmer while stirring for five minutes. Pre-grill one portabella cap. Stuff cap with about ½ inch of stuffing. Top with freshly grated Parmesan and place in convection oven at 450 degrees for 8 minutes. Garnish with finely shredded zucchini, carrot and sweet red pepper slaw.

Yields: 8-10 large portobello caps.

CATAHOULA'S

Box 351, 234 King Drive Grand Coteau, LA 70541 (888) 547-2275

John Slaughter, General Manager

In the heart of Cajun country and in the center of a rare rural historic district sits Catahoula's, a superbly renovated country store turned fine dining restaurant. Catahoula's, only 6 years old, has been featured in such publications as **Gourmet, Southern Living, Reader's Digest** *and* **USA Today.** *The cuisine can be described as South Louisiana with sophisticated influences. The seasonings and tastes are more interesting than traditional Louisiana "hot and spicy" flavors. Catahoula's is located 11 miles north of Lafayette just off Interstate 49, Exit 11 at Grand Coteau.*

Bill Schwanz, Executive Chef

SHRIMP ST. CHARLES

3	ounces butter and oil blend	1	teaspoon Creole seasoning
5	jumbo shrimp	1	cup Shiitake mushrooms, slivered
2	tablespoons roasted red pepper, diced		
2	tablespoon green onion, chopped	2	ounces freshly grated Parmesan cheese
2	tablespoons sundried tomatoes	1	ounce pesto
3	ounces quartered artichoke hearts	7	ounces cooked angel hair pasta

SAUCE:

2	ounces white wine	1	ounce lemon juice
4	ounces chicken stock	3	ounces béchamel sauce

In skillet heat 2-3 ounces butter-infused oil over medium-high heat. Add 5 large peeled and deveined shrimp and sauté 1 minute each side. Add next 6 ingredients and sauté about 3 minutes. Deglaze pan with white wine for about 30 seconds, then add

CLEMENTINE DINING & SPIRITS

113 E. Main St.
New Iberia, LA 70560
(337) 560-1007

Experience classic south Louisiana cuisine with a New Orleans flair. Clementine features a unique twist of such classics as corn and crab bisque and soft shell crab. Enjoy a tempting array of certified Black Angus steaks while soothing jazz sets the tone. Also indulge at our classic 1890's bar where Celmentine Hunter and other local artists' works are displayed. The name Clementine was chosen to pay tribute to owner, Wayne Peltier's favorite artist, Clementine Hunter.

Chef Joe Gonsoulin, Executive Chef

Chef Stuart Gonsuron

A chef who epitomizes the idea that food becomes art, his techniques enable the guest to experience taste and visual excellence. With a career expanding across the years and across the country, Chef Gonsoulin serves up dishes that are sure to please everyone.

__Career Highlights:__ Executive Chef – Chez Marcelle's Restaurant, Broussard, LA. The first Nouvelle Cajun Cuisine presented in the Lafayette area. Chef Joe cooked for the Louisiana Legislature in Washington, D.C. Chef Gonsoulin was the Executive Chef at the Old Bay Restaurant, New Brunswick, New Jersey. He relocated to New Jersey to open a Louisiana style restaurant. The restaurant was voted Best New Restaurant for 1988 in Central New Jersey by __New Jersey Magazine__. Chef Gonsoulin has received the Gold Medal (meat category) at the Acadiana Culinary Classic in 1985, the Bronze Medal (meat category) 1993 and the Silver Medal (seafood category) in 1994. Joe's seafood gumbo has won numerous awards at the World Famous Gumbo Cookoff.

ROASTED RED PEPPER AND WILD MUSHROOM BISQUE WITH CRABMEAT

CONTRIBUTED BY CHEF STUART GONSURON

4	tablespoons clarified butter	2	cups water reserved from Morels
1	large yellow onion – small diced	2	quarts heavy cream
1	tablespoon minced garlic	1	quart half-n-half
20	shiitake mushrooms sliced	2	teaspoons dried thyme
5	portobello mushrooms chopped	2	teaspoons granulated garlic
10	dried morels – rehydrated & sliced	2	bay leaves
8	red peppers – roasted & pureed	2	tablespoons crab base
		1	tablespoon chicken base

Sweat onions and garlic in butter. Add shiitake and portobello mushrooms and sauté for 5 minutes. Next add morels and pepper puree. When puree comes to a boil, add the reserved water, heavy cream, half-n-half, thyme, garlic and bay leaves. Simmer for 10 minutes, then add bases. Stir well and simmer for 10 more minutes. Thicken with blonde roux if desired.

Serves 10-12.

TUNA AU POIVRE

1	8-ounce tuna steak (sashimi grade)	1	cup heavy cream
	Kosher salt to taste	¼	cup chopped green onions
	Cracked black pepper to taste		Olive oil
½	cup brandy		Chopped parsley for garnish

Coat the bottom of a heated skillet with olive oil. Season tuna with salt and pepper and sear in skillet for 1 minute on each side. Remove from skillet and keep warm. Deglaze hot skillet with brandy then add green onions. When brandy is reduced almost completely, add heavy cream and reduce to desired consistency. Ladle sauce over tuna. Garnish with chopped parsley.

Serves 1.

CRISTIANO'S RISTORANTE LOUNGE & WINE BOUTIQUE

724 High Street
Houma, LA 70360
(985) 223-1130

Cristiano Raffignone, Chef/Owner

Starting at the age of 18, restaurant owner and businessman Cristiano Raffignone has worked in dozens of international locations, including Italy, London, Australia and New York City. Eventually, he settled in Houma and opened Cristiano's. While Cristiano's specializes in Italian cuisine, Raffignone admitted that he loves to involve Cajun as well as Asian touches into his traditional Italian dishes. Some of his most famous experiments have produced savory dishes like Ravioli Di Campagna (truffle ravioli with melted fontina cheese), Spaghetti Frutti Di Mare (crawfish, shrimp and scallops sautéed in extra virgin olive oil, garlic, red pepper flakes, white wine and tomato sauce) or Crespelle Al Granchio (crabmeat dressing rolled in crepes, served with a lite tomato and béchamel sauce). Cristiano's restaurant is stocked with comfortable sofas, beautiful works of art and antiques giving it a very homey atmosphere. Raffignone said that customers can also enjoy soft, live music every Thursday night in the Cristiano lounge.

FRANCESE (SALAD)

Heat skillet with 1 ounce of clarified butter. Toss in 1 ounce of pancetta bacon until crisp, then throw in 2 ounces of blue cheese and stir with tongs until cheese breaks down just a little. Let reduce to a creamy consistency. Pour mixture over 2 heads of fresh crisp frisee (Belgium endive, radicchio, or other assorted greens) and approximately 4 seasoned croutons on dish.

FRIED GREEN TOMATOES (ANTIPASTO)

(Breaded green tomatoes lightly pan fried, topped with lump crabmeat remoulade)

2   Fresh slices of green tomato about a ½ inch thick.

"NO EGG" EGG WASH:

1   cup cornstarch
2   cups all-purpose flour "seasoned" to individual's taste, mixed in iced club soda or water.

Place slices in seasoned flour completely covered on each side. Dust off excess flour and dip in wash. Then place slices into a mixture of Italian and Japanese (processed fine) breadcrumbs (approximately 2 cups of Italian and a ¾ cup of fine processed Japanese breadcrumbs) cover slices evenly on both sides. Fry slices until golden brown and crisp.

CRABMEAT REMOULADE:

1	pound white crabmeat	¼ teaspoon of Tabasco sauce
1	pound claw crabmeat	¼ teaspoon of Worcestershire
6	tablespoons of mayonnaise	A pinch of salt
½	tablespoon of ketchup	A pinch of cayenne pepper

Whisk all ingredients excluding crabmeat. Fold in one pound of white crabmeat and one pound of claw meat (after meat has been cleaned of shells and strained) into remoulade mixture. Place about a teaspoon of remoulade in the center of plate. Put a slice of fried tomato on top. Place a teaspoon of remoulade on each side of the bottom slice. Cut other tomato in half and wedge them on top of the 2 teaspoons of remoulade. Place another teaspoon in the center of the angled slices. Garnish top of dish with a small amount of spring medley, then place 3 slices of grape tomatoes in symmetry at the bottom of the dish and top with finely diced parsley and chives placed in center of the top of the remoulade.

Continued Page 118

SPAGHETTI FRUTTI DI MARE

Heat skillet with ½ cup of clarified butter. After butter turns clear, toss in a cup each of shrimp, scallops and crawfish, along with a ½ teaspoon of Kosher salt, minced garlic and crushed red pepper. Let seafood simmer until almost done. Deglaze with ⅔ cups of white wine and 2½ cups of pomodoro (tomato sauce). Let reduce to a sauce consistency, then toss in 6 cups of cooked spaghettini or desired pasta. Place on dish and garnish with finely diced parsley and basil.

CRESPELLE

(Italian pancake similar to a crepe)

CREPES:

1½	eggs	½	teaspoon of salt
1	cup of milk	1	tablespoon of
⅔	cup all purpose		butter
	flour		

To make crepes: In a bowl, beat the eggs, until foamy. Gradually beat in milk until blended. In a large bowl, stir together the flour and salt. Gradually whisk in the egg mixture. The batter should be as thin as heavy (double) cream. If it is too thick, add a little water. Cover and let rest for 30 minutes. Lightly brush a 6 to 8 inch crepe or omelet pan with a little of the butter. Heat the pan over medium heat. To test if it's hot enough, sprinkle in a drop or two of batter. If it sets quickly, the pan is ready. Stir the batter. Holding the pan in one hand, use a small ladle to pour in about 2 ounces of the batter. Immediately tilt the pan so that the batter spreads out evenly. There should be just enough to cover the bottom in a thin layer. Cook until just set and lightly browned around the edges, about one minute. With a spatula, flip the crepe over and cook the other side until speckled brown, about 30 seconds. Transfer the crepe to a plate. Repeat with the remaining batter, brushing the pan with more butter as needed. As the crepes are cooked, stack them, placing a strip of waxed paper between each layer. Let cool completely before filling.

D. I.'S RESTAURANT

6561 Evangeline Highway
Basile, LA 70515
(337) 432-5141

Daniel & Sherry Fruge, Owners

*This restaurant has won several first places in the "Crawfish Ettouffee Cook-Off in Eunice, LA. The restaurant has also been featured in the October 1999 issue of **Southern Living** magazine. D.I.'s restaurant presently seats 275. This Cajun family restaurant has had two major expansions. The second expansion included a bandstand and dance floor. The restaurant features live Cajun music nightly on Tuesday, Thursday, Friday and Saturday and a "Cajun jam session on Wednesday". Families enjoy dancing with young children to Cajun music while dining.*

ANGEL'S ON HORSEBACK
(APPETIZER)

8	fresh-shucked oysters	8	slices of bacon

Marinate oysters for ½ hour in Italian dressing and ½ teaspoon of hot sauce. Drain, wrap oyster in bacon and roll in Louisiana Fish Fry or fish flour. Deep fry (325 degrees) in oil till golden brown.

CRAWFISH BISQUE
(ENTRÉE)

1	medium onion	1	can Rotel tomatoes
1	medium bell pepper		

Sauté the above ingredients in 1 stick of margarine until transparent. Add 2 tablespoons of tomato paste and stir in 2 teaspoons of flour. Add salt and pepper. Add 5 cups of water and simmer. Add ½ cup of roux while simmering. Add 2 cups of clean crawfish tails and simmer till thick. Serve over rice, like a gumbo or soup effect.

Continued Page 119

BREAD PUDDING

DESSERT:

5 to 10	slices of bread	1	tablespoon
1	quart of milk		cinnamon
5	eggs	½	cup of raisins
2½	cups of sugar	½	cup pecans
⅓	cup of vanilla		(optional)

Tear slices of bread apart, place in greased 9 x 12-inch pan. Combine sugar, eggs, milk, vanilla and cinnamon and beat until blended. Pour over bread and sprinkle raisins. Bake at 350 degrees about 45 minutes or until firm. Slice when cool.

THE ORIGINAL DON'S SEAFOOD & STEAKHOUSE

301 East Vermilion Lafayette, LA 70501 (337) 235-3551

Ashby D. Landry, Sr., Owner
Ashby D. Landry, Jr., Owner

Take one look at the menu At Don's Seafood & Steakhouse and you will get a broad introduction to this region's most delicious dishes and their tantalizing names. Try one of the wonderful gumbos or crawfish étouffée, bisque or jambalaya, or tempt yourself with the stuffed red snapper, and surely you'll find yourself asking, "What is Don's secret?" The secret. That's what everyone wants to know. Just what is the secret behind the great food at Don's Seafood & Steakhouse? Well, there are many. First, all of the ingredients are the absolute freshest available, and our seafood is locally caught and bought so each dish is as fresh as it could possible be. Then there's our creativity in the kitchen — we're not afraid to improve on a good idea. And finally, there's the Landry family's 194 years of combined cooking experience.

The following recipes are from the Don's Seafood & Steakhouse cookbook:

CRAWFISH FETTUCCINI

By Emma Jeanne Carruth

3	pounds crawfish	2	large onions, chopped
3	sticks margarine		
2	rolls jalapeño cheese	1	large bell pepper, chopped
1	roll garlic cheese	3	ribs celery, chopped
1	package fettuccini noodles		
2	pints sour cream	4	ounces Kraft Shredded Swiss cheese

Sauté onions, bell pepper and celery. Add crawfish, jalapeño and garlic cheeses and sour cream. Mix in already cooked noodles. Pour into a prepared 9" x 13" casserole. Top with shredded cheese. Bake until cheese is melted.

Serves 6 to 8.

CRABMEAT A LA LANDRY

1	cup onions, chopped fine	1	cup cornflakes
⅓	cup celery, chopped fine	1	can evaporated milk
	Pinch of sage	1	pound white crabmeat
	Pinch of thyme	1	cup Ritz crackers, crumbled
	Pinch of nutmeg		
	Pinch of oregano	1	tablespoon flour
	Pinch of marjoram	1	teaspoon salt
¼	pound oleo or butter	½	teaspoon cayenne (red pepper)

Sauté onions and celery in oleo or butter until onions are wilted. Add sage, thyme, nutmeg, oregano, marjoram, salt, cayenne and flour. Add milk, stirring constantly. Toast the cornflakes and crumble; then mix with the crabmeat. Mix well. Combine crabmeat with the spices and put into ramekins or casseroles. Sprinkle with crumbled Ritz crackers. Add a pat of butter and bake for 20 to 25 minutes at 375 degrees.

Serves 6.

DUPUY'S OYSTER SHOP
108 South Main
Abbeville, LA 70510
(337) 893-2336

Jody & Tanya Hebert, Chef/Owners

Established by Joseph Dupuy in 1869. Mr. Dupuy harvested his own oysters and sold them for 5 cents a dozen! Joseph started a tradition, which continued through the next three generations – over 130 years of success in its original location! This restaurant is world famous for its oysters on the half-shell and outstanding seafood. This success continues today with the present owners, Jody and Tonya Hebert.

EGGPLANT DUPUY
(FRIED EGGPLANT TOPPED WITH A SHRIMP AND TASSO HERB CREAM SAUCE)

2	whole eggplants	2	tablespoons chopped parsley
5	cups breadcrumbs		
1	quart buttermilk	2	quarts heavy whipping cream
1	tablespoon salt		
1	tablespoon black pepper	1	cup flour
		½	cup melted margarine
3	cups diced tasso		
1	pound baby shrimp (peeled)	1	tablespoon minced garlic
2	tablespoons dry basil	2	quarts of vegetable oil
¼	cup chopped green onions		

Peel eggplant, slice in ¼-inch thick round medallions. Dip eggplant medallions in buttermilk, then in breadcrumbs (repeat twice). Set eggplant aside until later. In a medium-size pot pour heavy cream, tasso, dry basil, green onions, minced garlic, and chopped parsley on medium heat and let it cook for 15 minutes stirring occasionally. In a small bowl, mix melted margarine and flour to make a white roux mix until thick paste forms. Then with a small spoon add to sauce small amounts of white roux until slightly thick. Add shrimp, salt and pepper (to taste) to the sauce. Cook until shrimp are done. Fry eggplant in vegetable oil until golden brown. Place eggplant on plate, add shrimp, tasso and herb cream sauce on top of eggplant. Excellent appetizer for 8 or entrée for 4 (recommended to serve with pasta).

Continued Page 121

WHITE CHOCOLATE BREAD PUDDING TOPPED WITH FRANGELICA CREAM SAUCE

1	loaf white bread	¼	cup of vanilla extract
6	(2-ounce) cans of evaporated milk	5	eggs (beaten)
4	cups sugar	½	cup frangelica liqueur
2	cups of white chocolate chunks		

In small pot mix frangelica liqueur, 2 cans of evaporated milk, and 2 cups sugar. Let cook on low till it thickens a little. Set aside. In large bowl, bread into pieces. Pour 4 cans of evaporated milk on bread, then pour 2 cups sugar, 2 cups white chocolate chunks, ¼ cup vanilla extract, 5 eggs beaten and mix well. Soak for about 20 minutes and pour into baking pan. Bake on 350 degrees for 1 hour, let cool then cut in squares. Top with frangelica cream before serving.

Serves 10-12.

Joseph Jefferson House
Rip Van Winkle Gardens
New Iberia, Louisiana

FEZZO'S SEAFOOD, STEAKHOUSE & OYSTER BAR

2111 N. Cherokee Drive Crowley, LA 70526

The Story Behind the Name!

A long time ago when Phil's father was a young boy in Church Point, Louisiana he was very creative with his toys. His favorite toys were things he made with his mother's empty wooden spools. In Cajun French the word for these wooden spools is a fezzo. Everywhere he went he always had these spool toys with him. One day, the local postmaster began calling him Fezzo. A name he carried with him all of his life. In July 1979, Phil's family opened a grocery store in Rayne, Louisiana and called it Fezzo's Supermarket. Phil and Pat worked in the store for a long time. In July 1999, twenty years to the month later, Phil and Pat opened their first restaurant. When it came time to decide on the name it was clear. In honor of Phil's dad, they named it Fezzo's Seafood and Steakhouse.

Joshua Spell, Executive Chef

CREAMY CAJUN CRAWFISH & TASSO SAUCE

¼	pound smoked pork tasso	1	10-ounce can cream of mushroom Soup
2	pounds crawfish tails seasoned with ⅛ cup Fezzo's Cajun Seasoning	1	quart heavy whipping cream
¼	pound butter or margarine	1	cup shredded American cheese
1	cup diced onions	2	tablespoons cornstarch mixed with ½ cup water
¼	cup diced bell peppers		

Melt butter, then sauté onions and bell peppers. Dice tasso, then sauté with onions and bell peppers for 10 minutes. Add cream of mushroom soup. Add heavy whipping cream and cook for 20 minutes. Add seasoned crawfish. Thicken with cornstarch. Turn off and add shredded cheese. Serve over angel hair pasta.

Serves 6 to 8.

FLANAGAN'S

1111 Audubon Avenue
Thibodaux, LA 70301

Located between Nichols State University and Regional Medical Center, sits Thibodaux's premier dining experience "Flanagan's Creative Food and Drink". Established in 1983, Flanagan's has built a reputation for outstanding food in a casual yet refined atmosphere. A team of culinary experts are eager to create an excellent meal featuring Black Angus beef, only the freshest seafood available, pasta favorites and Cajun specialties headed by Executive Chef Kevin Templet. Under the leadership of General Manager Al Coffee, the restaurant also features an extensive wine menu and specialty bar drinks, such as Flanagan's own "Long Island Ice Tea". Recently awarded 4½ crawfish by **Gumbo** *Magazine, Flanagan's constantly strives for 100% customer satisfaction.*

BAR-B-QUE SHRIMP

20	large shrimp (peelings & heads-on)(10-12 per pound)	1½	tablespoons garlic
		12	ounces beer
2	tablespoons olive oil	1	tablespoon basil (dry)
	Salt & pepper Season-All	3	tablespoons green onions
2	tablespoons fresh, chopped rosemary	¼	cup bar-b-que sauce (smoky)
		½	stick butter

Heat olive oil in pan. Season shrimp with salt, pepper and Season-all. Place in skillet and cook on each side 2-3 minutes until pink almost all the way through. Add garlic. Let it cook for 1 minute. Deglaze with beer. Add basil and green onions. Add B-B-Q sauce and reduce by ⅓. Turn off fire and melt butter in sauce. Serve over toasted French bread slices.

SEAFOOD AU GRATIN

½	stick butter	1½	tablespoons garlic powder
½	large onion, diced		
2	pounds shrimp 90/110 peeled	½ to 1	teaspoon cayenne pepper
1	pound crawfish meat	1	teaspoon white pepper
1	pound claw crabmeat		Salt & pepper to taste
1	bunch green onions chopped	4	dashes hot sauce
1	pint half & half	For roux:	½ pound butter and 1¾ cup flour
2	tablespoons parsley		
1½	tablespoons onion powder	1	cup shredded Cheddar cheese

Melt butter and sauté onion. Add shrimp and sauté till almost done (4-5 minutes). Add crawfish and crabmeat and sauté 2 minutes. Add half & half. Add green onions, hot sauce and all dry seasonings. On side: make roux – melt butter and stir in flour. Stir constantly for 2 minutes and turn off fire. Bring seafood and half & half mixture to a simmer and slowly add small amounts of roux while stirring. Add roux until desired consistency is reached. Spoon in serving dishes and sprinkle Cheddar cheese over au gratin. Melt cheese in broiler. Serve with toasted French bread slices.

SOUTHERN PECAN CHICKEN CHAMPIGNON

4	boneless skinless chicken breast	3	tablespoons butter
4	ounces Southern Comfort whiskey	4	ounces sliced mushrooms
4	tablespoons diced onion	4	tablespoons roasted pecan pieces
2	cloves garlic minced	8	tablespoons pecan butter (see recipe below)
	Juice of ½ orange, seeds removed	12	ounces whipping cream
1	cup of all-purpose flour (seasoned to taste)	4	tablespoons chopped parsley
3	tablespoons olive oil		Salt & pepper to taste

Continued Page 123

PECAN BUTTER:

8	ounces sweet butter	1	pinch cayenne
3	basil leaves diced or 3 tablespoons dry basil	1	pinch blackening seasoning
2	tablespoons brown sugar	½	cup pecans

Mix all (pecan butter) ingredients together in a food processor. Roll in log shape in wax paper and refrigerate or freeze for future use.

Procedure: Marinate the chicken breast in 2 ounces Southern Comfort, diced onions, garlic and orange juice for 1 hour. Dredge in seasoned flour and pan fry in olive oil and butter mixture. After golden brown remove from skillet, finish cooking in oven then hold warm. Discard most of the oil from the skillet and deglaze with the marinade. Reduce for 2 to 3 minutes. Add mushrooms, roasted pecan pieces and pecan butter. Sauté mushrooms for 3 to 4 minutes; add additional 2 ounces of Southern Comfort and flame off. Add whipping cream and reduce to coat a spoon. Salt & pepper to taste. Fold in fresh parsley and spoon over panned chicken. This dish is excellent with your favorite stuffing or wild rice dish. For a more formal presentation serve this sauce with game hens, quail or duck.

Serves 4.

FREMIN'S
402 West 3rd Street Thibodaux, LA 70301

Nestled in the narrow streets of downtown Thibodaux, across from the historic Lafourche Parish Courthouse, sits Fremin's Restaurant, Thibodaux's newest Epicurean Delight. The building decorated in magnificent millwork, with mahogany bars, original long leaf pine floors, wrought iron balcony, beveled glass, pressed tin ceiling, Italian ceramic tile floors, and solid brass throughout the building, define the character and cornerstone of Fremin's philosophy. With a long history of personality, quality and tradition in the restaurant industry, this newest restaurant endeavor boasts "the new taste of Thibodaux" with a menu created by Corporate Chef Randy Barrios. The marriage of Creole style and Italian cooking come together in perfect harmony. The General Manager is Antonio Reymundo. Executive Chef Walter Grote heads up the culinary team.

ARTICHOKE & OYSTER SOUP

3	tablespoons butter	1	teaspoon dry thyme
3	tablespoons olive oil	3	ounces oyster liquor
1	medium onion (diced	40	artichoke heart quarters (chopped medium)
1	medium bell pepper (diced)	5	ounces dry sherry
2	ribs celery (diced)	18	oysters (chopped medium fine)
5	cloves garlic (minced)	3	tablespoons parsley (finely chopped)
1	teaspoon salt	4	ounces heavy cream
½	teaspoon black pepper	¼	teaspoon white pepper (level)
¼	teaspoon cayenne		Slurry of 1 ounce water and 3 teaspoons of cornstarch (level)
2	bay leaves		
8	tablespoons flour (level)		
8	cups (64-ounce) water		
3	tablespoons fish bouillon (level)		

Continued Page 124

Place first 10 items in heavy bottom sauce pot and sauté until translucent, approximately 8 – 10 minutes. Add flour and cook for 3 minutes. Add water and bring to a boil. Add fish bouillon, thyme and oyster liquor and simmer for 12 minutes. Add artichoke quarters and dry sherry. Simmer for 15 minutes. Add oysters and parsley and simmer for 6 more minutes. Add heavy cream and white pepper. Simmer with slurry, simmering for 2 minutes, then remove from heat.

Yield: ½ gallon.

CAJUN HOT BITES - CANE SKEWERED CHICKEN TENDERLOINS WITH A TABASCO GLAZE

60	1-ounce chicken tenderloins	6	tablespoons black pepper
4	large eggs	2	tablespoons cayenne pepper
4	tablespoons water		
4	tablespoons Tabasco hot sauce	1	gallon of oil to deep fry
8	cups flour	60	5-inch sugarcane skewers
6	tablespoons salt		

SAUCE:

6	tablespoons butter	6	tablespoons chipotle pepper sauce
3	ounces cane syrup		
16	ounces Tabasco pepper jelly	8	tablespoons water

Marinate the chicken tenderloins in the egg, water and Tabasco mixture for 30 minutes. Cut skewers from the meat of the sugarcane stick. Skewer the tenderloins on the cane sticks in and in and out crochet fashion. Mix together the flour, salt, black pepper and cayenne pepper. Bread the chicken kabobs in the seasoned flour mixture and deep fry at 360 degrees until golden brown and crispy. Drain on paper towel.

Glaze: Combine all sauce ingredients in a skillet and simmer for 3-4 minutes until glaze consistency. Toss the sugarcane skewered fried tenderloins in the hot glaze and serve by crossing the cane skewers in the center of service dish with cane leaves as garnish. Eat the chicken and chew the cane!

Serves 12

ABBEYVILLE PORK

1	each boneless pork loin (cut into 8-ounce portions)	1	green bell pepper
		1	pound crawfish (chopped)
2	each corn bread mix (follow instructions to bake)	2	bunches green onions
			Salt & pepper to baste
1	onion		

CANE SYRUP GLAZE:

2	cups cane syrup		Salt & pepper to taste
1	cup white wine		
1	pound butter		

Bake corn bread according to the package directions. Chop the onions and bell pepper. Sauté until lightly browned. Add chopped crawfish and sauté lightly. Finish with green onions. Season with salt and pepper.

Cane Syrup Glaze: Combine cane syrup and wine and start to reduce. Add the butter slowly to combine and cook down to sauce consistency.

Form a pocket in the pork "chop" and stuff with the cooled stuffing, using a pastry bag. Grill the pork to desired doneness and when almost cooked, glaze with the cane glaze.

Serves 6-8

SMOKED PORK FETTUCCINI

2	tablespoons olive oil	1	tablespoon brandy
		½	cup heavy cream
¼	each green, yellow and red bell peppers	1	teaspoon truffle oil
			Salt & pepper to taste
4	mushrooms (sliced)	6	ounces fettuccini pasta
4	ounces julienne pork loin smoked		
		1	tablespoon Parmesan cheese (grated)
4	each sun dried tomatoes (julienne)		

Cook pasta until al dente, shock & oil. Heat olive oil. Add mushrooms and bell peppers. Let sauté for 1 to 2 minutes. Add pork loin and tomatoes. Cook for an additional 2 to 3 minutes. Deglaze with 1 tablespoon of brandy. Add heavy cream and salt & pepper. Let reduce until sauce consistency. Add heated pasta and cook until pasta is coated with sauce. Twist pasta into bowl. Sprinkle with Parmesan cheese and drizzle over with truffle oil. Top with cracked black pepper.

Serves 1.

HANSON HOUSE

114 East Main Street
Franklin LA 70538-6164
(337) 828-3271

Bette and Caunse Kemper, Proprietors

Hanson House is a five bedroom antebellum home set on four acres in Franklin's historic district between Bayou Teche (of **Evangeline** *fame) and the Old Spanish Trail, one of the first coast to coast east west routes in American History. Hanson House has been in the family since 1852, with the current owner, Col. Clarence B. Kemper, Jr. the great-great-grandson of the man who made Hanson House the home that it is today: Albert Hanson, a lumber man and mill operator. The home is decorated in style appropriate to its use and growth over the 150 plus years that it has been in the family.*

The following recipes are served for breakfast at the Hanson House:

DATE NUT BREAD

2	cups brown sugar	2	teaspoons baking powder
¼	cup butter or oleo	1	teaspoon salt
2	eggs beaten	1	teaspoon vanilla
1¾	cup hot coffee	1	cup finely chopped nuts (toasted)
2	cups chopped dates		
3	cups flour		
1	teaspoon baking soda		

Mix the above ingredients thoroughly and bake for 1 hour at 350 degrees.

PEACH MARMALADE

12 to 15 peaches peeled		1	16-ounce can crushed pineapple
3	large ripe oranges		

Mix the items above in food processor (do not overmix). Add one cup of sugar to each cup of fruit. Cook slowly and stir often until thick. Process in sterile jars.

APPLE LOAF

4	cups Granny Smith apples – peeled & finely diced	1	cup butter, melted and cooled
2	cups sugar	3	cups all-purpose flour
¼	cup lemon juice Zest of one large lemon	2	teaspoons baking soda
1	cup finely chopped pecans (toasted)	1	teaspoon nutmeg
		2	large eggs
		1	teaspoon vanilla
		1	teaspoon salt

Mix apples, sugar, lemon juice and zest in a large bowl. Marinate approximately 2 hours.

Mix dry ingredients and stir into apples and add remaining ingredients. Mix well. Bake at 325 degrees for 1 to 1¼ hours in large pan. (45 minutes for miniatures). Cool. Refrigerate until serving time.

GREEK SPREAD

1	stick butter	½	teaspoon Tabasco
8	ounces cream cheese	1	teaspoon Lea & Perrin Worcestershire sauce
¼	cup chopped chives		
1	can chopped black olives	1	cup finely chopped toasted walnuts
⅓	cup chopped scallions		
½	teaspoon garlic powder		

Mix together and chill. Serve on toast points on melba toast with fruit plate.

ENGLISH APPLE PIE

8	apples pared and sliced (place in pie dish)	1	cup sugar Juice of one lemon Zest of one lemon
½	cup water		

Mix water, sugar, lemon juice and zest and pour over apples.

CRUMBLE:

1	cup brown sugar	½	cup butter
1	cup flour		

Sprinkle over apples and bake for 45 minutes to 1 hour at 325 degrees. Serve warm.

Eight servings.

HARBOR SEAFOOD RESTAURANT AND CATERING

500 Universe St.
Bayou Vista, LA 70380
(985) 395-3474

Mailing Address:
P. O. Box 2497
Patterson, LA 70392

Harbor Seafood is a casual dining family restaurant. They feature seafood, steaks, sandwiches, salads and Italian dishes.

CRAWFISH CASSEROLE
(AMY E. GROW, CHEF)

1	small block Velveeta cheese	1	can cream of mushroom soup
1	floret cup-up broccoli	1	cup onions, chopped
1	cup bell peppers	1	cup celery, chopped
1	cup mushrooms		
	Jalapeño peppers	3	cups cooked rice
1	pound crawfish with juice	1	cup crab boil
		1	stick unsalted butter

Melt Velveeta cheese and mushroom soup together in microwave. Cook rice. Sauté onions, bell peppers and celery in unsalted butter. Season crawfish as desired in a bowl of juice. Add crawfish to sautéed mixture. Sauté until crawfish are cooked. Add jalapeño peppers and mushrooms. Cook until soft. Add cooked rice and mix together in a 9 x 13 pan. Bake on 350 degrees for 25 minutes covered and then 25 minutes uncovered.

Serves 4 to 6 people.

BREAD PUDDING
(VIRGINIA BAILEY, CHEF)

1	9 x 13 pan	1½	loaves French bread
4	eggs		
3	cans evaporated milk	1	cup sugar
		3	tablespoons vanilla extract

Tear French bread into pieces. Add evaporated milk, eggs, sugar and vanilla extract. Stir well into a thick, soupy mixture. Bread should soak up majority of liquid. Add sugar and vanilla to taste if needed. Bake in oven on 350 degrees for 30 to 45 minutes, until firm (be sure not to dry out).

MERINGUE:

6	egg whites	¼	cup sugar

Beat egg whites until stiff. Add sugar slowly. Continue to beat until fluffy. Spread on bread pudding and bake until lightly brown.

Serves 10 to 12 people.

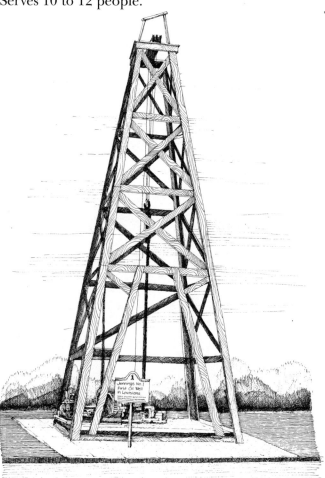

LAFAYETTE'S

1025 Kaliste Saloom Rd. Lafayette, LA 70508 (337) 216-9024

"Celebrating the food and history of Acadiana"

Lafayette's offers a full menu of Cajun favorites such as their world-championship seafood gumbo – loaded with shrimp, crab & crawfish, corn & crab bisque, Lafayette's Caesar salad, premiere seafood platters, Angus certified filets and ribeyes, Mississippi pond-raised catfish and fabulous desserts!

Brian Smith, Executive Chef

Chef Brian is a native of Lafayette, Louisiana. He began cooking at home with his mother, father, aunts, uncles and grandmother! He is a graduate of Lafayette Regional (graduated top of class in 1991!) Voted "Junior Chef of the Year" in 1991 by the ACF Lafayette chapter. His first culinary job was at The Hotel Acadiana. Chef Brian was the Executive Sous Chef at Prejeans Restaurant for 9 years before joining Lafayette's staff.

He has placed second 2 years in a row at the New Iberia Cook Off for gumbo and also placed second 1 year at the Ettoufee Cook Off. He has won numerous gold and silver medals at the Lafayette, Baton Rouge and Shreveport Classics. Chef Brian cooked with Chef James Graham at the James Beard Foundation.

LAFAYETTE'S CRAWFISH AND ARTICHOKE BISQUE

4	ounces butter	1	tablespoon fresh thyme
2	cups chopped onion	1	pound fresh peeled Louisiana crawfish
1	cup chopped bell pepper	2	pints chicken stock (rich)
½	cup chopped celery	1	quart heavy cream
¼	cup chopped garlic	8	ounces American sliced cheese
4	cups artichoke hearts (quartered)	2	ounces blonde roux
2	cups chopped fresh basil	4	tablespoons Cajun seasoning
½	cup chopped fresh oregano		

In a large sauce pot, cook onion, bell pepper, garlic and celery in 4 ounces of butter until onions are clear. Add artichoke hearts and herbs and simmer for 5 minutes. Add crawfish and seasoning and mix well. Add stock and simmer for 5 minutes. Add cream and simmer for 10 minutes. Fold in roux and simmer for 10 more minutes. Dissolve cheese and serve.

Serves 8-10.

SHRIMP AND TASSO PASTA

8	ounces butter	¼	cup celery
1	pound 26/30 count peeled shrimp	3	tablespoons minced garlic
8	ounces diced tasso	2	tablespoons Cajun seasoning
1	pound pasta	1½	cups white wine
1	cup onion		
½	cup bell pepper		

In a medium sauce pot, sauté tasso in 2 ounces of butter for 3 minutes. Add shrimp and cook for 3 minutes. Add onions, bell pepper, celery and garlic. Cook for 7 minutes. Add white wine and seasoning. Simmer for 2 minutes. Fold in butter on low heat until dissolved. Serve with angel hair pasta.

Serves 6.

LANDRY'S RESTAURANT OF NEW IBERIA

Highway 90 West at 675 (Jefferson Island Road) New Iberia, LA 70560 (337) 369-3772

Landry's Restaurant of New Iberia was founded in 1969 by E. G. Landry. David Landry, along with his wife Grace, purchased the business upon the death of his father and was the first to offer a seafood buffet in the New Iberia area. The restaurant offers a luncheon buffet serving home cooking Tuesday, Wednesday and Thursday and a seafood luncheon buffet on Friday. The Seafood Grand Buffet on Friday and Saturday evenings and Sunday at noon boasts a wide variety of fried seafood, étouffée, gumbo, pasta and boiled seafood when available. Landry's steaks are fresh and delicious. On Friday and Saturday evenings, guests can enjoy live Cajun music and dancing. The restaurant also offers banquet facilities for seating up to 175 people.

CRAWFISH ÉTOUFFÉE

2	pounds crawfish tails (cooked)	1	stick butter or margarine
2	large onions (diced)	2	tablespoons flour
2	medium bell peppers (diced)	1	cup water
2	stalks celery (diced)		Salt, black pepper and cayenne pepper to taste
2	cloves garlic (diced	¼	cup chopped onion tops

Cook chopped vegetables and seasonings in butter over low heat until tender, stirring often. Add crawfish tails and mix well. Add flour and mix until smooth. Add water and stir well. Add onion tops and remove from heat. Serve hot over rice.

BLACKENED CATFISH

| 4 | catfish fillets | Salt, black pepper, cayenne pepper, paprika and garlic powder. |
| 1 | stick butter | |

Sprinkle catfish fillets with seasonings, heavy on the paprika. Melt butter in black iron skillet. Place catfish fillets in butter. Let cook about 5 minutes on each side, turning once.

Serves 4.

CAJUN FISH

Place blackened catfish on a dish and top with crawfish étouffée for a delicious entrée.

LITTLE RIVER INN

833 East Main Street
New Iberia, LA 70560
(337) 367-7466

**Richard Hurst
Elaine Hurst Alderman
Owners**

Little River Inn is celebrating its 14th Anniversary in New Iberia, the Queen city of the Teche, serving fine Cajun cuisine, lobster and steaks in a casual, yet fine dining atmosphere, overlooking the famous Trappey Live Oak, circa 1640. Little River Inn features the largest menu in the area, banquet menus for private parties and comprehensive liquor and wine selections. It is owned and operated by the Hurst family who have successfully operated Poor Boy's Riverside Inn since 1932.

CRABMEAT REMOULADE

2	cups mayonnaise	2	tablespoons Creole mustard
¼	cup extra fine chopped onions	1	tablespoon paprika
¼	cup extra fine chopped celery	1	tablespoon minced garlic
1	tablespoon horseradish	1	pound lump crabmeat

Mix all ingredients, except for the crabmeat, in a large bowl. Fold in crabmeat and serve on a bed of lettuce. Also, great as a dip for boiled seafood. This is better made a day ahead so flavors blend – add crabmeat when ready to serve.

STUFFED CRAB DRESSING

1	cup chopped yellow onions	½	loaf French bread (chopped in blender, using pulse, into small pieces – not crumbs)
1	cup chopped celery		
2	ounces diced red pimientos		
1	tablespoon minced garlic	1	pound white crabmeat
1	tablespoon Worcestershire sauce		Salt, red pepper, white pepper and black pepper to taste
⅔	pound unsalted butter		

In a large saucepan, melt butter over low heat and add all ingredients except for crabmeat and bread. Cover and simmer until vegetables are soft and peanut butter colored (do not brown). Carefully (so as not to break the crabmeat) fold in crabmeat, cover and heat until crabmeat is hot. Remove from heat and carefully fold in bread – do not stir. Let cool, then use as you wish.

Serves 4 people.

Suggestions for use:
(1) Stuff crab shells with stuffing and bake in oven at 350 degrees for 20 minutes if stuffing is hot, or if stuffing is cold, cover stuffed crabs with aluminum foil, bake for 25 minutes covered, then uncover and bake 15 more minutes.
(2) Roll stuffing into balls, batter and fry, or bake and top with Parmesan cheese for an appetizer.

LITTLE RIVER INN BREAD PUDDING RECIPE

20	pieces of bread broken or torn into 2" x 2" pieces	1	teaspoon of nutmeg
4	cups of milk	2	tablespoons of baking soda
4	eggs	3	tablespoons of vanilla extract
8	ounces of cream of coconut	2	cups of granulated sugar
½	pound of melted butter	1	teaspoon of almond flavoring
2	tablespoons of ground cinnamon		

Grease a 12" x 15" baking pan and preheat oven to 400 degrees. Mix all ingredients, except bread, together until well mixed. Fold in bread until well coated. Pour mixture into baking pan and bake for 30 minutes. Remove from oven and fold in sides of mixture to middle. Spread mixture flat in pan, put back in oven and bake for 10 more minutes. Remove from oven and serve. Cover to refrigerate. For a firmer texture, continue baking until toothpick inserted in middle comes out clean.

~Little River Inn~

MAISON DABOVAL
A FRENCH BED AND BREAKFAST

305 East Louisiana Avenue
Rayne, Louisiana 70578
(337) 334-3489

Martha and Gene Royer, Proprietors

Martha and Gene Royer's home was featured on HGTV's "If Walls Could Talk." HGTV was inspired by the rich history of the home and the extensive renovation work done by Martha and Gene. The episode number is WCT-601. Maison Daboval has five bedrooms decorated with antiques. Each has a private bath and all have claw-footed bathtubs. Every morning a Cajun breakfast is served. Both French and English are spoken.

Once you have enjoyed Martha's Cajun Breakfast you will quickly start making plans to come back for another visit. Here are a couple of her recipes:

FROG CAPITOL OF THE WORLD

EGG SOUFFLÉ

18	slices of bread	1	bunch green onions chopped
20	eggs	1	pound grated mozzarella
2	pounds spicy breakfast sausage	½	pint milk or whipping cream
1	onion chopped	1	stick melted butter
½	chopped bell pepper		

Preheat oven to 350 degrees. Cut crust off bread, butter one side, put buttered side down in large 9x13 pan. Sauté sausage with vegetables until sausage is brown and vegetables are tender. Drain off excess fat. Layer meat and vegetable mixture with cheese. Repeat the process until all is used, approximately three layers. Pour beaten eggs, milk and melted butter over top. Refrigerate overnight. Bake for 1 hour until done.

Serves 8 to 10

SWEET POTATO MUFFINS

1¾	cups all-purpose flour	½	cup packed brown sugar
1	teaspoon baking soda	½	cup vegetable oil
½	teaspoon ground cinnamon	1	17-ounce can of sweet potatoes, drained & mashed
¼	teaspoon salt	½	cup chopped pecans
2	eggs	1	cup dates, chopped
1	cup sugar	¼	cup all purpose flour

Preheat oven to 350 degrees. Sift first four ingredients in a bowl. Combine eggs and next four ingredients in another bowl and mix well. Mix sweet potato mixture and dry ingredients together. Dust pecans and dates with the ¼ cup flour then add to muffin mixture. Grease muffin pans and bake for 27-30 minutes.

Makes 1½ dozen.

MIKE'S SEAFOOD RESTAURANT

15358 Highway 26
Jennings, LA 70546
(337) 616-0766

Mike Walker, Chef/Owner

Mike's Seafood, located ¼ mile north of Interstate 10 in Jennings, LA., specializes in seafood, steaks, gumbo, salads, pasta and Po-Boys. The restaurant has seating for 120 people and accepts all major credit cards. The restaurant is a member of the Louisiana Restaurant Association.

BLUEBERRY CONGEALED SALAD

2	(3-ounce) or 1 (6-ounce) package black cherry Jell-O gelatin
1	can prepared blueberry pie filling
1	cup chopped pecans
1	(8¼-ounce) can crushed pineapple (do not drain)
2	cups boiling water
1	tablespoon lemon juice

Spray Pam in casserole dish. Dissolve Jell-O gelatin in boiling water, add pineapple, blueberries, lemon juice and pecans. After mixture has gotten firm in refrigerator, add topping.

TOPPING:

½	pint Sour cream
¼	cup sugar (granulated)
1	(8-ounce) cream cheese
½	teaspoon vanilla extract

Soften cream cheese-blend sour cream and cream cheese. Add sugar and vanilla. Spread over Jell-O gelatin.

CRAWFISH BISQUE

½	cup parsley
1	cup Pet evaporated milk
3	eggs
1	tablespoon salt
1	tablespoon red cayenne pepper
½	cup parsley
1	can Ro-Tel tomatoes
1	(8-ounce) can tomato sauce
1	tablespoon liquid crab boil
3	cloves garlic, minced
2	quarts water

Heads: Clean about 150 crawfish heads and boil in large pot with 2 tablespoons of baking soda. Grind crawfish tails, onions, celery, bell peppers. In a large bowl, mix with remaining ingredients and stuff heads. Roll heads in flour. Bake at 350 degrees for 20 minutes.

Gravy: Make a roux. When roux is dark chocolate color, add onions, celery, bell pepper and garlic. Simmer on low heat until onions are clear. Add Ro-Tel, tomato sauce and liquid crab boil. Add 1 quart of water. Cook slowly for 30 minutes. Add crawfish tails, green onions and parsley. Add another quart of water. Cook until boiling. Put in heads, salt and red pepper to taste. Let simmer about 45 minutes. Serves 40-50.

Mike's Seafood Restaurant

Mr. Lester's Steakhouse

832 Martin Luther King Rd. Charenton, LA 70523 (800) 284-4386

Mr. Lester's Steakhouse, established in 1995 and located within Cypress Bayou Casino, is known throughout the state and beyond for it's prime beef, bold portions, extensive wine and cigar selection, exceptional service, friendly staff and unique and enticing décor and environment. With the amazing talents of Chef Scott McCue, Mr. Lester's continues to build customer loyalty and exceed guests' expectations. Chef Scott McCue, although born and raised in Tucson, Arizona, has not only adapted to the Cajun culture and its cuisine, but also has cultivated his talents to enhance traditional Cajun dishes as well as solely create unique and delicious recipes. Chef Scott McCue is an active and founding member of the Atchafalaya Basin Chapter of the American Culinary Federation and has attained many medals for his skills in the many facets of his profession.

Acadiana Creamy Crab Cakes

2	tablespoons whole butter		Salt to taste
⅔	cup diced yellow onions		Pinch of cayenne
⅓	cup diced sweet red pepper		Pinch of granulated garlic
⅓	cup chopped green onions		Pinch of ground black pepper
1	pound cream cheese	½	tablespoon chopped parsley
1	pound jumbo lump blue crabmeat		Dash of Tabasco hot sauce

Heat butter in sauté pan and sauté onions, peppers and green onions until soft. Let cool. Mix cream cheese and sautéed onion mixture until mixed well. Fold in crabmeat, parsley and dry ingredients. Add a dash of Tabasco hot sauce. Portion into 12 (4-ounce) cakes. Let firm up in refrigerator for 1 hour.

BREADING:

3	cups breadcrumbs (white)		Pinch of salt and cayenne pepper
1	tablespoon chopped parsley	2	cups egg wash
		2	cups all purpose flour

Final Method: Combine the breadcrumbs, parsley, salt and pepper. Remove crab cakes from cooler and first dust with the flour, then dip into the egg wash and last the bread crumb mixture. Pan-fry or deep-fry the cakes to a golden brown, let drain and serve.

Serves 12.

Filet Mignon Au Poive

TENDERLOIN:

12	each 6-ounce prime beef tenderloin filets	Kosher salt and ground pepper corn melange for seasoning

Method: Season all sides of the filet with salt and pepper and sear on a hot broiler, place into a preheated 500-degree oven and cook to desired temperature.

AU POIVE SAUCE:

3	cups fine cognac	2	tablespoons coarse ground pepper corn melange
4	cups demi glace		
4	cups heavy cream		Kosher salt to taste

Method: Heat a small sauce pot and add cognac, let alcohol burn off. Now add the cream and demi glace, let reduce to 4 cups, add pepper and salt to taste and reserve warm. When the filet is cooked, top with the Au Poive sauce and serve.

Serves 12.

Continued Page 133

WHITE CHOCOLATE BREAD PUDDING SOUFFLÉ

1	quart heavy whipping cream	2	tablespoons vanilla extract
1	pound white chocolate chopped	2	teaspoons cinnamon
8	each whole eggs	½	cup white rum
2	cups milk	3 to 4 loaves day-old French bread	
2	cups sugar granulated		

Bring heavy cream to a boil, stir in white chocolate until smooth. Mix all ingredients together, except bread, until fully incorporated. Using day-old French bread ground up or sliced thin, soak the bread in the custard for a couple of hours. Butter a large baking pan and fill the pan with the bread pudding. Bake in a 350-degree oven until the bread pudding is firm to the touch and golden brown on top. After bread pudding cools crumble some by hand into a bowl (about 6 cups). Make a basic meringue with egg whites and sugar, whip the meringue to stiff peaks and fold it into the crumbles bread pudding. Fill your 4 (6-ounce) soufflé dishes full and then the soufflé itself with meringue and bake at 350 degrees for about 40 minutes.

(Serves 15)

NASH'S RESTAURANT
101 East Second St. Broussard, LA 70518 (337) 839-9333

Nash Barreca Jr., Chef/Owner

Chef Nash Barreca is a third generation restaurateur following in his grandfather, Frank and his father Nash Sr., who owned the famous Frank's Steak House in New Orleans for forty-five years. He continued his profession as an Executive Chef with his brother David who owns and operates Barreca's Restaurant in Metairie, Louisiana. Still the favorite place in Metairie where the locals go to dine. Chef Nash came to Lafayette in 1999 with his wife Jenny, formerly from here, to establish Nash's Restaurant in an old historical home built in 1908 in Broussard, Louisiana, approximately 5 miles south of Lafayette off Hwy. 90. He brings with him old traditional recipes brought down from the Creole chefs that taught him since he was fifteen years of age at his grandfather and father's restaurant.

SHRIMP AND WHITE BEANS

1	pound great northern beans	4	ribs celery, chopped
½	pound ham or seasoning meat	8 to 10 cups of water	
1	tablespoon margarine	1	cup chicken broth
1	medium onion, finely chopped	1	tablespoon fresh parsley chopped
½	medium bell pepper, chopped		Salt and pepper to taste

In a stockpot, sauté down margarine, meat, seasoning and garlic. Add chicken broth and beans. Add 8 to 10 cups water. Let cook for two hours till beans are tender. Add parsley, salt and pepper to taste last. If necessary, add water while cooking.

After beans are cooked:

In a sauté pan: Sauté 1 tablespoon unsalted butter, ½ teaspoon fresh chopped garlic, 8 ounces peeled

Continued Page 134

shrimp (size optional), 2 ounces shrimp stock and 2 ounces green onions, chopped. Let simmer till the shrimp are cooked then add 8 ounces of your cooked white beans. Let simmer till heated stirring occasionally. Pour over steamed rice. Approximately 4 servings per sauté pan.

GRILLED EGGPLANT, TOMATO, FRESH MOZZARELLA, PORTABELLO MUSHROOMS AND FRESH BASIL SALAD

3	ea. ¼ inch sliced eggplant with skin on	3	ea. ¼ inch sliced fresh Mozzarella cheese
3	ea. ¼ inch sliced vine ripe or Creole tomatoes	2	tablespoons finely chopped fresh basil leaves
3	ea. ¼ inch slice Portabello mushrooms	2	cups freshly grown spring mix Extra virgin olive oil Balsamic vinegar

In a sauté pan coat a thin layer of extra virgin olive oil. Salt & pepper eggplant, tomatoes and portabello mushrooms. Grill all three vegetables in the same sauté pan on both sides. Remove from sauté pan and place on dry paper towel to dry. On a platter, lay your spring mix on top. Layer each vegetable and slices of fresh Mozzarella cheese rotating each vegetable. Sprinkle fresh sweet basil on top. **Options:** You can add grilled chicken, duck breast or fish to this salad also. A vinaigrette dressing such as balsamic or raspberry will complement this dish.

CHICKEN BRACIUOLINI

4	6-ounce boneless skinless chicken breasts	1	tablespoon grated Parmigiana cheese
2	slices prosciutto – julienne style	1	only whole artichokes canned, chopped (no juice)
1	boiled egg shredded	½	teaspoon granulated garlic
¼	cup Italian seasoned breadcrumbs		Pinch of ground rosemary
1	tablespoon extra virgin olive oil		Pinch of ground sage
¼	freshly squeezed lemon (no seeds)		Pinch of black ground pepper

In a mixing bowl add Italian seasoned breadcrumbs, lemon juice, Parmigiana cheese, granulated garlic, olive oil, rosemary, sage and black pepper. Mix well by hand rubbing together until the mix is moist. Set aside.

Flatten raw chicken breast to ¼ inch thickness. Layer the mixed breadcrumbs over the top of the chicken. Add chopped artichoke, boiled egg and prosciutto in layers on top of the bread crumb mix. Top with Mozzarella cheese and hand roll chicken stretching the sides and folding so that the ingredients inside will not fall out. Use a toothpick 1 or 2 to hold together. Place the chicken in a casserole dish and smother with marinara sauce (red gravy). Cover with foil and put into a 350-degree oven for 40 minutes. Take out and serve with angel hair pasta. *Optional – you may use baby veal or round steak instead of chicken. If using round steak cook for 1 hour till meat is tender.

Serves 4.

SHRIMP & CORN BISQUE

2	sticks unsalted butter	1	cup finely chopped celery
1	cup bleached all-purpose flour	½	red pepper hand diced
1	gallon shrimp stock	2	tablespoons granulated garlic
3	pounds medium size shrimp peeled & deveined (save shells for stock)	1	tablespoon fresh thyme chopped
2	#303 cans whole kernel corn or cream of corn	1	tablespoon fresh tarragon chopped
2	cups heavy cream	3	bay leaves
2	cups finely chopped onions	1	teaspoon granulated white pepper
		1	tablespoon fresh chopped parsley

Peel & devein shrimp (save peelings for stock). Boil shrimp in plain water and drain. Set aside. Boil shrimp peelings to make a stock. Use 1¼ gallons of water so that you have enough stock for your bisque. Strain and set aside. In a stockpot melt butter and add flour. Stir to make a white roux (10 minutes). Add 1 gallon of shrimp stock. Let come to a boil. Add heavy cream, corn, onion, celery, peppers, thyme, white pepper, garlic and bay leaves. Let come to a boil. Add 3 pounds of cooked shrimp. Let come to a boil. Let cook for 30 minutes after boiling. Add chopped tarragon and chopped parsley.

Yield: 8 servings

PAT'S OF HENDERSON

1500 Siebarth Drive
Lake Charles, LA 70615

Richard & Nancy Perioux, Owners

This restaurant has won numerous awards including: "Best Restaurant in Southwest Louisiana", "Best Cajun Restaurant", "Best place for a Business Lunch". "Best Gumbo", "Best Seafood" and "Best Cajun Dish"!

The Pat's products mentioned in the recipes may be ordered by calling 1-866-711-7287 or www.patsofhenderson.com.

SEAFOOD GUMBO

1	cup shrimp (peeled)	¼	cup onions (chopped)
1	cup crawfish tails	½	clove garlic (chopped)
1	cup raw oysters (pasteurized)		Season to taste with Pat's Spicy seasoning
¼	cup bell pepper (chopped)		
½	cup Pat's roux	2	quarts of water

Heat water till it starts to boil. Dissolve roux in water by stirring on medium heat. Add onions, bell peppers, garlic and ¼ cup of seasoning to roux mixture. Cook on low heat for 45 minutes. If more seasoning is needed add to desired taste. Serve over rice.

CHICKEN & SAUSAGE GUMBO

1	large hen, cut and season with all-purpose seasoning	2	cloves garlic, minced Pat's all-purpose seasoning
1	pound sausage, cut		
1	medium onion, chopped	3½	quarts of water
1	medium bell pepper, chopped	1	cup Pat's roux

Fry hen until light brown and set aside. In a separate pot, dissolve roux in water over medium heat. Add seasoning to taste. Add onions, bell pepper & garlic to the water and boil for 20 minutes. Add hen and sausage to the water mixture. Cook on medium for 1½ to 2 hours or until meat is tender. If more seasoning is needed add to desired taste.

Yield: 6 – 8.

JEAN LAFITTE RESTAURANT

501 W. College Street
Lake Charles, LA 70605
(337) 474-2730

SHRIMP SAUCE PIQUANTE

4	onions, finely chopped		Pinch of sugar
3	bell peppers, finely chopped	1	cup of water
1½	cups chopped parsley	2	pounds of peeled and deveined shrimp
½	cup of oil		Salt, black pepper and red pepper to taste
1	six ounce can of chilies tomato		

Sauté onions, bell pepper and half of the parsley in oil until onions are transparent; add chilies tomato, sugar and water and cook on low heat for 2 hours. Add shrimp and remaining parsley, salt, red pepper; and continue to cook for about 20 minutes. Serve over cooked rice in soup bowls. Makes 4 to 6 servings.

CATFISH COURTBOUILLON

3	large onions, chopped		Salt, black pepper and red pepper to taste
1	cup of chopped celery	2	tablespoons chopped parsley
3	cloves of garlic, minced	2	tablespoons chopped green onions
1	16-ounce can of tomatoes		
1	can of chilies tomato	1	cooked spoon of roux
2	quarts of water		
4	pounds of fish (catfish, redfish or red snapper)		

To your roux, add onions, celery and garlic and cook until onions are transparent. Add tomatoes and chilies tomato and cook slowly, stirring for 5 minutes. Add water and simmer for 1 hour. Season fish with salt, black pepper and red pepper and tomato sauce and cook on low heat about 15 minutes, without stirring. Add parsley and green onion tops about 5 minutes before serving. Serve over cooked rice in soup bowls. Makes 6 servings.

PREJEAN'S RESTAURANT

3480 I-49 North
Lafayette, LA 70507
(337) 896-3278

For a genuine Cajun experience go to Prejean's Restaurant. It is a large place with 350 seats, a 14-foot stuffed alligator called "Big Al" and a live Cajun band. Owner Bob Guilbeau can trace his Cajun heritage back to the founding of this region. Prejean's culinary team has won more culinary competitions, more medals and trophies than any restaurant in the South. The restaurant offers guests a wide array of seafood specialties, steaks and wild game dishes.

Chef Frederick Nonato attended the University of Southwestern Louisiana and the Delgado Community College where he studied Culinary Arts. He has worked in several of New Orleans finest restaurants; Kelsey's, Anacapri's, and Don's Seafood Hut. In 1996 he became Sous Chef at Kelsey's Restaurant in uptown New Orleans, alongside Executive Chef/Owner Randy Barlow, former apprentice of Chef Paul Prudhomme. He joined Team Prejean in 1998 and worked closely with former Executive Chef James Graham assisting in many prestigious events, such as, dinner at The James Beard House, The Washington Mardi Gras Ball and Governor Foster of Louisiana's Christmas Galas. He was named as the new Executive Chef in September, 2000.

PHEASANT, QUAIL ANDOUILLE GUMBO

2	pounds diced Andouille	10	quarts rich chicken stock
1	pound diced Cajun smoked sausage	3	tablespoons paprika
2½	cups diced onion	2	teaspoons black pepper
2	cups diced bell peppers	1	teaspoon white pepper
1	cup diced celery	1	teaspoon cayenne pepper
¼	cup corn oil	1	bay leaf
10	each de-boned quail	2	tablespoons Kitchen Bouquet
6	each pheasant breast		
1	teaspoon Tabasco hot sauce	22	cups dark roux
¾	cup onion tops		In a cast iron pot over

medium low heat, place ¼ cup corn oil. In a non-stick skillet brown each individual ingredient starting with the Andouille, then sausage, onion, etc. transferring each ingredient to the cast iron pot. Add seasoning, stock and then dissolve roux and bring to a boil for 40 minutes and serve over rice. Servings: 12 + leftovers.

CRAWFISH ÉTOUFFÉE

2	tablespoons butter	½	teaspoon garlic powder
2	tablespoons flour		
¾	cup chopped onion	½	teaspoon black pepper
½	cup chopped celery		
⅓	cup chopped green onion tops	3	tablespoons chicken bouillon
⅓	cup chopped green onion bulbs	4	cups water
1	cup butter	3	pounds crawfish tails
¼	cup chopped parsley	2	tablespoons chopped parsley
1	tablespoon paprika		Chopped green onion tops
1	teaspoon cayenne pepper		

Melt 2 tablespoons of butter in a small skillet. Stir in the flour. Cook over medium heat until brown to form a roux, stirring constantly; set aside. Sauté the onion, celery, green pepper and green onion bulbs in 1 cup of butter in a large saucepan until tender. Add ¼ cup parsley, paprika, cayenne, garlic powder, black pepper and bouillon and mix well. Cook for 2 minutes. Add the water and bring to a boil. Stir in the roux. Cook until thickened, stirring occasionally. Add the crawfish. Cook just until the crawfish are tender. Stir in 2 tablespoons parsley and green onion tops. Serve over steamed rice. Serves 12.

BREAD PUDDING WITH JACK DANIEL'S SAUCE

*All ingredients should be at room temperature.

INGREDIENTS (PUDDING)

3	loaves stale bread	¾	cup butter
4	cups milk	2	cups sugar
8	eggs	2	tablespoons vanilla
1	can evaporated milk	1	teaspoon cinnamon
⅓	can water	2	sticks butter, cut into pieces

Cut bread into cubes. Combine all ingredients except bread and butter. Mix well and pour over bread in a

Continued Page 137

large mixing bowl. Let bread soak in milk mixture for 15 minutes. Pour bread mixture into a buttered 9x13 pan. Top bread mixture with butter pieces. Bake at 325 degrees for 1 to 1½ hours, or until pudding mixture has risen about 1 inch.

INGREDIENTS: (SAUCE)

1	stick butter	2	ounces Jack
½	cup water		Daniel's whiskey
½	cup sugar		(Black Label)
2	tablespoons vanilla		

Mix sugar and water together until dissolved. Add butter and simmer until melted. Cook over high heat for 2 minutes. Add Jack Daniel's and simmer 3 to 5 minutes. Serve warm on top of bread pudding.

Servings: 25

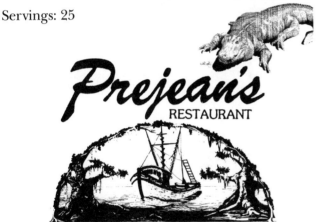

Prejean's RESTAURANT

Award-Winning Cajun Cuisine

PUJO ST. CAFÉ

901 Ryan Street
Lake Charles, LA 70601
(337) 439-2054

*This casual, yet elegant, restaurant is conveniently located just six blocks off I-10 in the heart of historical downtown Lake Charles. Housed in what once was the old Gordan's Drug Store, it comes highly recommended by the locals. As featured in **Southern Living** Magazine, Pujo St. Café offers courtyard dining, steaks, seafood, salads and pastas; complimented by a full bar and an excellent wine list.*

OYSTERS PUJO
(APPETIZER)

½	teaspoon olive oil,	2	ounces Southern Comfort bourbon
½	tablespoon minced garlic,	½	cup heavy whipping cream
½	tablespoon minced shallots,		Oysters
¾	cup minced tasso,		Flour
¾	cup minced smoked Gouda cheese,		Buttermilk
			Finely chopped pecans
4	cups fresh spinach,		Breadcrumbs
			Vegetable oil

Stuffing mixture: Sauté garlic, shallots and tasso in olive oil over high heat. After 3 minutes add Gouda cheese and cook another 3 minutes, add spinach and wilt down 1 minute. Deglaze with Southern Comfort bourbon. Add cream. Reduce by half and set aside.

Dust oysters with flour and dip in buttermilk, roll in ½ pecan and ½ breadcrumb mixture, that have been finely chopped, and fry for 1 to 2 minutes in vegetable oil. Place each oyster in a half shell and top with stuffing mixture and bake for 5 to 7 minutes at 400 degrees. Serve on a bed of greens garnished with a lemon twist. (Serves 6 to 8).

BREAD PUDDING WITH RUM SAUCE

¾	of a 20-ounce loaf of cheap white bread	5	eggs
		3½	cups milk
2½	cups sugar	2	tablespoons vanilla extract

In a large bowl tear bread into bite size pieces, add rest of ingredients and stir until mixed well. Spray a 9x13 pan with pan coating, pour mixture in pan and let stand at room temperature for about 45 minutes. Then bake at 350 degrees for 45 minutes or until center rises to golden brown. Let stand for 30 minutes before slicing.

RUM SAUCE:

¼	pound butter, at room temperature	1	egg
		¼	cup light rum
1	cup sugar		

Cream butter and sugar in mixer at high speed for about 5 minutes. On low speed add egg and continue to mix until egg is blended in completely. Then slowly add rum and mix for 3 minutes. Once all ingredients are incorporated continue to mix on high for 20 to 30 minutes. Serve atop warm bread pudding. Serves 12.

SNO'S SEAFOOD & STEAKHOUSE

13131 Airline Highway
Gonzales, LA 70797
(225) 647-2632

Todd & Candy Sheets, owners
Executive Chef David W. Tiner

Chef Tiner is a Louisiana native. He attended the Culinary Art Institute of Louisiana in 1995. Previous restaurant stints included Dajonel's as Sous Chef and Chef at Tezcuco Plantation Bed & Breakfast. Chef Tiner began working at Sno's Seafood in September, 1999 where he really developed his style of cooking, creating a combination of Cajun, Creole and French dishes. Chef Tiner claims that most of his best and creative dishes are made up on the spot!

SHRIMP DIABLO

24	each 26/30 count shrimp, peeled and deveined	1	teaspoon salt
2	whole eggs	1	pint ketchup
2	cups milk	½	teaspoon habanero chile **see note
2	cups flour	1	teaspoon chili powder
½	teaspoon habanero pepper *see note	1	teaspoon granulated garlic
1	teaspoon chili	2	sticks butter, melted
1	teaspoon granulated garlic		

Preheat enough oil for frying to 350 degrees. In a bowl combine milk and eggs and mix well. In another bowl combine flour and first set of seasonings, blend well. Dredge shrimp in flour mixture then into the egg wash and back into the flour mixture, fry until golden brown. In a food processor or blender combine the ketchup and seasonings, turn on high and slowly pour in butter. After blending, taste and adjust seasonings. Gently coat each shrimp in the blended mixture, place 6 to a plate garnished with green onions, serve with a side of blue cheese dressing for dipping.

*Habanero peppers are extremely hot, use sparingly.

**Habanero seasoning can be found at your local supermarket with the dried spices or specialty spices.

You can substitute the habanero for a less hot pepper such as cayenne or none at all if you are not heat tolerant. Yield: 4 servings.

CRAWFISH ÉTOUFFÉE

1	medium onion, diced	¼	cup green onion, sliced
1	medium bell pepper, diced	¼	teaspoon cayenne pepper
2	ribs celery, diced	1	teaspoon salt
¼	cup butter	1	teaspoon black pepper
2	pounds crawfish tails, whole	1	tablespoon granulated garlic
¼	teaspoon thyme	1	cup water
¼	teaspoon fresh parsley, chopped fine	½	cup butter
		½	cup flour

In a large pot or Dutch oven, melt the butter and sauté the vegetables until tender, add the crawfish tails and seasonings, cook until tender. Add the water and remaining butter, stir until the mixture comes to a boil, sprinkle the flour over the top of boiling mixture and whisk in, cook until thick (just a few minutes). Adjust the seasoning for salt and pepper to desired taste. Serve over hot rice with fresh French bread. Yield: 8 servings

CHOCOLATE BREAD PUDDING

1	loaf French bread, cut in 1-inch pieces	4	ounces half & half
3	whole eggs	1	tablespoon vanilla
2⅔	cups sugar	4	ounces butter, melted
12	ounces evaporated milk	1	teaspoon cinnamon
1	pound semisweet chocolate chips	½	teaspoon nutmeg

Preheat oven to 350 degrees. Cube bread and set aside. In a bowl combine sugar and eggs and mix well. In a small pot combine butter, milk, half & half and chocolate. Heat on medium until chocolate is melted and mixture is smooth, add vanilla and remove from heat. Slowly pour the chocolate mixture into the sugar mixture whisking the sugar constantly to prevent curdling eggs. Once combined place bread into a large bowl, pour the chocolate mixture over bread, gently toss to coat evenly, allow to set up for 5 minutes. Pour bread mixture into a 9x13 greased pan, sprinkle top with cinnamon and nutmeg. Bake for 20 minutes or until done. Serve warm or cold topped with chocolate syrup. Note* Fresh bread works the best, makes a moister pudding. Yield: 8 servings.

THAI CUISINE

607 B Kaliste Saloom Rd.
Lafayette, LA 70508

On Mogensen, Chef/Owner
Yai O'Neal, Chef/Owner
Toi Dailey, Chef/Owner

This authentic Thai restaurant offers an excellent alternative to the great Cajun cuisine in the area. Like Cajuns, Thai people enjoy a little spice in their life and the uniqueness and versatility of their cooking style will afford you an opportunity to enjoy an important part of their culture. Chefs On, Yai and Toi incorporate fresh herbs and spices into recipes from Southern, Central and Northeastern Thailand that have been passed down for generations. They are proud and pleased to share a small sampling of their cuisine.

RED CURRY
(GAENG DAENG)

1½	cups coconut milk	½	teaspoon sugar
1	tablespoon red curry paste	3-4	fresh Kaffir lime leaves
½	cup water or chicken stock	1	medium size red or green bell pepper sliced
12	ounces meat, your choice (beef, chicken, pork or shrimp)	2-3	sweet basil leaves
2	tablespoons fish sauce	1	tablespoon cooking oil

Heat wok and add oil and curry paste, stirring for 30 seconds. Add meat and cook until almost done. Add coconut milk and remaining ingredients and cook 2-3 minutes until meat is done. Add basil, remove from heat.

PAD THAI

12	ounces fresh flat rice noodles	½	cup ground roasted peanuts
1	cup bean sprouts	2	garlic cloves finely chopped
2	eggs (optional)	1	tablespoon chopped shallots
½	pound meat cut into small slivers, your choice (shrimp, pork, chicken)	4	tablespoons cooking oil
3	tablespoons chopped pickled radish	3	tablespoons fish sauce
1	cup tofu thinly sliced	4	tablespoons tamarind juice or vinegar

Heat cooking oil in a wok and sauté garlic. Add meat and cook until shrimp turns bright orange and chicken turns white. Add tofu and radish and fry until the tofu is nearly cooked. Continue to stir and slowly drizzle in the beaten eggs to form a fine ribbon of cooked egg. Add remaining ingredients except for bean sprouts and shallots and cook until noodles are done. Add half the bean sprouts and shallots and fry for about 30 seconds. Transfer to platter, sprinkle with peanuts and serve with bean sprouts.

Note: It is possible to use less oil than indicated by adding small amounts from time to time to keep the noodles from drying.

LEMON GRASS SOUP
(TOM YUM GOONG)

5	large shrimp shelled and de-veined	3	tablespoons fish sauce
3	cups chicken stock	5-6	Thai chilies, just broken with pestle
¾	cup mushrooms, halved	2-3	Kaffir lime leaves, torn
1	lemon grass stem, cut into short lengths	2	coriander plants, chopped coarsely
4	slices fresh galangal	1	shallot
5	tablespoons lime juice	1	dash MSG (optional)

Heat the stock to boiling. Add the lemon grass, galangal and Kaffir lime leaves. Return to boil, add shrimp and mushrooms and cook until shrimp is done. Season to taste with lime juice, fish sauce chilies and MSG. Add coriander and shallots. Remove from heat. Serve hot.

Author's Note: *Some of the above ingredients may not be available in your grocery store. Oriental grocery stores will more than likely stock these items. Check the glossary for definitions.*

THE PALACE CAFÉ

135 West Landry
Opelousas, LA 70570
(337) 942-2142

Tina D. Elder & Bill Walker, Owners

TINA'S VEGETABLE SOUP

1½	pounds diced beef or soup bone	3	carrots, chopped
3	quarts water	1	large bag mixed frozen vegetables
3	ribs celery, chopped	2	potatoes, cut in small pieces
2	large onions, chopped	1	can whole kernel corn
1	large bell pepper, chopped	½	cup shredded cabbage
1	(20-ounce can) crushed tomatoes		

In a 6 quart covered pot, add water, meat, onions, bell pepper, celery and tomatoes and boil for 2½ hours. Take soup meat from pot and remove from bone. Chop into bite sized pieces, discarding bone and fat. Return meat into broth, add potatoes and cabbage, cook ½ hour again. Then add frozen vegetables and corn during last 15 minutes of cooking.

Serves 8-10 people.

BEEF STEW

3	pounds cubed chuck roast	1	tablespoon cornstarch
2	onions, chopped	2	ribs celery, chopped
1	bell pepper, chopped	4	carrots, chopped

In a Dutch oven, brown the meat; add onions and bell pepper. Cook until tender. Add water. In a measuring cup, dissolve cornstarch in water; add to stew. Add celery and carrots: simmer vegetables until tender. Season with Tony's Creole Seasoning. Serve with boiled potatoes on the side.

Yield: 8 servings

BAKLAVA — STEVE DOUCAS ORIGINAL

SYRUP:

4	boiling cups water	3	cups sugar
2	lemons, clear juice only	1	pound honey

FILLING – PECAN

3	pounds ground pecans	3	tablespoons cinnamon
2½	cups sugar – white		

ALSO:

1½	standard packages. filo (phylo dough leaves)	1¼	pounds sweet butter – melted

Make a simple syrup by dissolving 3 cups sugar in 4 cups of boiling water. Simmer over medium low heat for 1 hour and 14 minutes (this is simple syrup). Add honey, bring to a slow boil. Mixture will foam, skim off foam until foam stops forming, add lemon juice. Allow syrup to cool to at least room temperature. (Can be made well ahead of time). Note: Add hot syrup to cold Baklava or cold syrup to hot Baklava but cold syrup to hot Bakalava is preferable.

Combine ground pecans, sugar and ground cinnamon until uniform. In a separate pan melt butter. Thaw filo (9 leaves), lay out ready to separate and use. Obtain an 18" x 13" pan. With a clean paintbrush, butter bottom and sides of the pan. Lay filo leaves one at a time on pan bottom, buttering each leaf completely, before adding another leaf, through out entire process. Place 8 filo leaves on bottom of pan. (Butter each leaf!) Add one third of pecan mixture to pan, smooth and pat down evenly. Add 4 more filo leaves, same procedure as above. Add second third of pecan mixture, smooth and pat down evenly. Add 4 more filo leaves, same procedure as before. Add last third of pecan mixture, smooth and pat evenly. Add 8 more filo leaves, same procedure as above. Be generous in adding butter to top layer. Place pan in refrigerator for about 45 minutes, or until butter through out surface hardens, evenly. Note: this step can be eliminated if desired. With a sharp (thin) knife, cut pan contents into diamond

Continued Page 141

shapes. On 18" length, cut into 10 to 13 rows, maintaining uniform shaping. Now make an angled cut from one corner to corner "cat-a-corner" from start. On both sides of first cut, make 4 to 5 cuts parallel to first cut (Diamond shape is result). Trim excess filo from sides of pan to give smooth appearance. Preheat oven to 375 degrees. Place pan in oven for 20 minutes. Lower heat to 350 degrees, cook for an additional 20 minutes. Lower heat to 325 degrees, cook and additional 20 minutes. Turn off heat, leave pan in oven an additional 20 minutes, top surface should be golden brown. Remove pan from oven, pour cool syrup onto hot Baklava evenly. Do not separate or serve Baklava until next day! Note: Cuts made in step 9 do not go to bottom of crust. Firmly re-cut in original grooves to bottom of pastry.

Yield: 20 servings

YELLOW BOWL RESTAURANT

Highway 182
Jeanerette, LA 70544
(337) 276-5512

Owned & Operated by:
T. K. & Colleen Roberts Hulin

In 1953, Tony and Margaret Roberts bought the Yellow Bowl, moving their family from Breaux Bridge to Jeanerette. Tony Roberts was a pioneer in moving the lowly crawfish onto the restaurant tables of Louisiana. He originated the ever famous fried crawfish, which remains our most sought after of all recipes. Margaret Roberts was a wonder in the kitchen, every meal reflecting the traditions and pride of the Bayou Teche area.

From 1988 to 2000, Neal and Kay Roberts, second generation owners, operated the Yellow Bowl, carrying on the prideful traditions started by Tony and Margaret Roberts. With the new millennium, brings a new look and a new Roberts as owner of the Yellow Bowl! T.K. and Colleen Roberts Hulin welcome you and promise continued superior service, with the guidance of Tony and Margaret Roberts, and the Yellow Bowl tradition of "good food with good friends".

Also, featured in Southern Living, Coastal Living and Ford Times.

CHEF FLOYD CLAVELLE'S SNAPPER AND GARLIC CREAM SAUCE

SAUCE:

½	quart of half and half	1	teaspoon thyme
½	cup each – Mozzarella, Romano, Cheddar and Parmesan cheese	1	teaspoon basil
		1	teaspoon Accent seasoning
		3	tablespoons chicken base
3	cloves minced garlic	1	cup shrimp stock

Add all ingredients and simmer for approximately 20 minutes or until cheeses are melted. Dissolve flour in small amount of water to thicken sauce. In a skillet, heat 2 tablespoons butter, ¼ cup water and 1 teaspoon lemon juice. Add skinless snapper fillet and cook on each side until fish flakes. Remove fish from skillet and pour ¼ cup cream sauce over. Garnish with parsley and serve.

HOLIDAY PUMPKIN CHEESECAKE

1½	cups graham cracker crumbs	3	eggs
2	tablespoons sugar	¾	teaspoon vanilla extract
¼	cup margarine, melted	1	cup sugar
1	teaspoon grated lemon rind	1	(15-ounce) can 100% pure pumpkin
3	packages cream cheese, softened		

SOUR CREAM TOPPING:

3	tablespoons sugar	1	16-ounce carton sour cream
½	teaspoon vanilla		

Mix on medium for 2 minutes.

Mix first 4 ingredients and press mixture firmly on the bottom of a 9-inch springform pan. Bake at 350 degrees for 5 minutes, then set aside. Beat cream cheese at high speed until fluffy. Gradually add sugar, then eggs, pumpkin and vanilla. Pour mixture into crust and bake at 375 degrees for 30-35 minutes. Spread sour cream topping on top of cheesecake and bake at 500 degrees until topping melts. Remove cheesecake from oven and let cool. Chill for eight hours before cutting.

Makes one cheesecake.

ALEXANDRIA – PINEVILLE In the very center of Louisiana you'll find the neighboring cities of Alexandria and Pineville, which hosted the famous Louisiana Maneuvers during World War II. You can stay at the palatial Hotel Bentley, known as "the Biltmore on the Bayous," which Generals Eisenhower, Clark and Patton turned into officers' quarters, while they mapped out the "war games" for the World War II maneuvers. Learn all about it at the Louisiana Maneuvers & Military Museum at Camp Beauregard in Pineville. Alexandria is also home to the circa 1800 Kent House, a fine example of French Colonial architecture. Take a historical walking tour of Alexandria and Pineville, sister cities with downtown areas facing each other across the Red River.

Alexandria is home to the 22-acre Alexandria Zoological Park - 500 animals including 20 endangered species. It has an Award-winning Louisiana Habitat Exhibit.

NATCHITOCHES was established in 1714 and is the oldest permanent settlement in the Louisiana Purchase Territories. The 33-block National Historic Landmark district is a shopper's paradise and a bed & breakfast lover's dream. Take a walking tour to get a close look at the lacy ironwork of the old Creole townhouses or board a vintage-style streetcar for a guided tour of the historic district and the filming sites of the movie *Steel Magnolias*. Revisit colonial days at Fort St. Jean Baptiste State Historic Site, a five-acre compound authentically re-created for original 1733 architects renderings. At the Cane River Creole National Historical Park you'll find Oakland and Magnolia plantations, where you can learn about French Creole architecture, cotton agriculture, slavery and tenancy systems, changing technologies, and social practices spanning the settlement's almost 300 years of history.

WINNFIELD is the home of the Louisiana Political Museum and Hall of Fame. Wander among lifelike statues and an impressive array of memorabilia of colorful Louisiana politicians including Winnfield's favorite sons, Louisiana Governors Huey P. Long, Oscar K. Allen and Earl K. Long.

MANY - West of Many, the 185,000-acre Toledo Bend Reservoir boasts some of the best birding, canoeing, hunting and fishing in the country. Along the shores of the reservoir are 32 marinas that offer a variety of services and accommodations. South of Many is the 4700 acre Hodges Gardens horticultural park and wildlife refuge, known as the World Famous Garden in the Forest. With 50 seasonally changed flower beds, a trophy bass fishing lake, hiking trails, cabins, and camping, the multi-level gardens here are truly interactive, not to mention magnificent.

LEESVILLE – In Leesville, named for Confederate General Robert E. Lee, stroll up the street to the Vernon Parish Courthouse. At nearby Fort Polk, learn all about the men of the 2nd Armored Cavalry Regiment who saved the famous Lippizaner stallions. The 2nd Cavalry is the oldest continuously serving regiment in the U.S. Army and has a fascinating history.

FERRIDAY – First cousins Jerry Lee Lewis, Mickey Gilley and Jimmy Swaggart grew up in the little town of Ferriday. It's true. Come visit their stomping grounds.

CAJUN LANDING

2728 MacArthur Drive
Alexandria, LA 71303
(318) 487-4913

*Voted #1 for Seafood Dining in Alexandria by the national publication **Where America Eats**. In addition to seafood, Cajun Landing also serves USDA choice steaks, chicken, catfish and burgers plus some of the best desserts in town. Cajun Landing is open 7 days a week for lunch and dinner.*

Lonnie & Sandy Lee McDonald, Owners

Chef Roy

CAJUN RICE MIX

1 pound hamburger meat	2½ ounces Lea & Perrin
1 pound ground pork	1 ounce Tabasco hot sauce
½ large onion, chopped	1 teaspoon Prudhomme's blackening seasoning
1 tablespoon granulated garlic	
¾ tablespoon black pepper	Cooked rice
1 tablespoon beef base	Chopped green onions for garnish

Sauté onions and add hamburger meat and pork to brown (thoroughly cook). Add garlic, black pepper, beef base, Lea & Perrin, Tabasco sauce and blackening seasoning. Mix with cooked rice thoroughly. Garnish with green onions. Serve warm.

Serves 4-6.

POTATO, LEEK AND ONION SOUP

5 tablespoons olive oil	1 large white onion, chopped
3 large leeks (white and pale green parts only) sliced	4 (14½-ounce) cans vegetable broth
1½ pounds potatoes, peeled and diced	3 large garlic cloves, chopped
	½ cup fresh chopped green onions

Heat olive oil in heavy large pot over medium-low heat. Add leeks, potatoes and onions. Sauté until onion is tender, stirring occasionally, about 12 minutes. Add broth and bring soup to a boil. Reduce heat to medium-low. Simmer until all vegetables are tender, about 20 minutes. Working in batches, puree 5 cups of soup in a blender. Return puree to soup in the pot. Season with salt and pepper.

Serves 6 to 8.

GARLIC BEURRE BLANC SAUCE

1½ cup chopped white ends (split) of green onions.	1½ cup white wine
	1 cup white vinegar
2 tablespoons chopped garlic	1 cup heavy cream
	2 # unsalted butter

Mix the onions, garlic, wine and vinegar and heat. Reduce but do not let onions and garlic brown) Add a pinch of pepper. Then add a cup of heavy cream. Add 2 pounds of unsalted butter, gradually. Bring to almost boil, then turn off. Pour through strainer.

Cajun Landing

CYPRESS BEND GOLF RESORT AND CONFERENCE CENTER

2000 Cypress Bend Parkway
Many, LA 71449
(877) 519-1500

Cypress Bend Golf Resort and Conference Center is located on Toledo Bend Lake, which rest along the borders of Louisiana and Texas. The lake is the fifth largest man-made reservoir in the United States with 186,000 acres of water and 1,200 miles of shoreline. Nestled in a forest of oak and pine trees, this resort will prove to be a tranquil refuge. You can sit awhile and admire azaleas, camellias, daylilies, all artfully designed into a breathtaking showcase of acres and acres of greenery and color. Sitting very comfortable on the banks of Toledo Bend Lake is some of the most beautiful landscaping you will ever see. Add into this an 18-hole championship golf course which is a charter member of the Louisiana Audubon Golf Trail and you've found the perfect spot for a meeting to convene. If golfing is not your game, enjoy fishing Toledo Bend Lake. Toledo Bend Lake is among the finest in fishing for bass, crappie and white perch.

Cypress Bend offers the perfect setting for meetings up to 350 people. With all of the amenities and technology you need to conduct successful meetings, seminars or executive retreats, we offer a refreshing atmosphere for conference and private business functions.

From bountiful American breakfast and theme luncheons buffets to gourmet Chef's Choice specials and fine dining in the evening, the Cypress Bend dining room will satisfy your every culinary craving in every way. Complete relaxation can be found at the Cypress Bend Spa and Gift Shoppe. Massage, facials and body wraps are available.

James McElroy, Executive Chef

A graduate of the Art Institute of Houston, James continued his training at the Culinary Institute of American at Greystone in St. Helena, CA. A veteran of the private club empire of ClubCorp., he was nominated as "Regional Chef of the Year" and Rising Star of the Year" for his work at the Willow Creek Country Club, the Deerwood Club and the Greenspoint Club in the Houston area. Specializing in fine dining, James has been awarded three bronze medals by the American Culinary Federation at competitions in Austin, TX, Indianapolis, IN and Orlando, FL. Presently employed as Executive Chef of Cypress Bend Golf Resort and Conference Center, James has brought to the resort a true fine dining experience for all guests.

Joel Aversing, Sous Chef

Joel has spent nearly a decade as a culinary professional. Fine dining establishments such as the Gourmet House in Rock Island, Illinois are among Joe's fine dining accomplishments. Joel trained under Chef Rupert Allerd while in Illinois. Noted for "evening out" beer dinners, Joel worked at the Blue Cat Brew Pub of Rock Island, Illinois. This upscale pub specialized in beer dinners that were designed to illustrate the marriage of fine cuisine and beer. Presently employed at Cypress Bend Golf Resort and Conference Center, Joel brings a repertoire of dishes that keep you hungry for more.

Continued Page 147

RED FISH PONTCHARTRAIN

1	redfish (any other fish can be substituted)	½	teaspoon garlic
		2	dashes Louisiana hot sauce
4	large sliced mushrooms	3	tablespoons Prudhomme's Redfish Blackening Spice
2	tablespoons crabmeat		
3	tablespoons fresh crawfish tails	½	tablespoon butter

FOR HOLLANDAISE:

2	large egg yolks		Salt and fresh cracked pepper to taste
1	teaspoon fresh lemon juice		
1	dash Louisiana Hot Sauce	¼	pound unsalted butter (melted)
2	teaspoons water		

In hot cast iron skillet blacken fish with blackening spice. Sauté crabmeat, crawfish, mushrooms garlic and hot sauce together, let simmer.

For Hollandaise: In a stainless steel bowl set over a pot of simmering water (do not let bowl touch the water), whisk yolks with the lemon juice, hot sauce and water until slightly yellow in color. Season with salt and pepper. Remove bowl from pot, and while whisking, add the melted butter, 1 tablespoon at a time, until it is full incorporated. The add the sautéed ingredients with the Hollandaise and simmer for about 30 seconds, giving time for the different flavors to melt together. Serve over the cooked fish. It can be garnished with sliced lemon and or fried leeks.

One serving.

ROASTED CORN AND POBLANO CHOWDER

1	onion (diced)	2	quarts heavy cream
4	poblano peppers	2½	cups milk
3	cups diced celery	½	tablespoon black pepper
5	cups whole kernel corn		
2	cups diced russet potatoes (cooked)	1	tablespoon garlic Tony Chachere's seasoning to taste
3	dashes Louisiana hot sauce	½	cup chicken stock

To roast the corn: Place corn on well-sprayed baking sheet. Cook at 350 degrees for 20 minutes, rotate and stir corn every ten minutes. Set aside.

To roast poblanos: Place pepper on the hottest part of the grill. Leave peppers on grill until all sides are relatively charred. Then place peppers in a container and tightly seal. Let pepper sit for about ten minutes then peel off the charred skin, seed and de-stem them. Set aside.

Take all diced vegetables and simmer with garlic, hot sauce and chicken stock. Once all the vegetables are soft, add the cream and milk. Bring to boil then simmer until chowder thickens. Add Tony's to taste with ½ tablespoon black pepper.

LASYONE'S MEAT PIE KITCHEN & RESTAURANT

622 Second Street
Natchitoches, LA 71457
(318) 352-3353

The Lasyone Family
James, Joann, Angela & Tina

Lasyone's Meat Pie Restaurant is the place to go for an authentic Creole/Cajun cuisine experience. A favorite with the locals and travelers alike, this family-owned and operated restaurant, famous for their meat pies, lets you feel like a real Louisiana native the moment you walk through the door and take in the aroma of good, down-home cooking! Lasyone's Meat Pie has been recognized and raved about by a score of magazines including **Southern Living, The New Yorker, Glamour Magazine** *and* **Gourmet Magazine***. It has also made its way on the national airwaves being featured by On the Road with Charles Kuralt and* **Good Morning America** *with Bryant Gumble.*

CRAWFISH ÉTOUFFÉE

3	cans chicken broth	1	teaspoon Accent
1	medium bell pepper, chopped	3	pods garlic, chopped
2	medium onions, chopped		Salt & pepper to taste
3	ribs celery, chopped	¼	teaspoon sweet basil
1	can cream of mushroom soup	¼	teaspoon poultry seasoning
1	medium can tomato sauce	1	teaspoon Worcestershire sauce
½	can water		
2	heaping tablespoons of plain flour (for roux)	1	teaspoon lemon juice
	Enough vegetable oil to make roux	1	pound crawfish tails (thawed)
1	tablespoon parsley flakes	½	cup green onion tops, chopped

Mix flour and oil together to make paste (roux). Put over medium heat and stir constantly until roux is brown. Do not burn. In a heavy Dutch oven, add all ingredients except crawfish and green onions. Let this cook until vegetables are tender. Add roux and let cook for 30 minutes over medium heat. Add crawfish and green onions and cook for 10 minutes longer. Do not over cook after adding crawfish. Serve over hot bed of rice.

Serves 4.

LASYONE'S RED BEANS & SAUSAGE

1	pound dry red kidney beans (picked & washed)	1	medium bell pepper, chopped
½	cup vegetable oil or bacon drippings	2	ribs of celery, chopped
½	cup dry parsley flakes	2	tablespoons sugar
10	cups water	¼	teaspoon red pepper
1	teaspoon Accent	1	cup chopped smoked sausage
2	teaspoons salt	1	teaspoon granulated garlic

In a 4-quart pot, combine all of the above ingredients except the smoked sausage. Add smoke sausage the last 30 minutes of cooking time. Cook approximately 2 hours or until beans are tender, on medium fire, uncovered. More water may be added as needed. Serve over fluffy, white rice. For additional sausage, cut smoked sausage in links and pan fry. Place on top of red beans and rice to serve.

Serves 6.

LEA'S

Highway 71
Lecompte, LA 71346
(318) 776-5178

Ann Johnson, owner

Established in 1928, Lea's has been a traditional place to stop not only for Louisiana residents, but for visitors from all over the world. Lea's restaurant is famous for its pies and Southern country cooking. Over 65,000 pies are baked annually! The pies are so famous that the Louisiana Legislature named the town of Lecompte, the Pie Capital of Louisiana because of Lea's. Lecompte has a pie festival every October with thousands of people attending. Lea Johnson was on the Johnny Carson Show when he was ninety-five years old because of a customer writing an article about his restaurant in the New Orleans paper. Lea's is in the Louisiana Restaurant Hall of Fame.

CORN SALAD

1	large red bell pepper, diced	¼	cup sugar
2	ribs of celery, diced	1	cup of sweet pickle relish
1	medium yellow onion, diced	4	cups of corn (frozen or canned)
2	whole peeled tomatoes, diced		Salt & pepper to taste

Mix all ingredients together and toss with salad dressing. Refrigerate for 3 hours or overnight. Serve cold.

NEW POTATOES WITH CREAM SAUCE

3 or 4	pounds of new red potatoes – quartered – not peeled	3	tablespoons cornstarch
1	stick butter		Salt & pepper to taste

Put potatoes in a large pot, and cover with lightly salted water. Cook until tender (about 5 minutes). Do not overcook. Drain off half the water. Cut up butter over hot potatoes. When melted, add evaporated milk. Make a paste with the cornstarch and a small amount of hot water. Add to potatoes to make a thick sauce. Add more salt if needed and black pepper to taste.

SWEET POTATO PIE

2	tablespoons softened butter	1½	cups cooked mashed sweet potatoes
¾	cup light brown sugar	½	teaspoon salt
3	large eggs	½	teaspoon nutmeg
1	cup evaporated milk	¼	teaspoon cloves
		¼	teaspoon cinnamon

Cream butter and sugar together. Add eggs. Add salt and spices. Add evaporated milk and mashed sweet potatoes. Bake at 425 degrees in a nine-inch unbaked pie shell until firm. This pie is good with toasted, chopped pecans on top or with whipped cream.

Established 1928
...A Louisiana Landmark and Tradition

LEESVILLE CAFÉ

114 South Third Street
Leesville, Louisiana 71446
(337) 392-2651

Dick Anna Bagents & Richard Bagents, Owners

The Leesville Café is located in the heart of the historic district and has been opened and closed many, many times over the years. The building was recently remodeled and the Bagents decided to try their hands in the restaurant business and opened the café in January, 2002. Although relatively new, the business has more than doubled since opening day.

POOR MAN'S FILET

2	pounds ground chuck
¼	cup minced green onion
¼	cup minced yellow onion
1	clove minced garlic
2	tablespoons Worcestershire sauce
	Dash of hot sauce
1	tablespoon chopped fresh flat leaf parsley
1	large egg (beaten)
1½	teaspoons salt
½	teaspoon black pepper
	Dash of red pepper
	Dash of white pepper
	4 to 8 slices uncooked bacon

Combine all ingredients except the bacon in a large bowl. When well combined, shape into 4 round burgers. Wrap 1 or 2 slices of bacon around each burger, securing with toothpicks. Grill or bake the burgers until fully cooked.

In a separate sauce pan, heat 1 cup of meat drippings (or beef stock) with ¾ cup butter and 2 tablespoons Worcestershire sauce and a dash of hot sauce. Remove toothpicks, cover burgers with sauce and serve.

4 servings.

CAFÉ CLASSIC CHICKEN SALAD

6	whole chicken breasts
1	whole yellow onion
2	stalks celery
1 to 1½	teaspoons salt
1	teaspoon white pepper
1	cup celery, finely chopped
½	cup green onions, finely chopped
⅓	cup yellow onions, finely chopped
¾	cup to 1 cup mayonnaise
¼	cup Dijon mustard
¼	cup chopped fresh flat leaf parsley
	Iceberg, red, green leaf lettuces (shredded)
	Fresh fruit such as seedless grapes, strawberries or apples

Place chicken breasts, whole onion and stalks of celery in pot and cover with water. Boil chicken until tender. Remove chicken and refrigerate until cool. Reserve stock for another use. When chicken has cooled, remove skin and bones. Chop breast meat into a large dice. Combine the chicken, celery, green onions, yellow onion, flat leaf parsley, mayonnaise, mustard, salt and white pepper. Mix well and chill before serving.

To serve, place whole leaves of green leaf lettuce on chilled plates. Top this with a combination of shredded lettuces. Mound one cup of chicken salad onto lettuce beds. Garnish with fresh fruit such as seedless green grapes, strawberries, etc.

Makes 6 entrée servings.

SLOW ROASTED BRISKET

1	(7- to 10-pound) brisket (well trimmed)
1	envelope Knorr onion soup mix
	Ground black, red and white peppers
	Texjoy steak seasoning

Wash and dry brisket. Generously season brisket with onion soup mix, ground black, red and white peppers and Texjoy steak seasoning. Place brisket in baking pan, cover with heavy-duty aluminum foil and marinate in the refrigerator for two days. Remove from the refrigerator and place the brisket in a 300-degree preheated oven for 30 minutes. Lower oven temperature to 250 degrees and bake for 5 to 6 hours. Pan drippings/juices combined with cooked rice complete this entrée.

6 to 10 servings.

MARINER'S SEAFOOD & STEAK HOUSE

On Beautiful Sibley Lake, Highway One Bypass

Post Office Box 2479
Natchitoches, LA 71458-2479
(318) 357-1220

When you visit Natchitoches, the flavor of Louisiana is only moments away at Mariner's Restaurant. This family-owned restaurant specializes in Cajun/Creole, fresh seafood and heavy aged beef. This restaurant is only minutes from downtown Natchitoches.

**Don and Jennifer Nichols,
Owners & Operators**

SEAFOOD GUMBO

7	ounces vegetable oil	1	teaspoon cayenne pepper (to taste)
1	cup flour	½	cup fresh parsley, chopped
1	bell pepper, chopped	½	cup green onions, chopped, tops & bottoms
1	large onion, chopped		
1	celery rib, chopped	1	pound lump crabmeat
2	quarts seafood stock	1	pound shrimp, already cooked, peeled and deveined
1	tablespoon salt (to taste)		
1	teaspoon black pepper (to taste)	1	pound crawfish tails, cooked

Cook flour and oil to a dark roux, but do not burn. Add chopped veggies (excluding parsley and green onions), to stop browning. Cook 10 minutes, stirring constantly. Add stock and seasonings. Bring to rolling boil, then reduce heat. Simmer for 1 hour. Add parsley and green onions and continue to cook for 4 more minutes. Add cooked crabmeat, shrimp and crawfish tails, bring almost to a boil, remove from heat and serve with steamed rice. This recipe will yield approximately 1 gallon of gumbo and you will need approximately 2 quarts of steamed, white rice to accompany the gumbo.

Should be enough for 8 – 10 people. Enjoy!

ANITA JONES
Provencal, LA

NATCHITOCHES STYLE MEAT PIES

2	tablespoons flour	6	green onions, chopped
1	tablespoon shortening	3	teaspoons chopped parsley
½	pound ground beef		Hot pepper sauce to taste
1½	pounds ground pork		
2	large onions, chopped		Salt & pepper to taste

Brown flour in shortening. Add other ingredients, salt & pepper. Cook thoroughly. Let cool completely. Overnight is best.

PASTRY:

6	cups flour	½	cup shortening
2	teaspoons baking powder	2	eggs
2	teaspoons salt		Milk (enough to moisten)

Sift flour, baking powder and salt. Cut in shortening; then add eggs. Add enough milk to make a stiff dough. Roll out very thin. Use a saucer to cut circles in dough. Dampen the edges of the circle with water. Fill the circle half full with cooked meat mixture. Fold dough over and crimp edges with a fork. Fry in deep fat until golden or bake in oven. May be frozen on a cookie sheet with each layer of pies separated by wax paper. Once frozen, the pies can be put in a zip-lock bag and eaten as needed. Pies may be made smaller by using something for a smaller circle.

Makes 18 large pies.

THE MAGNOLIA ROOM THE BAILEY HOTEL

200 West Magnolia
Bunkie, LA 71322
1-866-346-7111
www.baileyhotel.com

Mr. & Mrs. Thomas T. McNabb, Jr.
Becki L. Martin, Executive Chef

From the onset of the 2001 renovation of the Bailey Hotel, closed for nearly a half century, the Magnolia Room restaurant was the vanguard of the group spearheading the return to prominence by the hotel. Chef Becki was hired as lead chef to run the restaurant operation because of her vast culinary reputation with other restaurant/hotel groups. She has won numerous awards both nationally and internationally throughout the years and has demonstrated her expertise in catering to large functions including weddings, receptions and special events.

TOMATO & GOAT CHEESE SALAD WITH BASIL/KALAMATA OLIVE VINAIGRETTE

2	bags mixed gourmet salad greens
8	ripe tomatoes (preferably Roma)
16	ounces goat cheese (fresh if available)
1	red onion, sliced
1	recipe basil/Kalamata olive vinaigrette (recipes follows)

Place lettuce mix on chilled salad plates. Layer sliced tomato, goat cheese and red onion slices. Repeat layers if desired. Top with dressing.

Serves 4.

BASIL/KALAMATA OLIVE VINAIGRETTE

4	ounces fresh basil	½	cup red wine vinegar
4 to 5	cloves fresh garlic	1	teaspoon salt
¾	cup pitted Kalamata olives	½	teaspoon black pepper
1	cup extra virgin olive oil		

Combine all ingredients in a food processor or blender until smooth.

THE VERY BEST SEAFOOD GUMBO

Note: This recipe requires 2 days preparation time but is well worth the extra effort.

DAY 1:
Prepare stock and obtain fat for roux.

1	Long Island duckling, washed	2	cups water
	Salt and pepper to taste	1	large onion
	Granulated garlic to taste	4 to 5	stalks celery
			Several bay leaves
		4 to 5	whole carrots.

Preheat oven to 350 degrees. Season duckling with salt, pepper and granulated garlic. Place in roasting pan. Place cut up onion and other vegetables along with bay leaves inside duck cavity and around duck in pan. Roast for 2 hours or until skin is golden brown and crispy. Cool completely. De-bone duck (reserving meat for other uses). Place skin, bones and pan drippings in a large stock pot adding enough water to measure approximately 4 quarts. Simmer for 1 hour. Strain stock and discard bones and skin. Refrigerate liquid overnight.

DAY 2
Proceed with seafood gumbo:

4	onions diced	3	cloves garlic, chopped
1	stalk celery chopped	¼	cup butter or vegetable oil.
1½	cups chopped okra (may use frozen)		

Heat oil in large Dutch oven over medium heat, add vegetables and sauté until okra no longer ropes and color darkens. Frozen okra will not be as prone to roping as fresh. Set aside.

Continued Page 153

Prepare roux: Skim fat from duck stock. Add enough butter to duck fat to measure 2 cups. Heat fat in a large Dutch oven or heavy stockpot until it no longer sizzles (very hot). Rapidly whisk in 2 cups plain flour. You will need to work this flour in small amounts but work very quickly. (This is very hot and adheres to skin if splattered, so use extreme caution). Stirring constantly, over medium heat, cook until roux is the color of chocolate. DO NOT BURN the roux or you will have to start over from scratch. Add vegetable mixture to roux. You will need a large pot to complete the cooking of the gumbo and should end up in the largest available container as the total quantity will be approximately 2 gallons of gumbo. *Again exercise extreme caution when handling the roux.*

Add reserved duck stock and add the following seasonings:

	Salt to taste	1	teaspoon dried oregano
¼	teaspoon ground red pepper	1	teaspoon dried basil
¼	teaspoon ground white pepper	1	teaspoon dried thyme
½	teaspoon ground black pepper	1	can of regular Rotel tomatoes
1	tablespoon granulated garlic		

Simmer for 30 minutes on low heat. Stir in 2 pounds peeled & de-veined shrimp, 2 pounds crawfish tails and 1 pound of crab claw fingers. Simmer until seafood is done (shrimp should be pink and opaque). Stir in 2 quarts of oysters with juice. Simmer until oysters are plump, 5 to 10 minutes. Serve generous portion over rice as a main course.

Serves 10 to 12.

THE BAILEY HOTEL

HOSPITALITY SINCE 1907

LOUISIANA BAR-B-QUED SHRIMP

3 pounds large or jumbo shrimp, in shells

SAUCE:

1	pound butter	2	tablespoons granulated garlic powder
2	regular beers, not light beer		
1	teaspoon cayenne pepper	½	teaspoon ground oregano
½	teaspoon white pepper	½	teaspoon ground thyme
2	tablespoons Worcestershire sauce	½	teaspoon ground basil
	Juice from 2 lemons		Salt to taste

Melt butter, add beer and remaining ingredients, except shrimp. Bring to a rolling boil and add shrimp all at once. Stir to mix well. Reduce heat and simmer for 3-4 minutes. Serve shrimp and juice in bowls with crusty French bread for dipping. Provide plenty of napkins.

Serves 6.

ROAST DUCK AND ANDOUILLE PASTA

	Meat from 1 roast duck (reserved from seafood gumbo recipe)	½	teaspoon granulated garlic
1	pound sliced mushrooms	2	cups heavy cream
½	cup chopped green onions	½	cup shredded Parmesan cheese
½	stick butter	¼	cup dry red wine
½	teaspoon Cavender's Greek Seasoning	16	ounces pasta (bow-tie preferred) cooked al dente
		1	pound Andouille sausage

Melt butter in skillet, add mushrooms and Andouille sausage. Sauté until sausage and mushrooms are both done. Add green onions and continue cooking until onions wilt. Add duck and Cavanders Greek Seasoning. De-glaze pan with wine. Add heavy cream and reduce until mixture coats a spoon. Place warm pasta in large bowl or casserole. Add sauce and toss to coat pasta. Serve immediately with Parmesan cheese to taste.

Serves 4.

THE BENTLEY HOTEL

200 Desoto Street
Alexandria, LA 71301
(318) 448-9600

Located on the banks of the Red River stands the Hotel Bentley. This magnificent structure was built in 1908 with its New-Classical design. The colossal columns, Bedford limestone and terra cotta façade give entrance from its gallery to a grand lobby. A domed ceiling with stained glass highlights the interior gray marble columns and ornately styled mosaic tile floor. All are original from 1908.

Hotel Bentley became the focal point of all social life in Central Louisiana. With the beginning of World War II, Central Louisiana became the center of a nine-state area for the training of military personnel. Hotel Bentley became the center for families and visitors of the military. Many troop commanders lived at Hotel Bentley such as George Patton, Omar Bradley and Dwight Eisenhower. Many celebrities have been guests at Hotel Bentley, such as: John Wayne, Bob Hope, Mickey Rooney and Tommy Dorsey. In fact, most of the big bands of that era played from the bandstand in the Venetian Room at Hotel Bentley. Many politicians, such as Huey and Earl Long, were frequent guests at the Hotel Bentley. The hotel is listed on the National Register of Historic Places and is currently owned by Bob G. Dean Jr. of Baton Rouge and he has again renovated and modernized the hotel, still keeping the traditional elegance and romantic ambiance.

TOURNEDO BENTLEY

5	ounces beef tenderloin	2	ounces flour
4	ounces crawfish tails	2	ounces garlic
2	ounces bell pepper	4	bay leaves
2	ounces onion	½	cup of water
2	ounces celery	½	cup heavy cream
2	ounces butter	½	spoon cayenne
		2	teaspoons paprika

FOR ÉTOUFFÉE SAUCE:

Chop pepper, onions, celery and garlic. Melt 2 ounces butter in sauté pan until light brown. Add flour and stir flour and butter until it has a blond color. Add ½ cup of water, heavy cream, bay leaves, paprika, cayenne, garlic and crawfish. Stir ingredients. Let sauce thicken and simmer for 4½ minutes.

BEEF:

Cut 5 ounces medallion in half. Flour beef medallions and season with salt and pepper. Sauté in olive oil. Cook to preferred temperature and doneness. Pour etouffe sauce over beef.

Single serving.

THE LANDING RESTAURANT

530 Front Street
Natchitoches, LA 71457
(318) 352-1579

**Owned and operated by
Kent and Liz Gresham**

The Landing Restaurant was established in 1988. The Landing Restaurant only uses the freshest ingredients, vegetables and seafood. The steaks are aged USDA Black Angus choice and cut fresh in house. All of the spice mixtures are made in their own kitchen. The restaurant is open for lunch and dinner Tuesday through Saturday and for the Sunday Champagne Brunch Buffet. Closed Monday. Banquet facilities are available for receptions, weddings, parties or any special occasion.

EASY BEEF BRISKET

1	5-pound brisket of beef	3	ounces liquid smoke
	Celery salt		Worcestershire
	Garlic salt		sauce
	Onion powder		Salt & pepper

Spinkle brisket generously with celery salt, garlic salt and onion powder. Pour bottle of liquid over brisket , cover with foil and refrigerate overnight. When ready to cook, sprinkle lightly with salt and pepper. Sprinkle lots of Worcestershire sauce after the salt and pepper. Cover and bake at 275 degrees for 6 hours.

Serves 4 to 6.

BEEF STEW CROCKPOT

2	tablespoons vegetable oil	1	bay leaf
2	pounds beef stew meat cut into one-inch cubes	3	diced uncooked potatoes
¼	cup flour	1	stalk chopped celery
½	teaspoon black pepper	1	teaspoon paprika
1	teaspoon Worcestershire sauce	2	chopped onions
		2	teaspoons Kitchen Bouquet

In a Crock-pot place vegetable oil, meat, flour, salt and pepper. Stir to coat meat. Cook on low until meat and flour browns. Add all remaining ingredients and stir until well mixed. Cover and cook on low for about 10 hours or on high for 4 to 6 hours.

Serves 4 to 6.

BAKED CHICKEN & RICE

3	cups water	1	small onion chopped
6	cups of chicken broth	½	green bell pepper chopped
1	tablespoon butter	½	cup celery chopped
1	cup uncooked rice		8 to 10 pieces chicken

In a Dutch oven, bring water to a boil. Add chicken broth. Now add the other ingredients (except chicken) in the water. Season your chicken with salt and pepper and place on top of the rice and water mixture. Cook at 350 degrees for about 1½ hours.

Serves 4 to 6.

PORK CHOPS & POTATO BAKE

6	nice-size pork chops	¼	teaspoon Tabasco hot sauce
6 to 12	red potatoes cut in ½	¼	teaspoon Worcestershire sauce
1	can cream of mushroom soup		Salt & pepper to taste
1	can whole milk		

Using a Dutch oven, season the pork chops with salt and pepper and brown on both sides. Combine the soup, milk, Tabasco sauce and Worcestershire and set aside. Cut the potatoes and place right on top of the pork chops. Then pour the soup mixture on top of everything. Bake at 400 degrees for one hour and serve.

Serves 4 to 6.

TUNK'S CYPRESS INN

9507 Hwy. 28 west
Boyce, LA 71409
(Alexandria area)

This rustic, casual dining establishment was opened in 1978. Nestled on the edge of Kisatchie National Forest, customers dine overlooking beautiful Kincaid Lake. Tunk's features "Louisiana Cuisine" specializing in fresh gulf seafood and USDA Choice Steaks. Gumbo, alligator, crawfish and catfish are specialties of the house. This unique family eatery is home-owned and operated by the family of its founder, Tunk Andries.

Jimbo, Sandy and Scotty Thiels, owners

MISS MAYME'S SEAFOOD GUMBO

1	fryer (about 3½ pounds)	5	bay leaves
2	teaspoons salt	1	tablespoons garlic powder
1	teaspoon black pepper	¼	cup Worcestershire sauce
10	quarts water	3	cans whole tomatoes (8 ounces each) chopped
3	cups vegetable oil		
4½	cups all-purpose flour	2	tablespoons seafood base
3	cups onion, chopped		
2	cups celery, chopped	5	pounds medium-sized shrimp (peeled and deveined)
1½	cups bell pepper, chopped		
1	tablespoon chopped garlic	1	pound crabmeat
½	teaspoon red pepper	1½	pounds catfish fillets
1	teaspoon ground thyme		Salt & pepper to taste

Pour 10 quarts water into large stock pot. Place fryer, salt and pepper into pot. Boil until chicken is tender. Remove the chicken from stock and cool. In black iron pot heat the oil just under the smoking point (about 350 degrees). Gradually add flour with a wire ship until all is incorporated. Stir roux constantly over medium heat until it turns a dark brown color. Be careful not to burn! Add chopped vegetables to the roux and stir about 3-4 minutes. When vegetables soften, add contents of black pot to the chicken stock. Stir well. Add seasoning ingredients (garlic, red pepper, thyme, bay leaves, garlic powder and Worcestershire sauce). Add tomatoes and tomato sauce. Bring gumbo to a boil. Skim fat as it comes to the top. Reduce heat to simmer. Cook about 1½ hours, stirring often to avoid sticking. In two separate pots, cook gumbo crabs and catfish, (each covered with water and each with 1 tablespoon seafood base) until tender. Pour the stock from each of these pots into the gumbo pot. Pick crabmeat out and break fish into small pieces. Set aside. De-bone the chicken and chop. Set aside. Continue cooking and skimming the grease that rises to the top. Add shrimp, fish, crabmeat and chicken. Cook about 15-20 minutes. Add salt and pepper to taste. Serve over hot steamed rice.

Yield: 3 gallons.

TUNK'S CRAWFISH ÉTOUFFÉE

2	sticks oleo	1½	teaspoons paprika
1	cup onion, finely chopped	½	teaspoon minced garlic
½	cup celery, finely chopped	1	tablespoon Creole seasoning
½	cup bell pepper, finely chopped	¾	cup crawfish juice (add ¾ cup water to bag of crawfish tails to make juice)
1	can (10-ounce) Rotel tomatoes and green chilies (drain juice)		
2	cans cream of mushroom soup	¼	teaspoon Tabasco hot sauce
		1	pound crawfish tails, peeled

Sauté onion, celery and bell pepper in oleo about 10 minutes until just tender. Blend Rotel tomatoes and cream of mushroom soup in food processor. Add to onion mixture. Add remaining ingredients. Cook over medium heat about 20 minutes. Serve over steamed rice.

Makes 6 servings.

Continued Page 157

SNAPPER PONTCHARTRAIN

4 to 8-ounce red snapper fillets	¼	pound cooked lump crabmeat
4	tablespoons melted butter	¼	pound cooked, peeled crawfish tails
2	teaspoons Creole seasoning	4	tablespoons green onion tops, chopped
¼	pound cooked, peeled shrimp		

CHEESE SAUCE:

¼	pound (1 stick) butter	2	cups half & half cream
¼	cup flour	8	ounces Velveeta pasteurized cheese

On a buttered baking pan, place fish fillets skin side down. Brush with melted butter and sprinkle lightly with Creole seasoning. Bake in preheated 350-degree oven about 20 minutes until just done. While fish is baking, make cheese sauce. Melt butter in heavy saucepan over medium heat. Add flour, whisking until smooth. Cook about 4 minutes stirring constantly. Do not brown – remove from heat. Add half & half cream, whisking until smooth. Return saucepan to fire; cook until sauce thickens. Slowly add cheese. Blend until smooth - remove from heat. Add shrimp, crabmeat and crawfish tails to cheese sauce. Stir to mix. When fish is done, place on serving plates. Cover with warm seafood cheese sauce. Garnish with green onions. Serve immediately.

Makes 4 servings.

FRESH BERRY PIE

1	9" deep dish pie shell, baked		Fresh fruit such as:
1	can sweetened condensed milk	2	pounds strawberries, hulled OR
⅓	cup lemon juice	2	pints blueberries OR
1	8-ounce cream cheese, softened	2	pints blackberries
1	8-ounce tub Cool Whip topping		

Cream cheese in mixer until smooth. In separate bowl, mix condensed milk and lemon juice. Add to cream cheese. Beat until smooth. Add Cool Whip. In large bowl, fold in berries. Spoon into pie crust. Refrigerate.

Makes 1 pie.

9507 Hwy. 28 West
Boyce, LA 71409

SHREVEPORT – BOSSIER CITY The Red River separates Shreveport and Bossier City. This region is brimming with big-city excitement. The neon lights and fiber optics that turn the Texas Street Bridge into a fabulous urban sculpture are but a taste of the razzle-dazzle you'll find in the Shreveport – Bossier City area. It is the state's premier destination for gaming and horseracing. Besides the glitz and glitter of casino action there are other pleasures that await you. The American Rose Center, for example, features North America's largest rose garden with 118 acres of blooming beauty. The Center is headquarters for the American Rose Society. More than 20,000 roses are spectacularly planted in 60 individual gardens.

Savor fine dining and fabulous shopping on Shreveport's Line Avenue, or explore the antique galleries in the stately Fairfield Highland Historic District. Enjoy an evening of culture at the renowned Shreveport Symphony, or see what's playing at the ornate Strand Theatre, built in 1925. The Shreveport Symphony Orchestra is the oldest continuously performing orchestra in Louisiana. If you love classic cars, put the Ark-La-Tex Antique and Classic Vehicle Museum on your list. The Sports Museum of Champions is located on downtown Shreveport's riverfront. It features memorabilia of area athletes who have won national, international and world championships. Among those featured are Terry Bradshaw, Hal Sutton and Freddie Spencer.

If you're interested in the fine arts, the Southwest's largest collection of paintings and sculptures – including works by celebrated artists such as Frederic Remington and Charles M. Russell—can be explored at the R.W. Norton Art Gallery, located in a 40-acre landscaped park. The Louisiana State Exhibit Museum, housed in a unique neo-classical building, displays exhibits on the history and development of Louisiana including Native American artifacts, frescoes by famous muralist Conrad Albrizio, and more. Housed in an 1865 bank building, the Spring Street Museum features exhibits that will give you a glimpse of the dramatic 19th century history of Northwest Louisiana.

The Walter B. Jacobs Memorial Nature Park is dedicated to the preservation and study of nature, the park has interpretive exhibits, hiking trails and a designated picnic area.

Barksdale Air Force Base is located in Bossier City. At the Eighth Air Force Museum more than a dozen vintage aircraft can be examined. Displays here trace the noble history of both the Eighth Air Force and the Second Bomb Wing, which are stationed at Barksdale Air Force Base. Louisiana Downs is also located in Bossier City. The Sci-Port Discovery Center is located in Shreveport. The new 67,000 sq. ft. Center features 200+ hands-on experiences, 8 interactive discovery areas & IMAX Dome Theater.

MINDEN Superb hunting and fishing in Lake Bistineau, Caney lakes and Kisatchie Forest. Visit Minden's antebellum homes, Germantown Colony Museum and Dorcheat Historical Museum. Minden claims that its greatest asset is its warm and friendly people! Minden is located in Webster parish.

RUSTON The Louisiana Peach Festival is held here in early summer every year. At eclectic Follette Pottery, each piece comes complete with a catch recipe for such treats as "Whatever You Can Catch Crossing The Road Pie." Follette Pottery is the oldest pottery shop in Louisiana. Ruston is also home to Louisiana Tech University. The Ruston area is also perfect for lovers of the great outdoors. Record-breaking bass have been hauled in from the area's lakes. Grambling State University is also located in Lincoln parish.

MONROE – WEST MONROE The Quachita River separates the twin cities of Monroe and West Monroe. Monroe and West Monroe celebrate the Louisiana Folklife Festival every September. Explore the restaurants, boutique and specialty shops in the Historic Garden District Marketplace. West Monroe has famous Antique Alley where shoppers can peruse through treasures and collectibles such as stained glass, rare jade and ivory. Monroe is home to the Biedenharn Museum and Gardens. The Biedenharn home was the residence of the first bottler of *Coca-Cola*. Monroe is also home to The Louisiana

Purchase Gardens and Zoo. With 82 acres of landscaped gardens, arched bridges over meandering bayous and open grazing fields, one of the best animal collections available anywhere can be viewed by train or by boat. Big cats can be viewed from the 2000 foot elevated Catwalk. The Masur Museum of Art features a permanent art collection by acclaimed national and regional artists as well as special traveling exhibitions. The University of Louisiana at Monroe's Museum of Natural History has exhibits of mineral specimens from around the world as well as a variety of fossils including dinosaurs and Indian artifacts. Both Monroe and West Monroe are located in Quachita parish. The Monroe Civic Center schedules year round entertainment in the Arena. The West Monroe Convention center schedules year round events which include the West Monroe Gun & Knife Show, Northeast Antique Show & Sale, banquets, auctions and much more.

BASTROP is located in Morehouse parish. The Bastrop Main Street Program brings together the arts and historic sites. The restored court house serves as a centerpiece for the Main Street Program. The Snyder Museum houses historical Morehouse artifacts.

LAKE PROVIDENCE is located in Madison parish. It is home to the Louisiana Cotton Museum. This museum exhibits the history of cotton in the South. The exhibit includes a farmhouse, cabin, commissary, church, cotton field and gin. It also has an exhibit of music and instruments of the Delta Blues.

BERNICE is located in Union Parish. The Bernice Depot Museum features a restored 1899 railroad depot, a 1938 kid's caboose and park as well as articles and exhibits relating to the old railroad, the early town and parish. Lake D'Arbonne is located nearby in Farmerville. It is one of the finest fishing lakes in North Louisiana.

WINNSBORO is in Franklin parish. It is the home of the Franklin Parish Catfish Festival, Deep South Rodeo and Princess Theatre. The Catfish Festival is one of the largest festivals in the state. It is held in April each year.

SARAH ANDERSON HULL
Franklin Parish

Sarah Anderson Hull, a Franklin Parish native, is the owner/chef of The Deliberate Literate Bookstore and Café in Memphis, Tennessee. She developed the catfish and crawfish dish in recognition of the catfish industry and Catfish Festival in Franklin Parish. Sarah maintains ties to the parish with family and friends. The Catfish Festival is held the second Saturday in April each year.

SARAH'S PARTY RICE

1	stick butter	3	teaspoons chicken base (or 3 bouillon cubes)
1	cup long grain white rice	1	teaspoon vinegar
1	small onion, chopped	1	teaspoon salt
1	small bell pepper, chopped	1	small jar pimentos, drained
2	cups water		

Melt the butter in a skillet over low heat. Add chopped onion and bell pepper and cook until nearly transparent. Stir in the rice and sauté until well coated. Add the water and stir in bouillon cubes, vinegar and salt. Cook until cube dissolved. Add pimentos and mushrooms. Turn into a 1½ to 2 quart casserole dish. Cover and bake at 350 degrees for 45 minutes.

HULL HOUSE CATFISH WITH CRAWFISH SAUCE

4	catfish fillets		Juice ½ lemon
½	cup olive oil	⅛	teaspoon cayenne

Rinse catfish in bowl of water with a little lemon juice. Pat dry with paper towels. Marinate the catfish in the olive oil, lemon juice and cayenne pepper for at least 30 minutes before cooking.

CRAWFISH SAUCE

½	stick butter	1	tablespoon canned artichoke hearts, chopped
1	tablespoon green onions, chopped		
1	cup cream (half & half or whipping cream)	1	tablespoon chopped fresh parsley
2	tablespoons sherry	1	teaspoon capers

1	tablespoon pine nuts, toasted		Salt
1	cup crawfish tails, raw		Red pepper
3	tablespoons grated Asiago cheese (Fresh grated Parmesan can be substituted)	1	tablespoon chopped parsley for garnish

In a skillet, melt butter and add onions and cook until tender, 2 or 3 minutes. Add cream and sherry and cook over low heat until reduced by ⅓. Add remaining ingredients and cook until crawfish is done. Season with salt and red pepper to taste. Grill catfish (Sarah uses an electric smokeless grill in the kitchen). Place fillet on a plate and spoon sauce over the top. Garnish with remaining parsley and serve.

EGGPLANT CASSEROLE

1 or 2	small eggplants	1	tablespoon lemon juice
1	stick butter		Salt
1	small bunch green onions, sliced thinly, including tops		Red pepper
¼	cup chopped parsley		Soft breadcrumbs
1	cup shrimp, peeled and deveined (or ½ cup shrimp and ½ cup lump crabmeat)		Grated Asiago or Parmesan cheese

Split the eggplant in half lengthwise and place in a glass or stainless steel pan, add ½ inch water in pan. Bake at 350 degrees for about 30 minutes or until soft when squeezed. Let cool slightly and scrape pulp into a colander and drain. Chop the eggplant and set aside. While the eggplant is draining, melt the butter in a skillet. Add green onions and cook until tender. Add the eggplant and stir until hot and bubbly. Add parsley, shrimp and lemon juice. Add salt and red pepper flakes to taste. When the shrimp starts to turn pink, turn into individual casseroles. Top with breadcrumbs and cheese. Bake at 350 degrees until hot and bubbly.

Serves 3-4, depending on the size of the ramekins.

Note: Dish can be prepared omitting the breadcrumb /cheese mixture when ready to bake.

Continued Page 162

Quick Cherry Cake

1	egg	1	teaspoon cinnamon
1	cup sugar	1	(#303) can drained
⅓	cup oil		tart pie cherries*
1	teaspoon vanilla	½	cup chopped nuts
1	cup flour		
1	teaspoon soda		*Reserve 2 tablespoons
½	teaspoon salt		juice for glaze

Beat egg and add sugar slowly while beating. Add oil and vanilla. Add flour sifted with soda, salt and cinnamon. Mix well and fold in cherries and nuts. Pour into greased and floured pan (about 8"x12"x2"). Bake at 325 degrees for about 45 minutes.

GLAZE:

¾	cup powdered sugar	2	tablespoon reserved cherry juice
2	tablespoon butter, softened		

Blend well and pour over cake as soon as it comes from the oven. Sprinkle with nuts, if desired. This is quick and easy to prepare and can be used as a coffee cake or warm with ice cream as a dessert.

Slayden's Bar-B-Q

1401 N. Washington
Bastrop, LA 71220

Johnye Armistead, Owner

Slayden's Bar-B-Q celebrates its 40th anniversary this year. Established by Dan and Helen Slayden in 1962. The menu is simple and distinctive. Everything is homemade with top quality products. Our bar-b-que is original and unusual. Our beans and potato salad and pies are made from scratch. We take pride in being the oldest established family-owned restaurant in Morehouse Parish.

Slayden's Coconut Cream Pie

16	ounces milk	3	tablespoons cornstarch
3	egg yolks	1	10-inch pie shell, baked.
¼	cup butter		
⅓	cup sugar		
¾	cup coconut		

Heat milk. Beat egg yolks, sugar, vanilla and cornstarch. Add hot milk and butter and cook until thick. Add coconut and pour into pie shell. Beat the 3 egg whites until foamy. Add 5 tablespoons of sugar, pinch of salt, ¼ teaspoon cream of tartar and 1 teaspoon cornstarch. Continue to beat until stiff. Spread the meringue over the pie and bake until brown.

JAY & DEBBIE KAY'S RESTAURANT

8334 Highway 171
Grand Cane, LA 71032
(318) 933-8604

Mailing Address is:

724 Frank Burford Rd.
Keatchie, LA 71046

Jay & Debbie Burford, Owners

Jay and Debbie Kay's restaurant has been serving some of the best home-style cooking since November, 1995. The restaurant is located in historic Grand Cane in Desoto Parish. They boast that they have the best fried catfish in Louisiana! Customers are greeted each morning with the smell of Jay's fresh baked bread. The restaurant is also famous for their savory prime rib and Cajun gumbos and ettouffee.

PECAN PIE

1	cup dark Karo syrup		Pinch salt
½	cup sugar	1	teaspoon vanilla
3	eggs	1	cup chopped pecans
1	tablespoon margarine		

Heat syrup and margarine together over medium heat until margarine melts. Stir sugar and eggs together in bowl. Stir in salt. When margarine has melted, add syrup mixture to bowl. Stir in pecans and vanilla. Pour into unbaked pie shell. Place in preheated 400-degree oven for 10 minutes; then turn oven temperature down to 300 degrees for 45 minutes.

Makes one pie.

LEMON MERINGUE PIE

1½	cups sugar	3	tablespoons margarine
⅓	cup plus 1 tablespoon cornstarch	½	cup lemon juice
1½	cups water	2	drops yellow food color
3	egg yolks, slightly beaten		

Bake pie shell. Cool. Heat oven to 400 degrees. Mix sugar and cornstarch in a medium sauce pan. Gradually stir in water. Cook over medium heat, stirring constantly, until the mixture thickens and boils. Boil and stir for 1 minutes. Gradually stir at least half the hot mixture into the egg yolks; blend into the hot mixture in the saucepan. Boil and stir for 1 minute. Remove from heat and stir in margarine, lemon juice and food color. Immediately pour into pie shell. Heap the meringue onto the hot pie filling and spread over the filling carefully sealing the meringue to the edge of the crust to prevent shrinking or weeping. Bake about 10 minutes or until a golden brown.

PIE MERINGUE:

3	egg whites	6	tablespoons sugar
¼	teaspoon cream of tartar	½	teaspoon vanilla

Beat egg whites and cream of tartar until foamy. Beat in sugar, 1 tablespoon at a time and continue beating until stiff and glossy. Do not under beat! Beat in vanilla.

Makes one pie.

MS LUCY'S CLASSIC CAJUN – CULTURE & COOKING

17362 Zaunbrecher Road
Jones, LA 71250
(318) 823-2842

Lucy Henry Zaunbrecher, Chef & Author

*Born in the southwest Louisiana town of Gueydan, Lucy grew up on her parent's rice farm. At a young age, her mother, Mary Eloise Richard Henry, taught Lucy how to use the rice, poultry, beef, pork, vegetables and seafood indigenous to Louisiana to create simple, yet delicious, Cajun meals. In an effort to preserve her family's great recipes, Lucy compiled a cookbook called **Classic Cajun Culture and Cooking** in 1994. Her friends encouraged Lucy to start selling her cookbook on local television and result was her half-hour cooking show, **Ms. Lucy's Classic Cajun Culture and Cooking**. After two years on commercial TV, Lucy joined the Louisiana Public Broadcasting family of great cooks. The program was syndicated through the National Educational Telecommunications Association (NETA) to public television stations around the country. The following recipes are from her cookbook.*

SHRIMP CASSEROLE

1	pound peeled shrimp	1	10¾ ounce can cream of mushroom soup
¼	cup margarine		
½	cup chopped onion	½	10¾ ounce can Cheddar cheese soup
½	cup chopped green pepper		
½	cup chopped celery	2½	cups cooked long grain rice
¼	cup margarine		
		½	cup green onions

Sauté shrimp in margarine. Sauté onion, green pepper and celery in margarine. Add cream of mushroom soup, Cheddar cheese soup and shrimp. Mix. Add rice and green onions. Mix thoroughly. Pour into 9x13 inch casserole pan that has been sprayed with PAM vegetable spray. Bake at 350 degrees for 30-40 minutes.

Serves 8.

Note: ½ pound of smoked sausage, sliced thin may be added to casserole before baking. Serve hot.

CRABMEAT AU GRATIN

⅔	cup onion, chopped		Salt & pepper to taste
¼	cup bell pepper, chopped	3	cups lump crabmeat
½	cup butter or margarine	¼	cup parsley, chopped or minced
3	tablespoons of flour	½	cup grated cheese
1	small can evaporated milk	2	tablespoons paprika

Sauté onion and bell pepper, in margarine or butter. Slowly stir in flour, stirring constantly. Slowly stir in evaporated milk, stirring constantly. Add salt and pepper to taste, crab meat and parsley. Pour into individual foil crab shells or a casserole dish that has been sprayed with PAM vegetable spray. Sprinkle cheese and paprika over the top of casserole. Bake at 350 degrees until hot and bubbly about 20 minutes.

Serves 6.

BLUEBERRY PIE

8	ounce Philadelphia Cream Cheese	8	ounce Cool Whip topping
1	cup granulated sugar	1	pint raw fresh blueberries

Cream together the cream cheese and sugar. Add Cool Whip and mix well. Add blue berries and fold into cream cheese mixture. Pour mixture into a baked pie shell and refrigerate over night. Strawberries or peaches may be used as a substitute for the fruit.

PIE CRUST:

1⅓	cup plain flour	3	tablespoons cold water
½	teaspoon salt		
½	cup all vegetable shortening	½	cup pecan pieces

Sift flour and salt. Add vegetable shortening and cut in with a pastry cutter or two knives for pea-size consistency. Add water. Work in together. Roll out on lightly floured pastry board and put in a 9-inch pie pan. Bake at 350 degrees for about 10 minutes then sprinkle pecan pieces over the bottom of crust and continue to bake until the crust turns golden brown. Cool completely before adding filling.

COUNTRY PLACE RESTAURANT

1302 Country Club Circle
Minden, LA 71055

Tom McFarland, Chef/Owner

Tom McFarland has 27 years experience in cooking and catering services. He trained with a Greek chef as well as two chefs specializing in New Orleans cooking. Tom is known throughout the area for his quality and food presentation.

SOUTHWEST CHICKEN BREAST

5	5-ounce boneless, skinless chicken breast	2	medium tomatoes, chopped
1	onion, chopped	1	8-ounce package mushrooms
1	bell pepper, chopped		Cheddar and Monterey Jack cheeses, shredded

Season the chicken breasts to taste. Brown on each side until just done. Combine and sauté onion, bell pepper, tomatoes and mushrooms. Place breasts in oven proof pan and add sautéed condiments. Top with cheddar and Monterey Jack cheeses. Put in warm oven until cheese melts. Serve warm. Serves 5.

HOTWATER CORNBREAD

3	cups self-rising white cornmeal	3	eggs Oil

Add enough boiling water to cornmeal until moist – not wet. Add eggs and blend until smooth. Spoon in hot 350-degree oil and cook until golden brown on both sides. Serves 10.

BANANA BLUEBERRY PIE

2	Graham Crust pie shells	1	can blueberry pie filling

Blend: 1 8-ounce package cream cheese, 2 cups granulated sugar and 1 1# package Cool Whip topping. Slice 3 bananas into two graham crust pie shells. Spread ½ of the cheese mix, ½ can blueberry pie filling on top of cheese mix and ½ of the Cool Whip on top of each. Refrigerate until ready to serve. Makes 2 pies.

ATRIUM GRILLE

2001 Louisville Avenue
Monroe, LA 71210
(318) 325-0641

Hans Korrodi, Executive Chef

Born in the German-speaking region of northern Switzerland, Hans Korrodi came to the United States in 1969, after a tour in the Swiss Merchant Marine and having developed his cooking skills in prestigious establishments in Switzerland, Norway and England. After completing a sailor's apprenticeship on the Rhine River, he obtained a visa under the sponsorship of restaurateur and fellow Swiss Andres Meyer, who ran the famous Waterville Valley resort on White Mountain in Hew Hampshire. Korrodi served as assistant chef there and head chef in Vermont, and discovered Louisiana cuisine while on a vacation in New Orleans. It was here that "Chef" found his true calling, training at the posh Commander's Palace while simultaneously holding the Executive Chef spot at Brennan's in Houston. It was at the Palace where Chef learned from two other of Louisiana's great culinary artists, Paul Prudhomme and Ella Brennan, whom he credits as one of his greatest influences. In 1979, Chef decided to settle in West Monroe, Louisiana, catering for the Monroe/West Monroe municipalities. In 1986, he opened Chef Hans' Restaurant, which earned him that year's Louisiana Restaurateur of the Year award. In 1990, he resigned from his caterer's position and started another business, Chef Hans Gourmet Foods, Inc., where he is fulfilling his dream of sharing Louisiana's cuisine with the rest of the world.

Please Note: All of the Chef Han's products described in the following recipes may be purchased by contacting Chef Hans' Gourmet Foods, Inc., P. O. Box 3252, Monroe, LA 71210-3252 are by calling (318) 322-2334 or Fax (318) 322-2340

Continued Page 166

WILD RICE PILAF WITH OYSTERS AND SHRIMP CREOLE

2¼	cups water	½	cup green onions, chopped
1	package Chef Hans Wild Rice Mix	1	pint oysters
1	cup half & half milk and cream (can be substituted with milk)	½	pound shrimp, peeled & deveined
½	stick butter	1	tablespoon Worcestershire sauce
1	can mushroom soup		Chef Hans Creole Seasoning to taste

Preheat the oven to 300 degrees. Cook the Wild Rice Mix according to directions on package and set aside. Melt the butter in a saucepan and sauté the oysters and shrimp over medium heat for 3 minutes, stirring constantly. Add the mushrooms, green onions, Worcestershire sauce and half & half. Bring to a simmer and fold in the cooled wild rice blend. Place in a baking dish and bake for 20 minutes.

Serves 4.

WILD RICE SALAD

1	package Chef Hans Wild Rice Pilaf Mix	1	cup mayonnaise
2	eggs, hardboiled; one chopped, one sliced		Juice form ½ lemon
½	cup celery, chopped	1	tablespoon white vinegar
⅓	cup green bell peppers, chopped	1	teaspoon parsley, chopped

Cook Wild Rice Pilaf Mix according to directions on package and allow to cool completely. Mix mayonnaise, chopped egg, celery, bell pepper, lemon juice, vinegar and green onions. Combine with cooled rice and decorate with egg slices and parsley.

CHEF HANS' CRAWFISH IN HEAVEN

2	tablespoons butter	1	tablespoon Chef Hans' Creole Seasoning
1	cup finely chopped onion	1	tablespoon Chef Hans' Blackened Fish Seasoning
2	tablespoons flour		
2	cups milk	2	ounces dry white wine
1	pound cooked crawfish tails	1	ounce sherry
¼	cup half & half		Chef Hans' Hot Sauce to taste
½	cup finely chopped green onions		
1	tablespoon finely chopped parsley	8	ounces cooked angel hair pasta

Melt butter in saucepan over medium heat. Add onion. Cook until tender. Add flour, then stir continuously with wooden spoon for 2 minutes. Using wire whisk, add milk slowly. Simmer for 5 to 10 minutes on low heat. Add crawfish tails and half & half then fold crawfish into sauce. Add green onions, parsley, seasonings, wine and sherry. Add hot sauce to taste. Serve over angel hair pasta.

Serves 4 to 6.

Note: Shrimp can be substituted for crawfish.

CRAWFISH CARDINAL

1	pound crawfish tails	2	teaspoons paprika
2	tablespoons green onions, finely chopped		Salt, cayenne, black pepper, pepper sauce to taste
1	tablespoon chopped parsley	2	cups fish stock (or water)
2	tablespoons brown roux	1	ounce brandy
		1	ounce heavy cream

Cook roux and stock 10 minutes. Add other ingredients except cream. Mix thoroughly. Add cream. Serve with rice.

Serves 2 – 4.

HANS J. KORRODI
"1986 Restaurateur of the Year"

Continued Page 167

CHEF HANS' CRAWFISH ÉTOUFFÉE

¼	pound butter	1	tablespoon Chef Hans' Blackened Fish Seasoning
½	cup finely chopped onion		
½	cup chopped celery	1	pound peeled crawfish tails
½	cup chopped bell pepper	½	cup chopped green onions
1	teaspoon finely minced garlic	1	tablespoon finely chopped parsley
½	cup flour	1	ounce dry white wine
1	cup chopped tomatoes		Chef Hans' Hot Sauce to taste
2	cups water	3	cups cooked rice

Melt butter in saucepan over medium heat. Add onion, celery, peppers and garlic. Cook until tender, using a wooden spoon to stir. Add flour then stir constantly until mixture becomes light brown, blending with a wire whisk. Add tomatoes, water and seasoning. Simmer for 15 to 20 minutes. Add crawfish tails, green onions and parsley. Cook slowly for another 10 minutes. Add wine and hot sauce. Serve over rice.

Serves 4 to 6

Note: Shrimp can be substituted for crawfish.

VEAL "NEW ORLEANS"

24	ounces veal, sliced thin	½	pound sliced mushrooms
2	tablespoons chopped green onion	2	tablespoons butter or margarine
½	cup half & half	1	tablespoon flour
1	ounce white wine		Cayenne pepper & salt to taste
1	tablespoon chopped parsley		Coarse ground black pepper
4	artichoke hearts or bottoms, quartered		

Mix veal and flour. Melt butter in hot skillet. Add veal, stir and brown lightly. Add drained artichokes and mushrooms. Simmer 1 minute. Reduce heat to low and add green onions, parsley and wine. Mix well. Remove from heat. Add cream (Note: Do not cook after cream is added or ingredients will separate.) Season to taste with black pepper, salt, and cayenne pepper.

Serves 4.

CHEF HANS' SHRIMP REMOULADE

½	cup ketchup	1	tablespoon Creole (or Dijon) mustard
½	cup mayonnaise		
½	cup celery, finely chopped	1	tablespoon onion, finely chopped
2	tablespoons parsley, finely chopped	2	cloves garlic, finely chopped
2	tablespoons horseradish	½	medium dill pickle, finely chopped
2	tablespoons red wine vinegar	1	teaspoon Chef Hans' Hot Sauce
2	tablespoons salad oil	2	pounds shrimp, cooked, peeled and deveined

Combine all ingredients except shrimp and blend well with a wire whisk. (A food processor or blender may be used.) The flavors will be more intense if the sauce mixture is left standing for a while before serving. Shrimp Remoulade is traditionally served on a bed of lettuce. Place shrimp on lettuce and top with sauce. May also be used as a dip for shrimp or crawfish.

Serves 4 to 6

TURKEY GUMBO

6	tablespoons flour	½	cup oil
1	cup diced onions	4	cloves chopped garlic
¼	cup chopped green bell peppers		
½	cup chopped celery	1	8-ounce can tomato sauce
1	pound diced roast turkey	3	quarts water
¼	bunch chopped parsley	3	bay leaves
1	tablespoon Chef Hans' Creole Seasoning	1	can or 1 package frozen okra
			Salt & pepper to taste

Make a roux with flour and oil. Add garlic and cook until golden brown. Add onion, bell pepper and celery and cook until transparent. Add turkey and tomato sauce. Simmer 10 minutes, stir in water, and blend well. Add all other ingredients except okra. Cook 1 hour, add okra and cook 20 minutes. Serve in a soup bowl over steamed rice.

Yield: 1 gallon

ENOCH'S CAFÉ AND PUB

507 Louisville Avenue Monroe, Louisiana 71201 (318) 388-ENOC

"An Irish Pub with a Louisiana Attitude"

Doyle & Yvette Jeter, owners

Enoch's was first established on St. Patricks Day in 1980. Since then Enoch's has achieved legendary status in North Louisiana as a café, pub and live music venue. Everyone from Jerry Jeff Walker and Leon Russell to Zachary Richard have played Enoch's many stages. The newest and grandest Enoch's, our fourth location, is very much the Irish pub. Visitors from County Mayo and Cork have exclaimed they feel right at home. The Guinness doesn't hurt! These days you may very well find a trio from Ireland, or a Scottish piper filling the pub with Celtic sounds. Frequent musicians playing Enoch's include the Celtic Star, Beth Patterson, Sligo John Hennessey and The Conly's Irish Band. We never forget our Louisiana roots, so be prepared to hear some Cajun, country and rockabilly, as well. Enoch's grill still turns out some of the best pub grub found anywhere, and we still offer a wide variety of vegetarian sandwiches. On special nights you will find a crowd enjoying big bowls of Irish Stew, jambalaya, corned beef and cabbage or gumbo. It depends on the mood and the music.

ENOCH'S GUINNESS GRAVY

1	small onion, chopped		Cayenne pepper
½	stalk of celery, chopped		One bay leaf
⅓	cup fresh parsley, chopped		Oregano
½	small green bell pepper, chopped		Basil
1	medium can chopped mushrooms		Powdered thyme
	Garlic powder	2	cups of fresh beef stock
	Salt to taste	¼	cup of shredded roast beef
	Black pepper to taste	½	cup of brown sugar
		2	pints of Guinness Irish Stout
		½	cup vegetable oil
		½	cup roux

In a sauce pot, heat oil and sauté onions, green bell pepper, mushrooms and celery until soft. Add beef stock and shredded roast beef. Add all herbs and spices to taste. (A pinch of each will do with a triple pinch of garlic powder). Add 2 pints of Guinness Stout and brown sugar. Whisk all ingredients together and bring to a boil. Add roux a small amount at a time and whisk well. Simmer for 30 minutes. The gravy can be served on just about anything and can be used as a base for a great stew!

CRESCENT CITY CONNECTION

2102 Louisville Avenue
Monroe, LA 71210
(318) 324-1130

Bringing the World to Northeast Louisiana!

John E. Peters III, Chef/Owner

Since graduating from college Chef Peters' culinary experiences include stints at Enochs restaurant in Monroe and Commanders Palace in New Orleans, where he trained under the late Executive Chef Jamie Shannon, Sous-Chef Eman Loubier and Sous-Chef Gus Martin. During that period, Commanders Palace won the James Beard Award for "Outstanding Restaurant in the Country" for 1996 and the Zagat survey for Best in New Orleans '96! Upon returning to Monroe, he worked as Executive Chef at Warehouse No. 1 restaurant. On April 3, 2000, Chef Peters opened Crescent City Connection featuring Creole cuisine and Monroes' first and only sushi bar.

COTTONS ROASTED OYSTERS

24	fresh shucked oysters on the half-shell	1	cup chopped Andouille sausage or tasso
1	bunch green onions julienne style		Japanese breadcrumbs
1	red bell pepper cut into Brunoise dice (small dice)		Parmesan cheese Creole seasoning Kosher salt
½	cup chopped garlic Extra Virgin olive oil		Fresh cracked black pepper
24	thin slices of cooked artichoke hearts		

Lay oysters in their shell on a sheet pan. Put a pinch each of green onion, red bell pepper, Andouille sausage and garlic on each oyster. Squirt each oyster with extra virgin olive oil. Season each with Kosher salt, black pepper and Creole seasoning; top with Japanese breadcrumbs and Parmesan cheese; then roast in a 375 degree oven until oysters are just done.

Serves 4.

ESCARGOT SAUTÉ

	Canola oil	½ & ½	combo sage and rosemary (to equal 1 tablespoon fresh or ½ tablespoon dry)
	Creole seasoning		
	Salt & pepper		
1½	tablespoons garlic		
3	tablespoons green onion	½	cup white wine
16	sliced button mushrooms	½	cup Parmesan cheese
		2	cups heavy cream
		32	snails

Over high heat add oil to pan, then add escargot, garlic, green onions, herbs, and heat thoroughly. Add mushrooms and deglaze with white wine. Reduce by ⅔. Add heavy cream and reduce by half. Add Parmesan cheese, salt and pepper to taste. Garnish with Creole seasoning, Parmesan and parsley.

Serves 4.

SHRIMP AND ARTICHOKE SAUTÉ

2	pounds cooked linguini		Fresh ground black pepper
24	jumbo Gulf shrimp	¼	cup chopped garlic
24	pieces of quartered canned artichoke hearts	⅛	cup fresh julienne basil or your favorite herb
2	cups white wine	⅛	cup fresh chopped parsley
2	cups heavy cream		Parmesan cheese
	Creole seasoning		Canola oil
	Kosher salt		

Coat bottom of a large skillet (NOT IRON) with canola oil and heat on high until just before smoking. Carefully add shrimp, artichoke and garlic. Toss to sear on all sides and deglaze with the white wine, being careful as it may flame up a little. Then let reduce by half and add herbs, parsley, heavy cream and reduce by half again. Season with Creole seasoning, Kosher salt and black pepper. Toss in linguini, sprinkle with Parmesan cheese and serve.

Serves 4.

BUBBA LUIGI'S CAJUN & ITALIAN CUISINE

2105 North 7th Street
West Monroe, LA 71292
(318) 699-0234

Phyllis O'Toole, Executive Chef

SHRIMP DU CEIL

1	8-ounce package cream cheese
1	cup half & half
¼	cup sour cream
½	cup grated Parmigiano cheese
3	tablespoons Paul Prudhomme's Blackening Seasoning
2	tablespoons chopped garlic
1	cup diced green peppers and onions
1½	pounds small shrimp (40-50 count)

In a double boiler, combine cream cheese, half & half and sour cream. Cook until all ingredients are smoothly blended. Add seasoning, garlic, peppers, onions and cheese. Continue to cook until mixture has a thick, creamy consistency. Add shrimp and cook until shrimp are done. Serve over angel hair pasta with garlic bread.

Serves 4 to 6.

SHRIMP FRA DIAVLO

2	whole carrots (finely diced)
2	tablespoons chopped garlic
6	tablespoons olive oil
1	teaspoon crushed red pepper flakes
½	cup brandy
½	cup dry white wine
2	cups crushed Roma tomatoes
1	cup tomato sauce
½	cup porcini mushrooms
½	cup red bell pepper slices
½	cup green bell pepper slices
½	cup red onion slices
1 to 1½	pounds medium shrimp (31-35 count)

Toss shrimp and crushed red pepper flakes in a bowl until well coated and set aside. In a large skillet combine olive oil, garlic and finely diced carrots and sauté over medium heat until garlic starts to become sticky. Add shrimp mixture and continue to cook for about 5 minutes. Remove from heat. Pour brandy over shrimp and ignite (be careful!). Shake skillet gently until flames subsides. Return skillet to heat and add tomatoes, tomato sauce and wine. Simmer for about 20 minutes on low heat. Add peppers, onions and mushrooms during last 5 minutes of cooking. Serve over linguini or pasta of choice.

Serves 4-6

Martha Chaffin Miller 1993

TRENTON STREET CAFÉ

232 Trenton Street
West Monroe, LA 71291
(318) 322-1444

Trenton Street Café is owned and operated by Stuart and Sandy Spivey. They have been serving locals and tourist on Antique Alley in downtown West Monroe for 10 years. New Orleans style food is their specialty. Cooking experiences involve 4 years at USMC and culinary degree from Johnson & Wales University. They have received awards from New Star World's Taste of Northeast for Best Catfish and Best Seafood. Trenton Street Café has also been featured in Southern Living Magazine.

LOUISIANA HOT SAUCE

½	pound habanero peppers	¼	cup chopped garlic
½	pound cayenne peppers	1	cup chopped onions
½	cup sugar	¼	cup vinegar
⅓	cup salt	½	cup water

Combine all of the above ingredients and cook for 8 hours. Strain the liquid and can the sauce.

SHRIMP WITH LEMON AND WILD RICE

2	bell peppers, chopped	3	teaspoons lemon juice
1	cup onions, chopped	1	teaspoon Worcestershire sauce
3	teaspoons butter	½	teaspoon mustard
2	cups cooked wild rice	1	cup grated cheddar cheese
1	can cream of mushroom soup	1	pound raw peeled shrimp

Sauté vegetables, add rice, seasonings, cheese and shrimp. Pour into buttered casserole bowl. Bake at 375 degrees for 30 minutes. Top with cheese.

Serves 6 – 8

LOUISIANA HUSHPUPPIES

1¼	cups yellow cornmeal	1	teaspoon black pepper
½	cup all-purpose flour	1	onion diced
3	tablespoons baking powder	2	eggs, beaten
1	tablespoon sugar	½	cup milk
1	pinch of salt	½	cup kernel corn
		¼	cup green onions
		2	tablespoons jalapeño, diced

Mix dry ingredients. Mix wet ingredients. Combine ingredients. Fry tablespoon-size balls in hot grease (345 degrees for 2 minutes on each side).

ORANGE FRITTERS

2	eggs beaten	2	cups flour
½	cup sugar	2	teaspoons baking powder
2	tablespoons butter	½	teaspoon salt
1	tablespoon orange rind (grated)	½	cup orange juice

Beat eggs, add sugar, stir in butter and orange rind. Mix dry ingredients. Mix alternating dry ingredients and flour. Let stand for 15 minutes. Fry tablespoon-size balls at 350 degrees until done (2 minutes on each side).

KING CAKE

⅓	cup sugar	1	package dry active yeast
1	teaspoon salt	1	teaspoon vanilla flavoring
½	cup shortening	4	cups flour
2	large eggs		
1	cup milk at room temperature		

Cream sugar, salt and shortening well. Add eggs one at a time and continue to cream. Dissolve yeast to mixture of milk and flavoring and add to mix. Add flour and mix until smooth (80 degree) dough. Let dough rest for 1½ hours. Separate into 3 strips. Roll out strips and paint with vegetable oil. Add sugar and fold in. Plait the bread dough. Bake at 370 degrees for 12 to 15 minutes. Garnish with yellow, purple and green sugar.

Makes one cake.

TRENTON STREET BISTRO

Trenton Street
Ruston, LA 71270

Trenton Street Bistro is a new restaurant in historic downtown Ruston. We serve an eclectic menu within an intimate atmosphere. The owner, Debra Stall, is ever present with a smile and a happy word for customers. Her well-trained staff assists in providing excellent customer service and consistently serving exceptional food. Established in 2001, Trenton Street Bistro is ever striving to expand their imaginative menu and satisfy their customers.

GRILLED TOMATO AND CHICKEN SALAD WITH PLUM VINAIGRETTE

16	large tomatoes		Salt/pepper to
4	chicken breasts		taste
	(boneless skinless)	¾	pound smoked
1	loaf French bread		Gouda cheese
½	cup Italian	3	16-ounce bags
	seasoning		spring mix salad
1	cup olive oil		greens

Cut tomatoes into 1-inch thick steaks. Put onto a flat container, drizzle with half of the olive oil and salt and pepper to taste for 20 minutes, flipping once. Grill tomatoes for 2-3 minutes on each side. Grill chicken. Cut French bread into 2-inch croutons. Drizzle with olive oil and Italian seasoning and toast. Top croutons with smoked Gouda cheese and melt cheese. Toss salad in plum vinaigrette and place in center of plate. Place tomatoes on top of croutons and place 4 of each on a plate with spring mix and top with grilled chicken.

PLUM VINAIGRETTE

6	large red plums	½	cup olive oil
1	cup water		Salt and pepper to
1	cup sugar		taste
¼	white balsamic	1	lime
	vinegar		

Remove seeds from plums. Dissolve sugar in water to form simple syrup. Bring to a low boil, add plums. Cook until plums are mush and syrup is reduced by half (30-45 minutes). Place plum mixture in food processor and puree thoroughly. Add vinegar, olive oil, salt and pepper and lime. Mix until emulsified. Chill and serve.

Recipe by: Andrew Follette

FOLLETTE POTTERY

P. O. Box 766
1991 Pea Ridge Road
Ruston, LA 71270
(318) 251-1310

Libby and Kent Follette, owners

*Follette Pottery, nestled in the wooded hills of north Louisiana where spring water flows from the ground and wildlife abounds. Libby and Kent Follette have been making pottery to cook in, serve in and entertain with for over 30 years. Their pottery makes life a celebration. Included with each piece of pottery is one of their unique Louisiana recipes. The family recipes, representing the cuisine of north and south Louisiana are available in **The Follette Pottery Cookbook**. Kent and Libby have been guest chefs from Santa Barbara, California to Cambridge Springs, Pennsylvania. The Follettes have been featured in **Southern Living** and **Louisiana Life** magazines and have appeared on QVC. Kent appears regularly with Chef John Folse on PBS "A Taste of Louisiana." Follette Pottery can be found throughout the U. S. in the finest galleries and craft shops, but visiting the pottery is a real experience. Kent's fine Louisiana humor and Libby's warm southern charm make a visit to the pottery a memorable experience.*

The following recipes are from
The Follette Pottery Cookbook.

SPINACH LAURA

3	tablespoons flour	½	pint cottage cheese
½	stick butter, melted	1	teaspoon Creole
1	10-ounce package		seasoning
	spinach, thawed	½	cup feta cheese,
3	eggs, slightly		crumbled
	beaten		

Mix melted butter and flour over low heat. Add all ingredients except feta cheese and mix thoroughly. Fold into Follette Pottery baking dish. Sprinkle cheese over entire mixture. Place in cool oven. Bake at 350 degrees for 45 minutes.

Makes 6 servings

Continued Page 173

172

CRAWFISH DIP

1	cup finely chopped onions	½	cup finely chopped green onion
1	cup finely chopped celery	¼	cup butter
1	cup finely chopped bell pepper	½	pound crawfish tails, chopped
1	finely chopped jalapeño	½	pound crawfish tails, whole
½	cup finely chopped parsley	1	10-ounce can cream of mushroom soup Crackers or chips

Sauté chopped onions, celery, bell pepper, jalapeño pepper, parsley and green onions in butter for 10 minutes. Add crawfish tails and soup. Cook for 10 minutes, stirring frequently. Add salt and pepper to taste. Serve with crackers or chips in a Follette Pottery chip and dip set!

Makes 12 servings

CATFISH ALMONDINE

4	large catfish fillets (or other suitable fish)	⅓	cup cooking oil
		¼	cup butter
½	cup all-purpose flour	⅔	cup slivered almonds
1	teaspoon Creole seasoning	2	tablespoons chopped parsley

Rinse fish and pat dry. Grease four Follette Pottery individual fish bakers. Dredge fillets in flour. Sprinkle with Creole seasoning. Pan fry in cooking oil until fish is golden brown and flaky. Place in fish baker and put in warm (225 degrees) oven to keep warm while preparing almonds. Pour off remaining oil from skillet and melt butter in same skillet. Add almonds and sauté 2 to 3 minutes, until crunchy. Pour almonds over fillet, garnish with lemon slices and parsley.

Makes 4 servings

DUMB BUNNIES PEACH COBBLER

2	cups flour	1½	cups of famous Ruston peaches
4	teaspoons baking powder	1	8-ounce container non-dairy whipped topping
1	teaspoon salt		
2	cups sugar		
2	teaspoons vanilla		

Combine flour, baking powder, salt, sugar, vanilla, milk and butter. Pour into greased Follette Pottery giant pie dish. Cover with peaches. Place in a cool oven and bake 45 minutes at 350 degrees. Serve warm topped with non-dairy topping.

Makes 6 servings

JANE'S CREAMY LEMON MERINGUE PIE

1	pie crust, baked 10 minutes	½	cup lemon juice
3	eggs, separated	3	drops yellow food coloring
1	14-ounce can sweetened condensed milk	¼	teaspoon cream of tartar
		⅓	cup sugar

In mixing bowl, combine egg yolks, sweetened condensed milk, lemon juice and food coloring. Pour into baked pie crust. Beat egg whites and cream of tartar to soft peaks. Add sugar and beat until stiff. Spread over pie filling. Seal to edges. Bake 12 to 15 minutes at 350 degrees. Cool and chill several hours.

Makes 6 servings

ATHENIAN DELIGHTS

6535 Line Avenue
Shreveport, LA 71106
(318) 868-5282

Nikos & Julie Fotakos, Proprietors

Athenian Delights is located on Shreveport's exclusive Line Avenue. It's beautiful murals make you feel as if you have journeyed to Greece for a romantic dinner. Athenian was established in 1996 by Nikos and wife, Julie. Nikos moved to the United States in 1995 and longed for a taste of home so he opened this quaint corner café. Athenian offers Mediterranean sandwiches and pastas for lunch and a full Mediterranean kitchen for dinner specializing in fresh fish and lamb chops. An extensive wine list and cocktails are available.

PASTITSIO
(GREEN MACARONI BAKED IN A DISH WITH GROUND MEAT, ONION, TOMATO SAUCE AND CHEESE.)

1	kilo of macaroni	1	kilo of ground meat
2	large onions finely chopped		
½	cup of oil	2	cups of mashed potatoes
	Salt	½	cup of butter for macaroni
10	cups of milk		
1	cup of flour 3 cups of grated cheese		Pepper
		1	cup of butter
		8	eggs

Put meat and chopped onions in frying pan with a little water. Cook till water is absorbed, stirring once or twice. Pour the oil in and brown the meat. Add salt and pepper (to taste). Put in the tomatoes and allow the ingredients to boil on a low heat. Boil water in a big saucepan, add salt and put in macaroni. When boiled, drain and spread half of it in a baking pan. Sprinkle with grated cheese and spread over it an even layer of the meat mixture. Spread on the rest of the macaroni, sprinkled with cheese and pour over it half of the cup of melted butter.

Prepare the béchamel sauce in the following way: Put l cup of butter on to heat and when it is heated add flour and stir with a wooden spoon. Add the milk, stirring continuously to avoid lumps. *A further precaution is that the milk should have been warmed beforehand.* Then add the cheese (keeping aside 2 tablespoons) and a little salt. As soon as the sauce thickens, beat the eggs well and add them slowly to the sauce.

Pour the sauce over the contents of the baking pan, spreading it evenly and sprinkle it with the 2 tablespoons of cheese that has been kept back. This will make the crust of the sauce crisp. Bake in moderate oven for 30 to 40 minutes until browned. The ingredients for this recipe are suitable for a large baking tin, for cooking in an electric oven.

ATHENIAN DELIGHTS

DOMINIC'S ITALIAN RESTAURANT

1409 East 70th Street
Shreveport, LA 71105

DOMINIC'S OF NATCHITOCHES

805 Washington St.
Natchitoches, LA 71457

For thirty-five years it has been a pleasure and a passion of mine to be in the restaurant business. I worked in a restaurant while a young college student in Ruston, LA in 1965. After graduating from college I continued in the restaurant business. My father and mother, Mr. & Mrs. Joseph B. Cordaro (deceased) raised 11 children. My mother was an excellent chef and I attribute my love for cooking from her. I also trained under the legendary chef and personality, Ernest Palmisano, Sr. Both of these people had an impact on my career by giving me a wide variety of culinary experiences and different avenues to explore in the food industry. I have also had the opportunity of serving such celebrities as The President of the United States Bill Clinton, Tom Landry, Tommy Lasorda, Terry Bradshaw, Hal Sutton, David Toms, Shreveport Mayor Keith Hightower, Mr. & Mrs. John Manno, Sr., two prominent north Louisiana businessmen from Ruston, James Davison and Lucius McGehee and their families, Doug Thornton (G.M. of the Superdome, a native of Shreveport, has his own chair in the restaurant), Dr. Charlie Roberts (President of LSU Alumni), Sam Butera (legendary saxophonist from New Orleans), Mrs. Dalton (Sugar) Woods and various other state and local officials.

We plan to feature 3 specialty items: our famous Italian salad, angel hair pasta with crawfish tails and Italian donuts called Spingees. "Cuz" has been our theme as it means family to us. We invite you to join us so that we can embrace you as we have done so for 35 years.

Dominic Cordaro, Chef/Owner

THE ITALIAN SALAD
(OUR PRIDE!)

This salad from the beginning has been our signature. We have always felt that a salad of this nature should set the tone for the meal. This particular salad starts out with three kinds of lettuce: iceberg, Boston and romaine blended with fresh basil, cherry tomatoes, herbs, spices and mixed with our Italian salad dressing (recipe follows). The salad is then topped with my homemade olive mix and accented with a wedge of lemon and a roll of provolone cheese.

ITALIAN SALAD DRESSING

¼ cup pure virgin olive oil
2 tablespoons red wine vinegar
Hint of sugar
Squeeze of lemon
Chopped basil
Salt & pepper to taste

ANGEL HAIR PASTA WITH CRAWFISH TAILS

1 pound peeled crawfish tails
1 pound angle hair pasta
1 medium tomato wedge
1 cup fresh zucchini, cut
1 cup yellow squash, cut
1 tablespoon fresh minced garlic
1 pinch oregano
6 basil leaves
¼ cup fresh parsley, chopped
¼ cup olive oil
Dash of lemon pepper
Squeeze of lemon juice
Romano cheese for topping

Cook pasta and set aside. Pour olive oil in a large skillet. Combine the rest of the ingredients, except the lemon pepper and lemon juice, in skillet. Sauté for about 8 minutes. While sautéing, add lemon pepper and lemon juice. Stir ingredients gently. Put individual servings of pasta on plates and top with sauté mix. Sprinkle with Romano cheese. Serve hot. Yield: 6 servings

MAMA LOU'S SPINGEES
(ITALIAN DONUTS)

2 cups of flour (sifted 3 times)
2 teaspoons of baking powder
1 teaspoon salt
3 eggs
1 tablespoon sugar
1 cup milk
Vegetable oil for frying
Cinnamon to taste

Mix ingredients in large bowl until you have a semi-liquid batter. Pour vegetable oil in a deep skillet for frying the donuts. Heat oil until hot, but not boiling. Drop donut mixture by the spoonful into hot oil and cook until golden brown. Remove donuts from the oil. The donuts are then served hot with confectioners sugar or honey.

BELLA FRESCA RESTAURANT

6307 Line Avenue
Shreveport, LA 71106
(318) 865-6307 phone
(318) 865-6362 fax

"Festive Fare, Swanky Setting, Great Service"
Southern Living Magazine

David Bridges, Chef/Owner

Chef Bridges was raised in New Orleans and graduated from the New England Culinary Institute in 1994. He has honed his culinary skills in Florida, St. Croix, U.S. Virgin Islands and New Orleans.

KOREAN BBQ OYSTERS
(APPETIZER)

3	tablespoons tomato paste	½	cup olive oil
4	garlic cloves	2	tablespoons fresh grated ginger
3	shallots		
¼	cup cilantro	1	teaspoon cayenne pepper
1	teaspoon ground pepper	¼	cup white sugar
½	cup rice vinegar	2	lemons juiced
4	tablespoons white vinegar	¾	cup teriyaki
		½	cup soy sauce
½	cup brown sugar	6	dashes Tabasco sauce
½	cup sesame oil	24	oysters in the shell

Combine ingredients (except the oysters) in a food processor to make BBQ sauce. Shuck oysters leaving them in the shell. Place 1 tablespoon of BBQ sauce on top of each shucked oyster. Place oysters on top of the grill. When the oysters start to bubble cook for 30 seconds then serve.

Serves 8 (3 per person).

GRILLED TUNA WITH MASHED TURNIPS AND CABERNET WITH FOIE GRAS SAUCE

8   6-ounce pieces of #1 yellow fin tuna

FOR SAUCE:

2	cups Cabernet wine	½	pound foie gras
4	cloves garlic		Salt and pepper to taste
4	stems of thyme		

Place wine, garlic and thyme into a pot. Reduce wine to ¾ cup. Remove thyme and place wine and garlic into blender. While blender is running add cubes of foie gras until all the foie gras is emulsified into the sauce. Keep warm.

FOR TURNIPS:

6	cups chopped turnips (peeled)	¼	pound butter
½	cup heavy cream	2	cups peeled and quartered potatoes
½	cup water		

In a pot, place turnips, cream, water and butter. Cover pot and steam on medium heat until turnips are tender. Place potatoes in a separate pot, cover with salted water and boil until done. Strain potatoes.

FOR DISH:

Season tuna with salt and pepper. Grill tuna to desired temperature. Divide mashed turnips onto 8 plates. Place one piece of tuna on top of the turnips and pour sauce around. Garnish with fried garlic slices or fried leeks and serve. Serves 8.

WHITE CHOCOLATE/MACADAMIA CRÈME BRÛLÉE

1	quart heavy cream	4	ounces chopped macadamia nuts
8	ounces white chocolate	8	tablespoons unrefined sugar or sugar in the raw
8	egg yolks		

Preheat oven to 325 degrees. Place white chocolate into a stainless steel bowl. Place cream into a pot and bring to a simmer. Pour cream over chocolate and stir until mixture is smooth. Temper in egg yolks. Divide mixture into eight 6-ounce soufflé cups. Place 1 tablespoon of macadamia nuts into each cup. Bake in a pan with a water bath for 40 minutes or until the custard looks firm. Take out of the oven and let the custard cool for 15 minutes. Sprinkle 1 tablespoon of sugar on top of each custard. Caramelize the sugar using a blowtorch or a salamander and serve. Serves 8.

THE GLENWOOD VILLAGE & TEAROOM
"SPECIALISTS IN VICTORIAN TEA LUNCHEONS"

3310 Line Avenue
Shreveport, Louisiana 71104

Proprietress, Sharon Gale McCullar

Nestled in amidst fine English antiques and china, gourmet teas, and ladies accessories, The Glenwood Tearoom has been featured in Southern Living Magazine, Weekend Getaways in Louisiana & Mississippi, and Destinations Travel Magazine. Tearoom specialties include a Victorian Era Shepherd's Pie with Nutmeg Potato Crust, Puree a la Frankfort Soup, Lemon Blueberry Scones, Sticky Toffee Pudding with Caramel Sauce, handmade Champagne Truffles and Victoria's Trifle. Guests may choose traditional afternoon tea medleys or select from the a la carte luncheon menu.

BONNE FEMME SOUP

1	cucumber, peeled, seeded, sliced	4	tablespoons cornstarch mixed with ⅓ cup water
4	leaves of Boston lettuce, shredded	½	cup each chopped cooked ham and chicken
2	tablespoons butter		
1	cup white onion, chopped	1	teaspoon chervil
⅛	teaspoon pepper	¼	teaspoon nutmeg
1	teaspoon raw sugar	6	cups chicken broth
		2	cups heavy cream

In a medium saucepan, melt butter and sauté cucumber, lettuce and onion until soft. Puree vegetables in food processor. Return puree to double boiler; add meats, broth, cream, sugar and seasonings. Simmer on low heat 30 minutes. Add cornstarch mixture and continue cooking over low heat until soup thickens and comes just to a boil. Serve immediately garnished with sippets of toast.

Serves 8

MANDARIN CHICKEN AND ALMOND TEA FINGER SANDWICHES

¾	cup finely chopped cooked chicken breast	1	3-ounce package of cream cheese, softened
½	cup canned mandarin oranges, drained (reserve liquid)	¼	cup heavy cream
		2	tablespoons of reserved mandarin juice
¼	cup sliced, darkly toasted almonds	6	slices very thin white sandwich bread

Combine chicken, mandarin oranges and almonds; set aside. With electric mixer, whip cream cheese until light and fluffy; add heavy cream and reserved mandarin juice. Continue beating until very light in texture. Fold in chicken mixture. To assemble sandwiches, spread ½ cup of mixture on each of three slices of bread. Top with remaining bread. With electric knife, trim crusts and cut each sandwich into four triangles. Refrigerate, covered with damp paper towels, until ready to serve.

Makes 12 tea sandwiches.

THE GLENWOOD VILLAGE
AND TEAROOM

Continued Page 178

Hazelnut Scones with Lathering Cream & Lemon Honey

2	cups all-purpose flour	2	large eggs, lightly beaten
2	teaspoons baking powder	½	cup heavy cream
¼	teaspoon salt	1½	tablespoons Frangelico liqueur
½	cup sugar	1	tablespoon sugar for garnish
½	cup chopped hazelnuts	18	whole hazelnuts for garnish

Sift dry ingredients together in a bowl. Add butter and work into dry ingredients until crumbly. Stir in chopped hazelnuts. Combine eggs, cream and liqueur; add to dry ingredients, stirring just until moistened. Roll dough to ¾ inch thickness on a lightly floured surface. Cut with a 2½ inch daisy or heart shaped cutter, and place on light greased baking sheets. Sprinkle tops generously with sugar and place a hazelnut in each center. Bake at 350 degrees for 15 minutes. Serve with Hazelnut Lathering Cream and Lemon Honey.

Makes 1 dozen scones.

LATHERING CREAM

1	cup heavy cream	1	tablespoon Frangelico liqueur
¼	cup sifted powdered sugar	½ to 1	teaspoon grated lemon rind

Beat cream at medium speed until foamy; gradually add powdered sugar, beating at high speed until stiff peaks form. Gently fold in liqueur and lemon rind.

Makes 2 cups.

LEMON HONEY

4	large eggs	½	cup freshly squeezed lemon juice
2	egg yolks		
2	cups sugar		
1	tablespoon grated lemon rind	¼	cup unsalted butter.

Combine all ingredients except butter in double boiler; cook, stirring regularly, until as thick as honey. Add butter and allow to melt into lemon honey. Cool.

Makes 2½ cups.

JUMBO GULF CRABMEAT WITH CABBAGE

1	small Chinese cabbage	2	teaspoons Dijon mustard, grainy style preferably
¾	cup diced bell peppers		Few drops of Tabasco hot sauce
¾	cup mayonnaise, homemade preferably		A dash of curry powder
3	tablespoons cider vinegar, can be substituted by lemon juice		Freshly ground black pepper
¾	teaspoon dried tarragon	1	pound jumbo lump crabmeat, flaked and picked over to remove any cartilage
2	tablespoons ketchup		

Remove 8 large leaves of the cabbage, plunge them in a large pot of boiling water and blanch until softened. Drain and cool down in ice water. Quarter and core the remaining cabbage and shred to make about 2

Continued Page 179

cups. Save the rest for another use. Whisking the mayonnaise constantly, add the vinegar (or lemon juice), the tarragon, ketchup, Dijon mustard, Tabasco sauce, curry powder and black pepper. Blend very well. Add the shredded cabbage and toss, add the crabmeat and toss again. Remove the cores of the blanched cabbage leaves. Lay the leaves on a cutting board and fill each of them with ¼ cup of the crab mixture. Roll up the leaves to enclose the filling. Using a serrated knife, cut each roll into 4 pieces.

Serves 8.

SAUTÉED DUCK WITH PRUNES, MADEIRA AND CORIANDER SEEDS

Note: Duck is delicious, but too often it's rejected as too fatty or too complicated to cook. In the following recipe you'll soon see that it's as easy as roasting a chicken!

24	pitted prunes	3	ducks (5 pounds each)
2	cups Madeira wine		
6	teaspoons coriander seeds	½	pound unsalted butter
		2	cups of duck broth

In a small bowl, cover the prunes with the Madeira wine, let soak for at least 8 hours. De-bone the ducks and trim the excess fat. Start a duck stock with the bones. Heat a heavy skillet over high heat for two minutes, then add the coriander seeds. Cook, tossing, until golden brown (about 1 minute). On a work surface, crush the seeds slightly with the back of a heavy knife, set aside. Lightly sprinkle both sides of the duck pieces with salt and pepper. In a heavy sauté pan melt some butter over moderate high heat. Add the duck, skin sides down. Cook until the skin is light brown (about 4 minutes), then bake in oven preheated at 400 degrees until medium rare. (do not turn the duck during all the cooking). Transfer the cooked duck to a platter and keep warm while preparing the sauce. Pour off all the fat from the pan and add the soaked prunes and Madeira. Boil rapidly until reduce to 1 cup. Add the stock and let reduce to 2 cups. Turn off the heat, whisk in the remaining butter to thicken the sauce. Set aside. At this point you have several options. You can serve all the pieces of duck covered with the sauce or serve sauce on the side, or peel off the skin and serve sauce on the side.

MAPLE SYRUP MOUSSE WITH ORANGE ZEST

An easy recipe with an unusual flavor that can be prepared ahead to the point it is time to add the whipped cream. Use high quality maple syrup for best result.

½	cup of high quality maple syrup	1	orange
4	egg yolks	1½	cups heavy cream

Using a peeler knife, peel the orange and cut the skin into thin sticks (julienne). Place into a small pan and cover with cold water and bring to a boil. Drain and set aside. Over moderate heat and in a double boiler, combine and whisk the maple syrup, egg yolks and salt. Cook until the mixture is thick enough to coat the back of a spoon. Remove the top of the double boiler and place it over a bowl of ice. Stir to cool and add the orange "julienne". In a medium bowl whip the cream until peaks form. Fold into the maple mixture. The mousse can be served at once or preferable refrigerated 2 hours.

Servings: 8

OLIVE STREET BISTRO

1027 Olive Street
Shreveport, LA 71101
(318) 221-4517

"Come and enjoy real Mediterranean Style Food at this locally-owned restaurant"

Giuseppe Brucia, Executive Chef/Owner

Giuseppe Basciano, Chef De Cuisine

INSALATA DI FINOCCHI E ARANCE

2	large ripe oranges	2	tablespoons walnuts or pecans, chopped
2	fennel (anise) bulbs Juice from ½ lemon		
2	tablespoons honey	3	tablespoons extra virgin olive oil
2	tablespoons Grand Marnier		Kosher salt to taste Black pepper
1	tablespoon tarragon, chopped		

Peel the orange and remove all of the white pith from the flesh and save the juice. Cut the oranges into segments. Thinly slice the fennel. Put in a bowl with the orange segments. Add all the other ingredients and mix well. Put the mixture in the refrigerator for 10 minutes. Serve in individual bowl.

SPAGHETTI ALA PEPPINO

8	anchovies	6	tomatoes (blanch skin off, dice & remove seeds)
4	tablespoons water (Put water in small pot, add anchovies until dissolved on low heat and sieve – set aside)	2	tablespoons capers
		¾	cup pitted black olives
		2	tablespoons Italian parsley, chopped
4	tablespoons extra virgin olive oil	1	jalapeño, chopped
4	chopped garlic cloves	1	pound Italian spaghetti Kosher salt to taste

In a skillet sauté the oil, garlic, parsley and jalapeños and cook until light brown. Add tomatoes, capers, olives and anchovies and simmer for 15 minutes. Cook the spaghetti al dente in boiling salted water, drain and then add to the skillet. Mix and serve.

CARPACCIO DI FILETTO DI BUE BISTRO

1	10-ounce filet of beef	2	tablespoons Parmigiano shredded (per person)
¼	cup pesto sauce		
¼	lemon		Black pepper to taste

Place the beef in a freezer for 3 hours or long enough to be lightly frozen. Cut the meat into fine slices and arrange on 4 individual plates. Pour the basil sauce (recipe below) and lemon juice over the beef slices. Add shredded Parmigiano cheese to each plate. Serve with toast or country bread.

Serves 4

BASIL SAUCE:

1	bunch of basil	2	tablespoons extra virgin olive oil
1	clove of garlic		Kosher salt to taste
2	tablespoons pine nuts		Pepper to taste

Wash the basil and allow to drain. Pat dry and chop in blender with the garlic, pine nuts, and Kosher salt. Slowly add the oil to the blender until the mixture is creamy.

CHIANTI RESTAURANT

6535 Line Avenue
Shreveport, LA 71106

Executive Chef Enrico Giacalone

Owners Enrico and Nino Giacalone, Italian born brothers, transcending family culture and traditions with training in fine dining, opened Chianti Restaurant in the fall of 1987, during which period the local economy could only support a "red and white check" tablecloth style restaurant. With great success, Chianti featured a vast menu that included the most popular "Regional Italian" food fare. As the years went by, the local economy improved and Enrico and Nino slowly evolved the restaurant to fine dining by redecorating, and offering the much more sophisticated and renowned "Northern Italian Cuisine". With continued success in maintaining a clientele with the most discriminating taste, Enrico introduced signature dishes that have become popular among the locals and he would like to share a few with you. He hopes you enjoy them!

SCALOPPINI DI VITELLO ALLE NOCI & MORE
(VEAL SCALOPPINI WITH NUTS & BERRIES)
Yield: Two Entrees

6	1-ounce scaloppini of white veal, pounded lightly	2	tablespoons unsalted butter
1½	tablespoons of roasted slivered almonds	1	medium size shallot
6	medium size mushrooms sliced	2	ounces blackberry brandy
2	dozen large blackberries washed and patted dry	1	ounce dry white wine
		1	pint heavy whipping cream Salt & pepper to taste

In a large skillet, sauté the veal with the butter, at medium heat, for a minute on each side. Remove the veal (medium rare), set it on a plate and cover it. Turn the heat source to high, and in the same skillet, add more butter if needed, then add the sliced mushrooms, the blackberries, the almonds and the shallots; sauté the ingredients for a minute. Add the blackberry brandy and carefully make it flame with a match, add the wine and let all the liquid reduce to half its size. Add the cream and cook the sauce until you have it reduced to a medium thickness consistency. Add the scaloppini to the sauce to reheat for a minute, place three each on two plates, pour the sauce over and serve immediately.

INVOLTINI DI MELANZANA
(EGGPLANT SLICES ROLLED WITH RICOTTA CHEESE)
Yield: Appetizer for two

4	slices of eggplant (sliced lengthwise ¼ inch thick)	1	ounce grated or shredded Parmesan cheese
1	tablespoon chopped garlic	2	ounces shredded mozzarella cheese
2	tablespoons chopped Italian parsley	1	ounce grated pecorino cheese (optional for sharpness)
3	tablespoons extra virgin olive oil	8	ounces simple tomato sauce Salt & pepper to taste
6	ounces ricotta cheese		

Prepare the "simple tomato sauce" and keep warm. Sprinkle the slices of eggplant with salt, and place them in a colander to purge its bitterness. Prepare a marinade with the olive oil, the garlic, one tablespoon of parsley and a little sale and pepper. After twenty minutes, pat dry the slices of eggplant and place them onto a plate with the marinade, making sure that both sides of each slice is coated with it. In a bowl, mix together the ricotta, Parmesan, mozzarella and pecorino. Add a little salt and pepper to taste. Grill the slices of eggplant until soft, and then lay them onto a greased sheet pan. Divide the cheese mixture into equal parts for each of the eggplant slices and roll each one. Leave them in the same pan, cover with aluminum foil and place in a preheated oven at 350 degrees for ten minutes. With a ladle put enough tomato sauce to line the bottom of two plates, place two eggplant rolls in each plate, sprinkle with the remaining parsley, grated pecorino cheese (optional) and serve.

Continued Page 182

"SIMPLE TOMATO SAUCE"

1	14.5-ounce can whole peeled tomatoes crushed by hand	1	tablespoon chopped garlic
2	tablespoons extra virgin olive oil	2	tablespoons chopped fresh basil
		1	teaspoon sugar Salt & pepper to taste

In a 2-quart saucepan over medium heat, put the olive oil and cook the garlic softly for a few minutes without browning it. Add the crushed tomatoes, the basil, the sugar, salt and pepper. Bring to a boil and simmer for ten minutes. Puree the sauce in a blender and return to pan to keep warm.

GERALD SAVOIE'S

2400 East 70th Street
Shreveport, LA 71105
(318) 797-3010

"Shreveport's Real Cajun Restaurant" - Serving the finest in Cajun Cuisine. Come and enjoy the "Cajun Casual" Atmosphere. The restaurant is open 7 days a week and offers patio dining. Catering available.

RED SNAPPER A LA' GERALD

1	8-ounce red snapper fillet per person	6	ounces jumbo lump crabmeat per person

Season the snapper with red pepper, garlic powder and a little salt. (Too much salt will make the snapper chewy.) Cook snapper in an old iron skillet with real butter. (Season prior to cooking) After flipping the snapper, place the crabmeat in the same skillet with the same seasoning and butter. Do not burn the butter. When the snapper is done (about 5 minutes), place the crabmeat on the snapper. Serve immediately.

FERTITTA'S 6301 RESTAURANT

6301 Line Avenue
Shreveport, LA 71100

Joe Fertitta, owner

CHOPPED SALAD

1	head – Romaine, shaved	5	pieces – Cooked bacon, chopped
1	each – Vine Ripe Tomato, small dice	4	ounces – Smoked tomato dressing
½	each – Red onion small dice		Garnish: 1 each – Potato, julienne & fried OR 2 cans – Shoestring potatoes
2	each – Hard boiled egg – chopped		

Combine all ingredients in a medium mixing bowl. Gently toss until all ingredients are thoroughly combined. Shape the salad in a compact tower on chilled plates. Top each salad with the shoe string potatoes for garnish. Serve immediately. Servings: 5.

SMOKED TOMATO DRESSING

4	each – Roma tomatoes, halved & smoked	3	dashes – Tabasco sauce
6	ounces - tomato puree		Kosher salt – to taste
1	cup sour cream		Fresh ground black pepper - to taste
1	cup mayonnaise	1	each – Range Top Smoker
1	tablespoon – garlic, minced	1	ounce – Pecan shells
3	dashes – Worcestershire sauce		

NOTE: If you do not have a range top smoker, replace the smoked Roma tomatoes with: 1 cup – Ketchup and 2 dashes of liquid smoke. Cut tomatoes in half, lengthwise and place in a range top smoker with 1 ounce of pecan shells. Set smoker over a medium-high flame on a gas range. Smoke for approximately 10 minutes. Remove tomatoes from

Continued Page 183

smoker and cool to room temperature. Meanwhile, in a medium-size mixing bowl combine all other ingredients and whisk together until thoroughly combined and creamy. Next place cooled tomatoes in a food processor and puree. Finally, add smoked tomato puree to dressing mixture and whisk together. Adjust seasoning with salt and pepper. Refrigerate until needed. Servings: 5

CRAB TOPPED PORTABELLA AU GRATIN

5	each – marinated & grilled portabellas	½	cup – shredded Parmesan cheese
2	pounds – jumbo lump crab	1	bunch – scallions, sliced
3	ounces – Pommery cream sauce* (recipe follows)	1	roasted pepper, peeled & julienne cut
5	slices – baby Swiss cheese		

Using a medium-size mixing bowl, gently toss the jumbo lump crab and pommery cream sauce together. Set aside. Arrange the portabellas, cap side down, on a non-stick sheet pan. Evenly distribute the crab mixture onto the center of cap. Place one slice of the baby Swiss cheese on top of each assembled crab-portabella. Sprinkle the scallions and arrange the roasted peppers on top of the Swiss cheese. Next, evenly distribute the Parmesan cheese on top of the crab-portabellas. Bake in a 400-degree oven for approximately 25 minutes or until golden brown on top. Serve immediately. Servings: 5

POMMERY CREAM SAUCE

2	cups – white wine	2	tablespoons – Creole (grain) mustard
2	cups – heavy cream		
1	each - shallot, minced	2	teaspoons – Old Bay Seasoning
			Salt – as needed

In a medium-sized saucepan, combine white wine and shallots. Bring to a boil and reduce by half. Whisk heavy cream into wine reduction and lower heat to medium-high. Let the sauce reduce by half. Once it has reduced it will be thick enough to coat a spoon (nappe consistency). Remove from heat. At this point, whisk in the Creole mustard and Old Bay seasoning. Adjust seasoning with Kosher salt. Chill the sauce until use. Makes 1 pint

MARINATED & GRILLED PORTABELLA

5	Portabellas, stems removed	¼	cup – Lite soy sauce
½	cup extra virgin olive oil	2	cloves – garlic, minced
¼	cup – balsamic vinegar		Kosher salt to taste
			Fresh cracked black pepper to taste

Remove the stem of the portabella with a paring knife. Using a spoon, scrape away the undercarriage (dark brown fronds) from under the cap. In a small mixing bowl, whisk together the oil, vinegar, soy sauce, garlic, salt and pepper. Set the cleaned portabellas in a medium-sized pan. Pour the marinade over the mushrooms and coat evenly. Let marinate for approximately 10 minutes. **Note: *Do not let the mushrooms marinate too long otherwise the flavor of the marinade will overpower the overall taste of the dish.*** Once the mushrooms have marinated, grill over a medium-high flame. Grill on each side for approximately 2-3 minutes. (Or until a grill mark is made). Be careful not to overcook the portabellas. The final cooking process is completed once they are assembled with the crab mixture and baked in the oven. Once grilled, set aside until it has cooled to room temperature. Servings: 5.

LEMON CRUNCH PIE

PIE CRUST:		LEMON FILLING:	
1	cup – sugar	3	cans – sweetened condensed milk
1½	cups – Graham cracker crumbs	½	teaspoon – lemon extract
3	cups – shredded coconut	1	cup – fresh lemon juice
1	cup – all purpose flour	3	each – eggs, beaten
1	cup – butter, melted		

For the crust: In a medium mixing bowl, combine all dry ingredients. Form a "well" in the center of the dry ingredients and pour the melted butter into it. Mix together until well combined. Use half of the crust mixture to line a non-stick, 9-inch pie pan. Reserve the remaining crust to top the pie. Lemon Filling: Whisk all ingredients together until well blended. Pour filling mixture into lined pie shell. Evenly distribute the remaining pie crust on top of the pie. Bake in a preheated 325 degree oven for 25 minutes…Or until top is firm to the touch and toasted brown. Once the pie has baked, let cool on a baker's rack until it has reached room temperature, then refrigerate overnight (or for 24 hours) to let it set. Serve with whipped cream and fresh raspberries. Makes 1 9-inch pie.

CRAWFISH ENCHILADAS

1½	pounds crawfish tails	1	teaspoon ground cumin
1	whole jumbo yellow onion (diced)	1	teaspoon garlic powder
½	cup chopped fresh jalapeno peppers	1	teaspoon ground black pepper
2	ounces white Zinfandel	1½	cups of diced fresh tomatoes
1	pack of corn tortilla		

Sauté the onions and jalapeno peppers in a saucepan until they are transparent. Add the tomatoes and all other ingredients and sauté for an additional 3 minutes. Remove from heat. Heat tortillas in an ungreased skillet for 10 seconds each. Take heated tortillas and spoon in 3 ounces of the crawfish mixture and roll. Place in a 9x13-inch oven pan. Top enchiladas with sauce. Cover with Cheddar cheese and heat in oven until cheese is melted. Serve hot.

CHICKEN TORTILLA SOUP

3	jalapeños finely chopped	1	16-ounce can whole peeled tomatoes
1	16-ounce can tomato juice	1½	ounces chicken base paste
½	gallon water	2	raw (8- to 10-ounce) skinless chicken breast
1	potato (cubed)		
1	yellow squash		
¼	head of cabbage	1	zucchini (cubed)
⅓	cup rice	4	ribs of celery
1	tablespoon black pepper	1	carrot
		1	onion
1	tablespoon cumin	1	tablespoon garlic powder

In a large stockpot, add the following: water, tomatoes, chicken, tomato juice, spices, jalapenos and chicken base. Bring to a boil, add remaining ingredients then lower temperature to let simmer for 10 to 15 minutes. After it has simmered, you should use a potato masher to stir contents until all chicken has been broken up and spread throughout the soup. It is then ready to serve.

Continued Page 185

GRILLED FISH OR SHRIMP TACOS

TACO SAUCE:

½ cup mayonnaise
½ cup plain yogurt
½ red onion, chopped
¼ teaspoon white pepper
1 ounce Chardonnay wine

½ tablespoon of minced garlic
½ teaspoon chicken base paste
¼ teaspoon horseradish
1 tablespoon Creole mustard

In a metal mixing bowl, add all ingredients, mix and refrigerate until needed.

PICO DE GALLO:

½ diced onion
2 diced bell peppers
3 diced fresh tomatoes
1 diced jalapeno
1 ounce olive oil

1 ounce chopped cilantro
1 ounce garlic powder
½ teaspoon black pepper
¼ teaspoon salt

Mix all ingredients in a large mixing bowl and refrigerate until needed.

To start your tacos, first you must determine which seafood to use. When using fish it should be a light tasting fish such as tilapia or trout. The shrimp should be a nice size but not huge (either 26-30's or 21-25's). When using fresh fish fillets or shrimp, you should grill them using a lemon pepper sauce and a little butter. After grilling, remove and place on tray. Take corn tortillas and heat on skillet for 10 seconds on each side, then form tortilla into taco shape in your hand. Ladle about 1 ounce of taco sauce in the bottom of each shell. Place about 4 ounces of fish or grilled shrimp in the shell and cover with finely shredded lettuce and a little finely shredded red cabbage. Top with Pico de Gallo and serve.

SUPERIOR GRILL™

UNCLE EARL'S PEA PATCH CAFÉ

108 Abel
Winnfield, LA 71483
(318) 628-3560

Audrey Lewis, Chef

The Pea Patch Café is located inside the Pea Patch Art Gallery and Antique Mall in historic downtown Winnfield, the home of three of Louisiana's governors. Their cook, Audrey Lewis, specializes in southern cooking including black-eyed peas and cornbread, a sure favorite of their hometown governor, Earl Long. It is his farm, the Pea Patch, that gives the unique business it's name. They also serve sandwiches, salads, and desserts. Dine in for a delightful hometown atmosphere amidst beautiful antiques and artwork by owner Gail Shelton. They are open for lunch on Tuesday through Friday from 11:00 AM – 2:00 PM

BLACK-EYED PEAS AND CORNBREAD:

4	cups dry peas	1	teaspoon Tony
2	tablespoons salt		Chachere's
1	teaspoon garlic		seasoning
	powder	½	teaspoon pepper

Rinse dry peas and place in crockpot and cover with water. Add seasoning and cook on high for 6 hours or on low for about 12. These can also be cooked on the stove, boiling them for about 30-45 minutes, or until tender. Serves 8-10. The peas are high in fiber and low in fat. They are best served over rice, with buttermilk cornbread and fresh coleslaw.

BUTTERMILK CORNBREAD:

1	cup white or yellow cornmeal	1	teaspoon salt
½	cup flour	½	teaspoon soda
2	teaspoons baking powder	1	egg
		1	cup buttermilk

Heat oil in baking pan or iron skillet in 400-degree oven. Mix dry ingredients. Add egg and buttermilk. Pour in pan when hot, and bake for 15 minutes.

SAWDUST PIE

1	graham cracker crust	½	teaspoon nutmeg
1½	cups sugar	3	eggs
1	cup buttermilk	3	tablespoons margarine (melted)
1	teaspoon vanilla	3	tablespoons flour
½	teaspoon cinnamon		

Mix and pour into crust. Bake at 350 degrees for 45-50 minutes. Serve with whipped cream and graham cracker crumb topping.

Makes 1 pie.

JESSE'S STEAK & SEAFOOD

3942 Front Street
Winnsboro, LA 71295
(318) 435-9948

Nell Book, Owner

PEE WEE'S CRAWFISH CASSEROLE

5 pounds crawfish tails	2 tablespoons Tony's Creole seasoning
4 cups chopped celery	2 tablespoons salt
4 cups chopped bell pepper	1 pound package of spaghetti noodles
2 cups chopped green onions	1 pound margarine
2 (49½-ounce) cans of mushroom soup	1 large #10 can of Cheddar cheese sauce

Boil noodles. Sauté onions, bell pepper and celery in margarine until tender. Add mushroom soup and cheese. Bring to a slow boil. Then add boiled noodles and crawfish. Season to taste. Put in large pan and bake in oven at 350 degrees for 15 minutes.

Serves 25 to 30 people.

BREAD PUDDING

PUDDING:

2 loaves of bread (white or honey wheat)	6 cups milk

Cover bread with 6 cups of milk.

6 cups of sugar	Cinnamon (optional) (to your taste)
4 tablespoons vanilla flavoring	
6 eggs	

Mix all of the above ingredients together. Pour into a 12 x 20 buttered pan and bake at 350 degrees for 45 minutes (for golden brown crust).

SAUCE:

2 sticks of butter	3 tablespoons Amaretto rum (optional)
2 cups of sugar	
6 whole eggs (whipped)	

In saucepan, combine butter and sugar until melted, stirring frequently. Remove from heat, stir in whipped eggs until mixture thickens. Add Amaretto rum if desired. Pour sauce over baked pudding.

Serves 20 to 25 people.

WATERFRONT GRILL

5201 DeSiard
Monroe, LA 71203
(318) 345-0064

Sam & Don Weems, Chef/Owners

The Waterfront Grill overlooks the beautiful Bayou DeSiard. The restaurant opened in February, 1997 to rave reviews! The popular restaurant features catfish, shrimp, oysters, beef, chicken and all types of seafood – "none of it fried". Waterfront Grill was featured in Southern Living Magazine in 2001. Don Weems was recently selected as "2002 Restaurateur of the Year" by the Louisiana Restaurant Association!

GRILLED CHICKEN AND TOMATO BASIL CREAM SAUCE OVER BOWTIE PASTA

1	14oz. can crushed tomatoes
1	14oz. can diced tomatoes
1	quart heavy whipping cream
½	cup dried basil
⅓	cup oregano
	Salt & crushed red pepper to taste
⅓	cup white wine
⅓	cup diced garlic
⅓	cup butter
1	cup grated Parmesan cheese
6	boneless, skinless chicken breasts – grilled & diced
6	cups cooked bowtie pasta

Simmer tomatoes with 1 cup of water over low heat for 1½ hours. While simmering, add basil, oregano, salt, crushed red pepper and white wine. Add heavy whipping cream and set over low heat. Roast garlic in skillet with butter for 1 to 2 minutes. (Do not let it brown) Add garlic to tomato sauce. Remove from heat. Add Parmesan cheese. Add layer of chicken over pasta. Top with sauce.

Serves 6 – 8.

WINE AND HERB BAKED CATFISH WITH WILD RICE

2	cups melted butter	12	(3-5oz.) catfish fillets
½	cup white wine		Tony Chachere's seasoning
½	cup olive oil		
¼	cup parsley flakes		
⅓	cup diced garlic	1	box Uncle Ben's long grain wild rice (cooked according to directions)
2	tablespoons crushed red pepper		
1	tablespoon salt		

Sauté garlic in melted butter. Add wine, olive oil, oregano, parsley flakes and red pepper. Lightly season catfish with Tony Chachere's seasoning. Bake at 500 degrees for approximately 15 minutes until done in a baking dish. Whisk butter mixture until blended and pour over catfish and bake until mixture bubbles around edges. Serve over bed of wild rice. Spoon juice over the catfish and rice.

Serves 8-10.

"The Finest in Grilled Catfish, Seafood & Steaks"

Glossary

Aioli ~ A garlic mayonnaise from France usually served with seafood.

Ancho ~ A fairly mild red chili pepper.

Andouille ~ (Fr) A thick Acadian sausage of lean smoked pork, ranging from bland to very peppery.

Anise ~ An herb that tastes like licorice. It is often used in pastries, cheeses, etc.

Antipasto ~ An antipasto is an appetizer that is generally served before pasta.

Appareil ~ (Fr) A mixture of ingredients already prepared for use in a recipe.

Arborio rice ~ An Italian medium-grain rice that is used frequently for risotto.

Arugula ~ A leafy salad herb that has an aromatic peppery flavor.

Bain-marie ~ **(Water bath)** consists of a bowl placed over a bowl of boiling hot water to gently cook the sauce, etc. without over-cooking.

Balsamic vinegar ~ Balsamic vinegar is a very fine aged vinegar made in Modena, Italy. It is expensive but is the favorite vinegar of most Louisiana chefs because of its sweet, mellow flavor.

Basil ~ An aromatic herb widely used in Mediterranean cooking. It is used in pesto sauce, salads and cooking fish.

Basmati rice ~ A long-grain rice with a nutty flavor.

Bay ~ Dried bay leaves are used frequently in poultry, fish and meat dishes as well as stocks and soups.

Béarnaise ~ One of the classic French sauces. It is made with emulsified egg yolks, butter, fresh herbs and shallots. It is often served with poultry, grilled fish and meat.

Béchamel ~ It is also one of the basic French sauces. It is a sauce made from white roux, milk or cream, onions and seasonings.

Beignet ~ A French word for batter dipped fried fritters, usually sweet like a doughnut.

Beurre blanc ~ It is a white butter sauce made from shallots, white wine vinegar and white wine that has been reduced and thickened with heavy cream and unsalted butter.

Salt and ground white pepper to taste.

Beurre manie ~ A paste of flour and butter used to thicken sauces.

Bisque ~ A thick seafood soup usually made from oysters, shrimp or lobster and thickened with cream.

Blanch ~ The purpose is to loosen the skin on a fruit or vegetable by placing it in hot water for a few minutes and then in to cold water to stop the cooking process.

Bon Appetit! ~ Literally, good appetite or "Enjoy!"

Boudin ~ A peppery, pale-brown link of pork meat, liver, onions and other seasonings. Rice is usually what binds the fillings of this richly seasoned sausage.

Braise ~ The slow cooking of food in a tight container with a flavoring liquid equal to about half the amount of the main ingredient.

Brie ~ A soft cows' milk cheese made in the French region of Brie.

Brûlée ~ A French word for "burnt" and refers to a caramelized coating of sugar, such as a topping for crème brulee.

Bruschetta ~ Toasted bread slices rubbed with garlic and drizzled with new green olive oil.

Café au Lait ~ Coffee and chicory blend with milk; usually a half-and-half mixture of hot coffee and hot milk.

Cajun ~ Slang for Acadians, the French-speaking people who migrated to South Louisiana from Nova Scotia in the 18th century. Cajuns were happily removed from city life, preferring a rustic life along the bayous. The term now applies to the people, the culture and the cooking.

Glossary

Culinary Terms Frequently Used by Louisiana Chefs

Cannelloni ~ Italian pasta tubes filled with ricotta cheese, chocolate, etc.

Caper ~ The pickled bud of a flowering caper plant. It is found on the Mediterranean coast. Capers are often used as a condiment in salads, used in making tartare sauce and as a seasoning in broiling fish.

Capon ~ A castrated male chicken.

Caramel ~ Sugar "caramelizes" when dissolved in water and boiled to a golden brown color.

Cardamom ~ A member of the ginger family. It has a spicy flavor and is used in Indian and Middle Eastern dishes.

Cayenne pepper ~ Red chili pepper that is dried and ground fine for home use.

Cèpe ~ (Also called porcini) These delicious earthy treasures are members of the *Boletus edulis* species of wild mushroom.

Chaurice ~ A highly spiced pork or beef sausage used in Cajun cooking.

Chervil ~ An herb belonging to the parsley family. It is best used fresh because of its delicate flavor.

Chicory ~ An herb, the roots of whish are dried, ground and roasted and used to flavor coffee.

Chiffonade ~ Leafy vegetables such as spinach and lettuce cut into thin strips.

Chipotle ~ A brownish-red chili pepper that has been dried and smoked and sometimes canned. This chili pepper has a smoky flavor and is very hot.

Chive ~ A member of the onion family used in flavoring foods.

Chutney ~ A sweet and/or sour seasoning that can be made from fruits and vegetables and flavored with many kinds of spices.

Cilantro ~ A fresh coriander leaf.

Clarified butter ~ Butter that has been heated to remove the impurities.

Clarify ~ To remove all impurities.

Condiment ~ Any seasoning, spice, sauce, relish, etc. used to enhance food at the table.

Consommé ~ A clear strained stock, usually clarified, made from poultry, fish, meat or game and flavored with vegetables.

Coriander ~ A member of the carrot family. Fresh coriander is also called cilantro. This herb is prized for its dried seeds and fresh leaves and is used in similar ways to parsley.

Coulis ~ A thick sauce or puree made from cooked vegetables, fruits, etc.

Courtbouillon ~ A rich, spicy soup, or stew, made with fish fillet, tomatoes, onions and sometimes mixed vegetables.

Couscous ~ Traditional couscous is generally made from coarsely ground semolina, a wheat flour used for pasta. It is popular in the Mediterranean areas of Morocco and Algeria. It is often served over vegetables or meats along with sauces.

Crème Brûlée A custard made from eggs and covered with a "burnt" layer of sugar which has caramelized in the oven.

Crème faîche ~ It is often made from un-pasteurized cream with an additive such as yogurt which gives it a distinctive flavor.

Crevette ~ It is a French word for shrimp.

Creole ~ The word originally described those people of mixed French and Spanish blood who migrated from Europe or were born in Southeast Louisiana. The term has expanded and now embraces a type of cuisine and a style of architecture.

Cumin ~ A spice from the seeds of the cumin plant. It is often used in making pickles, chutneys and especially in curries.

Currant ~ A delicious fruit used to make jams and jellies. It is also used as a glaze for meats. The red variety is widely used.

Culinary Terms Frequently Used by Louisiana Chefs

Curry ~ A mixture of spices widely used in preparing and cooking meats and vegetables. It is often used in Indian cooking.

Daikon ~ A large radish.

Deglacer ~ A process of dissolving cooking juices left in a pan where meats or poultry have been cooked. This is achieved by adding liquids such as stock or wines to the sediment and then reducing it to half the volume. The sauce is the strained and seasoned.

Demi-glace ~ A brown sauce boiled and reduced by half.

Dente, al ~ Vegetables cooked until they are firm and crunchy.

Dijon mustard ~ Mustard made from a white wine base.

Dill ~ An herb used with vinegar to pickle cucumbers. It is also used to flavor foods.

Dirty Rice ~ Pan-fried leftover cooked rice sautéed with green peppers, onions, celery, stock, liver, giblets and many other ingredients.

Dredge ~ To coat food with a dry ingredient such as breadcrumbs, cornmeal or flour.

Dungeness crab ~ A large rock crab found in the Pacific Northwest.

Étouffée ~ A succulent, tangy tomato-based sauce. Crawfish Etouffee and Shrimp Etouffee are delicious New Orleans specialties.

Fagioli ~ The Italian word for beans.

Fais do do ~ The name for a lively party where traditional Cajun dance is performed.

Farfalle ~ "Butterfly"-shaped pasta

Fennel ~ A vegetable bulb or herb with a spicy flavor. It is often used in soups and salads.

Feta cheese ~ A soft and crumbly goat's milk cheese often used in salads and Greek dishes.

Filé powder ~ Sassafras leaves that have been dried and used in the final stages to thicken gumbo. Okra can also be used to thicken gumbo instead of file powder.

Filo ~ (phyllo) A very thin dough that contains little fat and is used for strudel, baklava and other pastries.

Flan ~ An open custard tart made in a mold. Caramel cream custard is a popular flan dessert.

Foie gras ~ The enlarged liver of a fattened or force-fed goose.

Frais, fraîche ~ Fresh

Fraise ~ Strawberry.

Fumet ~ Liquid that gives flavor and body to sauces and stocks. **Fish fumet** is used to poach fish fillets. It is made from dry white wine, fish stock, and bouquet garni.

Garde manger ~ Pantry area where a cold buffet can be prepared.

Garnish ~ A small amount of a flavorful, edible ingredient added as trimmings to compliment the main dish and enhance its appearance

Ginger ~ A spice from a rhizome of a plant native to China. It is used fresh in Chinese cooking, but can also be used dried or ground.

Glace ~ (Fr) ice cream; also used for cake icing.

Glaze ~ It is used as a coating to give a shiny appearance to roasts, poultry, custards, jams and jellies.

Glutinous rice ~ Sticky rice used by the Japanese to make sushi and rice cakes.

Gorgonzola ~ A strong Italian blue cheese.

Gratons ~ The Acadian-French word for fatty pork skins fried in lard (also known as Cracklings).

Grillades ~ Squares of braised beef or veal. Grillades and grits is a popular local breakfast.

Glossary

Culinary Terms Frequently Used by Louisiana Chefs

Guava ~ A tropical fruit shrub. It makes delicious jellies.

Gumbo ~ A Cajun or Creole soup thickened with okra or filé powder. Gumbo is an African word for okra.

Habañero ~ An extremely hot chili pepper, oval-shaped and smaller than the jalapeno. The color changes from green to orange and red upon ripening. It is used in stews and sauces.

Haddock ~ It is closely related to a cod but smaller and thin-skinned. It is excellent broiled in butter.

Halibut ~ The largest member of the flounder family. It can be smoked, broiled or grilled.

Herbsaint ~ Anise liqueur – tastes like licorice.

Hoisin sauce ~ It is used in Chinese cooking to flavor sauces and marinades. It is a thick brown sauce made from soybeans, garlic, sugar and salt.

Hollandaise ~ It is one of the classic sauces in French cooking. It is made from an emulsion of hot clarified butter and eggs lightly heated until it begins to have the consistency of a smooth custard. It also contains lemons and shallots.

Haricot vert ~ Green string beans

Infuse ~ To soak spices, herbs, or vegetables in a liquid to extract their flavor.

Jalapeño ~ A very hot green chili pepper generally used fresh, but also available canned.

Jambalaya ~ A Cajun dish of rice, shrimp, crawfish, sausage, chicken and beans, seasoned with Creole spices.

Julienne ~ Vegetables cut into thin strips.

Kalamata ~ Kalamata are large black Greek olives.

Kale ~ A frilly, leafy vegetable of the cabbage family.

King Cake ~ A ring-shaped pastry decorated with colored sugar in the traditional Mardi Gras colors, purple, green and gold, that represent justice, faith and power. A small plastic baby is hidden inside the cake and the person who finds it must provide the next King Cake.

Lagniappe ~ This word is Cajun for "something extra," like the extra doughnut in a baker's dozen. An unexpected nice surprise.

Leek ~ A member of the onion family. Leeks are used in soups, casseroles, etc.

Loganberry ~ Similar to a blackberry and raspberry. It can be served with cream as a dessert, a filling for tarts or as a cream pudding.

Mandoline ~ A tool use to cut vegetables evenly into thick or thin slices.

Mango ~ A delicious, sweet tropical fruit served as desserts and also used in cooking preserves and chutneys.

Marinade ~ A liquid, including seasonings, to flavor and tenderize fish, meat and poultry before cooking.

Marinara ~ A tomato sauce flavored with herbs and garlic, usually served with pasta.

Merlot ~ A red-wine grape that produces a fruity flavor.

Mesclun ~ A mixture of wild salad leaves and herbs. They are generally served with dressing containing walnut or olive oil and wine vinegar.

Mirepoix ~ A mixture of cut vegetables—usually carrot, onion, celery and sometimes ham or bacon—used to flavor sauces and as a bed on which to braise meat.

Mirin ~ A sweet and syrupy Japanese rice wine used for cooking.

Mirliton ~ A hard-shelled squash.

Mornay ~ A classic French sauce; béchamel sauce to which egg yolks, cream and cheese are added.

Culinary Terms Frequently Used by Louisiana Chefs

Muffuletta ~ This huge sandwich is made up of thick layers of several different types of Italian meats, cheeses and a layer of olive salad. Served on special Muffuletta bread.

Oregano ~ Oregano is an herb very similar to marjoram but more pungent. It is widely used in Greek and Italian cooking.

Orzo ~ Rice-shaped pasta.

Panache ~ French to describe something mixed or multicolored such as salads, fruit or ice cream.

Pancetta ~ Italian bacon that is sometimes rolled into a solid round.

Paprika ~ A variety of red bell pepper that has been dried and powdered and made into a cooking spice. It is used in making Hungarian goulash, etc.

Penne ~ tube-shaped pasta cut on the diagonal.

Peperonata ~ An Italian dish of bell peppers, tomatoes, onions and garlic cooked in olive oil. It can be served hot or cold.

Peperoncino ~ A hot red chili pepper served fresh or dried.

Peperoni ~ A Italian salami of pork and beef seasoned with hot red peppers.

Phyllo ~ See filo.

Piccante Sauce ~ Hot spicy tomato-based sauce.

Piccata ~ Veal scallop.

Plantain ~ A tropical fruit similar to the banana.

Po-Boy ~ This sandwich started out as an inexpensive meal for poor boys. There are fried oyster po-boys, shrimp po-boys and others. All are served on French bread.

Poisson ~ French for fish.

Poivre ~ French for pepper.

Pomodoro ~ Italian for tomato.

Porcino ~ Italian for a wild mushroom.

Portobello mushroom ~ A large cultivated field mushroom which has a firm texture and is ideal for grilling and as a meat substitute.

Praline ~ A sweet candy patty. The main ingredients are sugar, water and pecans.

Prawn ~ A large shrimp.

Prosciutto ~ Italian ham cured by salting and air drying.

Puree ~ Food that is pounded, finely chopped, or processed through a blender or strained through a sieve to achieve a smooth consistency.

Quiche ~ A custard-filled tart with a savory flavor.

Radicchio ~ A reddish member of the chicory family used as a garnish or for salad.

Ratatouille ~ A mixture of tomatoes, eggplants, zucchini, bell peppers and onions cooked in olive oil. It can be served hot or cold.

Reduce ~ To boil down a liquid to thicken its consistency and concentrate its flavor.

Red Beans and Rice ~ Red beans cooked in seasonings and spices and usually with chunks of sausage and ham—served over a bed of rice.

Relleno ~ stuffing

Remoulade ~ One of the classic French sauces. It is made from mayonnaise seasoned with chopped eggs and gherkins, parsley, capers, tarragon and shallots. It is served with shellfish, vegetables and cold meats.

Rice wine ~ Distilled from fermented rice.

Ricotta ~ The word ricotta means "re-cooked" in Italian. It is a soft cheese made from whey. It has a slight sweet taste.

Rigatoni ~ Italian macaroni .

Risotto ~ An Italian arborio rice dish simmered slowly.

Glossary

Culinary Terms Frequently Used by Louisiana Chefs

Roghan josh ~ A spicy lamb dish from India, red in color and served with rice.

Roulade ~ French for a rolled slice of meat or piece of fish filled with a savory stuffing.

Rosemary ~ A shrub with aromatic needle-like leaves. It is used fresh or dried as an herb, especially with lamb, pork and veal.

Rouille ~ A spicy red pepper and garlic mayonnaise.

Roux ~ (Fr) A mixture of flour and fat (usually butter or shortening) cooked together slowly to form a thickening agent for sauces, gumbos, and other soups.

Sec ~ means dry.

Shallot ~ A sweet member of the onion family. It has a more delicate flavor than regular onions. It is used extensively in French cooking.

Shiitake ~ It is a dark brown mushroom with a meaty flavor. It is available both fresh and dried. It was originally from Japan but is now cultivated in both America and Europe.

Sommelier (Fr) Wine Steward

Sorrel A leafy plant often used in salads, soups, omelets, purees and sauces. It has a distinct lemon taste.

Sweat ~ To cook in a little fat (in a covered pot) over very low heat, so that the food exudes some of its juice without browning: used especially with vegetables.

Tartare ~ Tartare sauce is made with mayonnaise, egg yolks, chopped onions, capers and chives. It is often served with fish, meat and poultry.

Tasso ~ A highly seasoned Cajun sausage made from pork.

Thyme ~ A herb with a pungent smell that belongs to the same family as mint. It is used in soups, stocks, casseroles and stews.

Timbale ~ (Fr) Metal mold shaped like a drum.

Tofu ~ It is a white Japanese bean curd made from minced soy beans boiled in water then strained and coagulated with sea water. It is soft and easily digested.

Tomatillo ~ Mexican fruit related to the tomato. It is often used in salsa, salads, sauces, etc.

Tournedos ~ A trimmed cut of beef or veal fillet.

Veal ~ The meat of milk-fed baby beef.

Vermicelli ~ A thin Italian pasta.

Vinaigrette ~ A basic dressing of oil and vinegar with salt, pepper, herbs and sometimes mustard.

White sauce ~ Béchamel or veloute sauce, both made from roux.

Zabaglione ~ A rich Italian custard made of egg yolks beaten with Marsala wine and sugar until very thick.

Zest ~ The outer skin of citrus where the important oils have accumulated.

Index

Index

Fine Dining

Mississippi Style

by John M. Bailey

Chefs of the Hospitality State

Fine Dining
Tennessee Style

by John M. Bailey

Chefs of the Volunteer State

PLEASE SEND ME:

_____ copies of **Fine Dining Tennessee Style**   @ $29.95 each $ _____

_____ copies of **Fine Dining Mississippi Style**   @ $29.95 each $ _____

_____ copies of **Fine Dining Louisiana Style**   @ $29.95 each $ _____

Tennessee residents add sales tax @ $ 2.77 each $ _____

Add shipping & handling @ $ 6.50 each $ _____

Total Enclosed $ _____

Mail cookbook(s) to:

Name _____

Address _____

(NO PO BOX NUMBERS PLEASE)

City_____ State _____ Zip_____

Make checks payable to Starr★Toof.

Charge to   ☐ Visa   ☐ MasterCard   Valid thru _____

Account Number _____ Signature _____

Mail to: Toof Cookbooks
Starr★Toof
670 South Cooper Street
Memphis, Tennessee 38104

PLEASE SEND ME:

_____ copies of **Fine Dining Tennessee Style**   @ $29.95 each $ _____

_____ copies of **Fine Dining Mississippi Style**   @ $29.95 each $ _____

_____ copies of **Fine Dining Louisiana Style**   @ $29.95 each $ _____

Tennessee residents add sales tax @ $ 2.77 each $ _____

Add shipping & handling @ $ 6.50 each $ _____

Total Enclosed $ _____

Mail cookbook(s) to:

Name _____

Address _____

(NO PO BOX NUMBERS PLEASE)

City_____ State _____ Zip_____

Make checks payable to Starr★Toof.

Charge to   ☐ Visa   ☐ MasterCard   Valid thru _____

Account Number _____ Signature _____

Mail to: Toof Cookbooks
Starr★Toof
670 South Cooper Street
Memphis, Tennessee 38104

Nottoway Plantation
The largest plantation home in the South ~ White Castle